David Hiser

Paul

Jackie + Jonathan
Thank you
for your generous
hospitality — your
home town + families
are wonderful!
love
Mum

"9/07"

To Jackie and Jonathan
Thanks so much for
the Greatest of visits
to the UK. xxx ooo
and Cheerio
Barbara

aspen's rugged splendor

Exploring the Human and Natural Histories of the Maroon and Castle Creek Valleys

ERG Press | Aspen, Colorado

aspen's rugged splendor

ERG Press | Aspen, Colorado

Written by PAUL ANDERSEN

with LOUIS DAWSON III *&* JAY COWAN

Photographed by DAVID HISER

and other photographers as credited

Conceptualized by BOB LEWIS

Made possible by MICHAEL STRANAHAN

Designed by CURT CARPENTER

Aspen's Rugged Splendor
Exploring the Human and Natural Histories of the
Maroon & Castle Creek Valleys

ERG Press © 2007

Text by Paul Andersen,
with Louis Dawson III and Jay Cowan

All photos by David Hiser, except where noted

Maps and design by Curt Carpenter

DISTRIBUTED BY WHO Press • www.whopress.com

FIRST PRINTING • August, 2007

ISBN: 978-1-882426-25-6

PRINTED IN CANADA

COVER **From 17,000 feet on a late winter afternoon, looking southeast over North Maroon Peak, lower left, to West and East Maroon Creek Valleys**

FRONTISPIECE **A party of women on horseback from the late 1800s pauses on Pearl Pass, the ridgeline southern border of Pitkin County.** ASPEN HISTORICAL SOCIETY PHOTO

TITLE **Climbers atop Sievers Mountain look across Maroon Creek Valley to 14,018' Pyramid Peak. Behind them is West Maroon Pass, a popular hiking route to Crested Butte.**

Contents

ACKNOWLEDGMENTS

ASPEN'S RUGGED SPLENDOR was underwritten by the Environmental Research Group (ERG), a small, nonprofit organization based in Aspen that relies on supporters and volunteers who give freely of their time, funding and expertise. This book would not have been possible without them.

Information for the Geology chapter was furnished in large part through interviews and field studies by noted geologist Bruce Bryant. This soft-spoken but authoritative scientist mapped the geology of much of the Aspen area in the 1960s and published, in 1988, through the United States Geological Survey, a definitive treatise: *The Geologic Story of the Aspen Region*. Since 1995, Bryant has been Scientist Emeritus with the USGS. Acknowledgment also goes to David Laing and Nicholas Lampiris for the detailed geological descriptions in their book, *Aspen High Country: The Geology*.

Lou Dawson and Jay Cowan, free-lance writers in the Roaring Fork Valley, contributed comprehensive original histories on mountaineering and Aspen Highlands, respectively. Andre Wille, an Aspen-born biologist, school teacher, and mountaineer, collaborated on the ecology section with his independent research. He contributed especially to the global warming section through his field observations.

Historical sources were many and varied. Some were uncovered in the archives of the Aspen Historical Society or among long-forgotten issues of the *Aspen Times* and the *Ashcroft Journal*. Much of the historical information came from studiously researched and scholarly histories of Aspen and environs written by Malcolm Rohrbough, Len Shoemaker, Mary Eshbaugh Hayes, Lysa Wegman-French, Frank Wentworth and Muriel Sibell Wolle. Special thanks to Ramona Markalunas for her careful review of the history text and her devotion to the historical preservation of Ashcroft and other sites. A debt of gratitude is due Larry Fredrick, an Aspen historian who read the manuscript for historical accuracy and helped set the record straight. Thanks also to Bruce Gordon and his organization, EcoFlight, for contributing several hours of flight time for aerial photography.

Once a book is written, there comes the long, hard process of proofreading and editing. Hensley Peterson, a long-time friend of the Environmental Research Group, volunteered many hours to perform this laborious and focused chore. She reviewed the text, offered invaluable insights, and persevered through several drafts. The publishers owe Hensley a great debt, plus a pair of bifocals.

Finally, we acknowledge all of those who have labored in the interest of preserving the pristine wilderness encompassing both valleys. Without dedicated visionaries willing to draw the line on human development, this vast and beautiful landscape would not have endured as an inspiring legacy to conservation. ❖

Dedication

The Mace clan at Ashcroft in the mid-1950s.

THIS BOOK is dedicated to the Mace family in recognition of their stewardship of the upper Castle Creek Valley. Over fifty years ago, they built their home in Ashcroft; they called it Toklat and they made it sacred.

Toklat is a landmark that has served as a rustic lodge, comforting home, art gallery, and today as a nature center for the Aspen Center for Environmental Studies. Throughout their long tenure as the only full-time residents of Ashcroft, the Maces have cultivated in themselves and in others voluntary simplicity, uncompromising respect for the land, and deep sympathy for the wildlife around them.

The Maces have made a lasting impression upon the landscape in Ashcroft and upon the culture of Aspen. They replanted dozens of species of native grasses in the meadows surrounding their home and cultivated respect for wild nature in the Roaring Fork Valley. Many have been touched by their words and by the lasting value of their work. ❖

WAR CRY ON A PRAYER FEATHER

Who speaks for animals who cannot talk?

Who sees for flowers which are blind?

Who guards the river which has but one course?

Who represents the mountain in time?

Who comes here to argue for the life of beavers?

Who will tell of the importance of snails?

Who has seen the mantis shed his skin?

Who believes in butterfly wings?

I am nature's advocate

Ten million birds

Ten million trees

Ten million animals

Ten million fish

Are mine.

I will fight you in this room

And out of it

I will dare you to define

Progress

On the face of a dime.

—NANCY WOOD • Dedicated to Stuart Mace •1977

The gorges or canyons
cut by Maroon and Castle Creeks and their branches
are probably without a parallel for ruggedness, depth,
and picturesque beauty in any portion of the West.
The great variety of colors of the rocks,
the remarkable and unique forms of the peaks,
and the extreme ruggedness,
all conspire to impress the beholder
with wonder.

F.W. Hayden • 1874

The cosmos unfolds above the Maroon Bells.

Introduction

AN ARROWHEAD found near Pearl Pass in the summer of 2003 is a touchstone to the past, a link to the first people to ever see this country twelve to fifteen thousand years ago. They moved along the Great Plains at the edge of the foothills tracking the warming sun south from the frozen north where a temporary land bridge had allowed their forebears to cross the Bering Straits from Asia.

They pursued the buffalo, a moving banquet, and they followed the river valleys, their life-giving highways. Small migrating bands foraged into the foothills for food. They climbed into the mountains on trails made by their cloven-hoofed prey. They followed streams until they reached mountain glaciers clinging to cirques and arêtes.

The feet of man tamped the soil. The eyes of man prodded the dark timber. The arms of man carried weapons and tools. The mind of man sought the means of survival. The soul of man wrestled with the mysteries of life and death.

Beneath a swirl of stars around a campfire, a small community gathered and stared skyward into the infinite. The fire crackled and sparks mingled with the stars. The distant reaches of space projected light too ancient for understanding. Pictures emerged from the glimmering cosmic palette and a fertile intelligence leaped beyond the senses and attempted to rationalize the taunting abstractions of being.

Today, we gaze at the same stars and ponder the same cosmos. We marvel at the grandeur of the Maroon Bells, listen to birdcalls in a verdant aspen grove, surprise a deer in a wildflower meadow, study distant mountain ranges from high peaks. We interpret the story of geology in rock strata millions of years old and feel the thrill of life in the diversity of flora and fauna. We read the story of man etched in wagon roads across mountainsides, in mine tunnels plumbing the depths of the earth, and in forlorn ghost towns that echo the voices of the past.

Aspen's Rugged Splendor opens with a tribute to conservation and environment, then delves into geology and the forces that built and carved the mountains. It describes the natural world, the tragic plight of the Ute Indians, and the ages of exploration, settlement, commerce and recreation.

Bob Lewis, the initiator of this book and its companion, *East of Aspen: A Field Guide to Independence Pass*, once observed while standing before the Maroon Bells: "Time and space are the only constants here. All else—mountains, rivers, human enterprise—is transient, temporary, and must inevitably yield to vast, eternal forces." Bob smiled at the notion, musing on eternity.

Aspen's Rugged Splendor describes two valleys that convene at the Roaring Fork River only a quarter mile apart, but whose headwaters encompass a vast wilderness of peaks, basins and valleys. This book is a guide to understanding these two distinctly different valleys. It invites personal exploration and contemplation of our place within the dynamic natural world—a place ultimately defined by time and space. ❖

1 Guardians of Grandeur

CONSERVATION AND ENVIRONMENT

C ONSIDER the Castle and Maroon Creek Valleys as two sides of a triangle radiating out from its point at the Highway 82 roundabout. The third side of the triangle traces the high ridge of the Elk Mountain Range divide. Within this triangle is a vast expanse of rugged mountains, high altitude lakes, rushing streams, wildflower meadows and deep forests. This vast mountain redoubt provides a great escape from the fast pace of contemporary life by offering a complete immersion in the living world of wild nature. Thanks to the vision and commitment of local guardians, these wild lands are part of an ongoing legacy.

During the early years of settlement by white Europeans, these valleys were rarely appreciated for their wilderness values. They were a treasure trove of silver, timber, wildlife and grazing lands and were valued more for material wealth than for the esoteric values cherished today. Men tamed the wild lands to make them profitable; they killed game for sport and survival; they plowed and irrigated the land to make it produce; they grazed the land with cattle and sheep; they industrialized the land with steam and hydroelectric power.

After the Silver Crash of 1893 and the slow decline of silver production in the Elk Range, outdoor recreation attracted increasing numbers. By the 1950s, skiing put Aspen on the map, mountain climbing became popular and culture imbued Aspen with art.

By the 1960s, recreation had eclipsed resource extraction as the region's dominant economic force. The stunning beauty of the Elk Mountains had worked their magic and inspired a lasting ethic of conservation and environmental awareness.

LEFT **Green Gentian or Monument Plant,** *Frasera speciosa,* **at the south end of Maroon Lake. One of our most spectacular wildflowers, it may wait several decades to push up a flow-covered stalk 5-7' tall.**

RIGHT **The inter-faith Aspen Chapel beneath the Tiehack runs on Buttermilk ski area, was built in 1969 at the junction of Castle Creek and Maroon Creek roads. Its large public parking area is a good meeting place and car-pooling point for groups venturing up both valleys.**

WILDERNESS CHAMPIONS

I N 1964, the Wilderness Workshop was founded to defend wilderness values threatened by logging, mining and tourism. Co-founders Dottie Fox, Joy Caudill and Connie Harvey determined that preserving the wild lands surrounding Aspen was a cause worth fighting for. Today, with only two percent of the land mass of the lower forty-eight states designated as wilderness, their mission proved visionary.

Thanks to the efforts of the Wilderness Workshop, the Maroon and Castle Creek Valleys are encompassed by the 180,000-acre Maroon Bells-Snowmass Wilderness, which includes six of Colorado's fifty-four "Fourteeners."

"We got together and wrote letters," said Connie Harvey. "At first we had no organization, then it grew organically. We all knew that if you didn't have wilderness, there could be road building, logging, dams, water diversions, power lines, ski areas; all kinds of things. Wilderness also provides habitat protection."

Before the official designation by the United States Congress under the Wilderness Act of 1964, the area had been protected administratively since the 1950s for its obvious wilderness attributes. Despite major industrial activity in Castle Creek Valley during the mining boom of the 1800s, the region was left comparatively unspoiled. And because there was little mining in the Maroon Creek Valley, it was also pristine.

"In order to preserve the land in its natural state it is absolutely necessary to have the kind of protection afforded by official wilderness areas," added Harvey. "It is wonderful to feel that it is safe, that this is one battle we won't have to go on fighting. It's something I'm very proud of because it was very important."

Wilderness champions (L TO R) **Joy Caudill, Dottie Fox and Connie Harvey**

T HE MAROON BELLS-SNOWMASS WILDERNESS began with about 80,000 acres, but was more than doubled in 1980, thanks again to the Wilderness Workshop. "Wilderness is a tremendous asset," said Dottie Fox, an artist and avid hiker who passed away in 2006. "It protects our air and water and gives us one of the most pristine environments in the whole country."

The Wilderness Act prohibits motorized vehicles and mechanical contrivances from wilderness. Transportation must be on foot or horseback only; even bicycles and wheelchairs are banned from wilderness. No cabins may be constructed and no-impact camping is required. Travel through wilderness may be rigorous on rough trails with no bridges or signs. Challenges and risks are part of the experience. In sum, wilderness demands that individuals be attuned to nature's larger presence and that their sojourns are described by physical effort and awe.

Wilderness guarantees protection of the land, but it also draws increasing numbers of visitors who seek the solace and serenity of the vanishing wilds. In the 1970s, as the Maroon Bells-Snowmass Wilderness became increasingly popular, the impacts of visitation intensified. Further legal and regulatory measures had to be taken to save the area from being literally loved to death.

In the decade leading up to 1977, the Maroon Creek Valley had been overrun with cars. Each summer a quarter of a million visitors brought traffic congestion, noise and pollution. Automobile exhaust was killing vegetation and fouling the air. Car exhaust was akin to human breath tainting the cave paintings of Lascaux or fading Michaelangelo's mural on the ceiling of the Sistine Chapel.

As a result, on July 23, 1977, automobiles were banned from the Maroon Creek

These simple wooden signs mark entry into priceless ground—that's open to everyone.

Valley during summer months. Anyone wishing to visit Maroon Lake was required to ride a bus from the parking lot at Aspen Highlands.

"The purpose of the Maroon Valley bus service," explained then Pitkin County Commissioner Michael Kinsley, "is to maximize your enjoyment of the natural wonders of the valley while minimizing impact on this heavily used area. It is an attempt by an environmentally conscious community to preserve the beauty of the area for all to enjoy."

Bus passengers were provided with a written description of the delicate biology of the valley. The Wilderness Workshop provided volunteer guides to ride the buses and describe the features enroute to Maroon Lake. Education was successfully linked with an appreciation for the valley's ecological preservation.

The bus program worked. In the decade following the road closure "The Bells" became even more popular as record numbers flocked to a protected valley. The impacts of visitation were so daunting that the Forest Service actively discouraged publishing commercial photographs of the Maroon Bells. It was reasoned that too many people would be drawn to the valley, lured by the singular beauty of these iconic peaks, which are still among the most photographed mountains in the world.

The Maroon Bells–Snowmass Wilderness may exemplify Rocky Mountain splendor better than any other Wilderness in Colorado: 100 miles of trails lead over nine passes above 12,000 feet; vast regions lie above the tree line; long glacial valleys point the way to glistening alpine lakes; and six peaks rise above 14,000 feet.

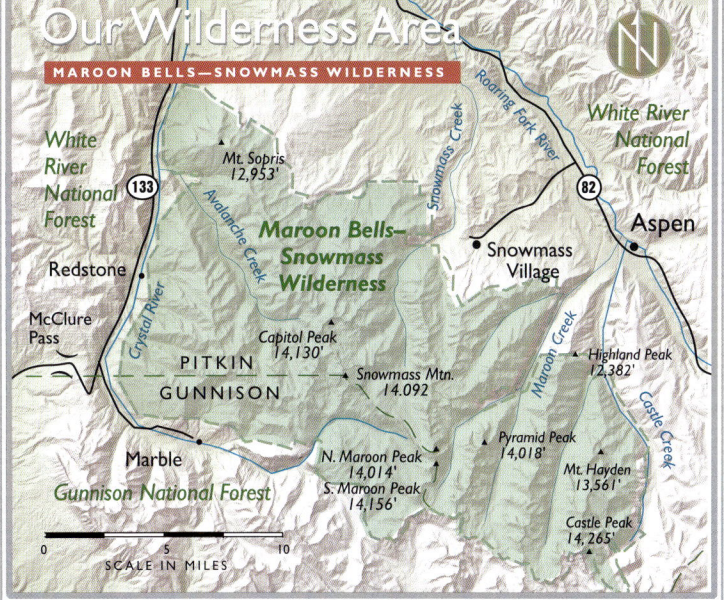

CONSERVATION PHILOSOPHERS

Stuart Mace in 1966

THE CASTLE AND MAROON CREEK Valleys are alluring for their scenic beauty, but also for what they provide in wilderness values. These values have inspired hundreds, perhaps thousands, with appreciation for wild places and a closeness to the creative force of nature. Few visitors see these wild lands without realizing a sense of scale that humbles them.

Conservation philosophy has deep roots in Aspen, but few practitioners have pursued it with the personal commitment and soulful devotion of a staunch wilderness advocate named Stuart Mace, whose home was adjacent to the ghost town of Ashcroft and to whom this book is dedicated. Tenacious, contentious and deeply committed to wild nature, Mace started in the early 1950s spearheading a preservation campaign based on his deep philosophical beliefs. "The mountains cut man down to his proper size," he insisted. "They are a constant reminder of where I belong and where I fit into things."

Bob Lewis, another visionary wilderness advocate, began in the 1970s looking at the Castle and Maroon Creek Valleys as parts of the larger Elk Range, enlarging the conservation challenge. Lewis advocated for a holistic perspective that expanded the scope of land management from individual drainages to the entire range in what he said should become a "bioregion."

Bob Lewis in 2004

Lewis, an Aspen biologist who passed away in 2006, determined that when Pitkin County was split apart from Gunnison County in 1881, an erroneous ecological division occurred. By drawing the county line along the divide ridge of the Elk Range, the Elks were, in effect, bisected. The U.S. Forest Service has followed this division in managing two different forest agencies—the White River and Gunnison National Forests.

Biologically, the Elk Mountains constitute a single bioregion that should be managed as a single entity, maintained Lewis. By parceling the Elk Range into two geographic areas, land managers sometimes fail to address critical linkages. The Elk Range, said Lewis, should be seen as a unified whole: 'The Elk Mountain Bioregion.'

Bob Lewis proposed these boundaries for the Elk Mountain Bioregion.

MELTING A GLACIER

SCIENTISTS Bruce Bryant and Andre Wille have been looking at the Elk Range with a global perspective. Their individual observations have provided evidence that global warming may already be impacting the Elk Range. Their independent studies in the Maroon Creek Valley reveal that a remnant Pleistocene glacier from the last major ice age is visibly shrinking.

Pyramid Peak (14,018 feet) divides East and West Maroon Creeks. Seen from Highway 82, Pyramid is the dominant mountain in the Maroon Creek Valley and one of the most challenging climbs of all the Colorado "Fourteeners." The standard route to the summit involves a steep ascent into a cirque at the base of Pyramid's nearly vertical north face. Sheltered in this shadowed cirque is the melting glacier.

Hikers walking over the floor of this glacial cirque find travel difficult because it is covered by jagged rock. While crossing this rugged obstacle course, one might never guess the true nature of the cirque floor; it spreads across a layer of ancient, flowing ice nearly 100 feet thick. This feature is called a "rock glacier" because the ice is covered by fallen rock accumulated over millennia, all of which moves with the elastic flow of the glacier beneath. The rock glacier, according to observations in the 1960s by geologist Bruce Bryant, has been moving downhill at about 2.2 feet per year.

The "head," or uppermost part of the Pyramid Peak rock glacier, reaches to about 12,000 feet. Its "foot" drops off steeply at 11,400 feet. The layer of rock and soil covering the ice six to ten feet thick acts as an insulating blanket, explaining why this glacial ice has lasted for 10,000 years.

The most striking feature of this rock glacier is a depression that has grown into a large crater with a melt-water pond. On sunny summer days, rocks continually break loose from the supporting ice, which is melting away beneath them.

Glaciers around the world—in the Himalayas, the Andes, Greenland, and the Alps—are receding. On the Quelcaya ice cap in Peru, recent measurements have shown that one glacier has retreated over 500 feet per year. It is predicted that the ice cap atop Africa's Mt. Kilimanjaro will be completely melted by 2020.

In recent years, the warmest global temperatures on record presage dramatic changes, not only in the rock glacier beneath Pyramid Peak, but in the local ski industry. Former Aspen Skiing Company President Pat O'Donnell described the potential impacts from global warming in a letter he wrote to President George W. Bush on June 13, 2001:

Bruce Bryant

"As President/CEO of one of the largest ski resorts in the United States, I am particularly concerned about the potential effects of climate change on our business. The best scientific studies available suggest that resort skiing in Colorado will virtually disappear by the year 2100. This would be catastrophic for Colorado's economy and for the tens of thousands of employees who depend on this industry for their livelihood."

According to records kept by the City of Aspen, average high temperatures in Aspen have climbed significantly in the past three decades. In 1949, there were eighty frost-free days. In 2003, there were over 100 days without frost—a 20 percent increase. In 1997, Aspen's climate swing hit a warming peak with 130 frost-free days.

WHILE A GENERAL WARMING TREND is in keeping with global warming studies conducted at the Goddard Institute for Space Studies (part of NASA) and the U.S. National Oceanic and Atmospheric Administration (NOAA), the dramatic increases recorded in Aspen are more abrupt, possibly due to extreme fluctuations caused by altitude and latitude.

According to John Katzenberger, director of the Aspen Global Change Institute, increasing levels of carbon dioxide and other gases in the atmosphere are raising global temperatures. "Many of us in the climate world think the western U.S. will be warmer, and this means that unless it gets very much wetter, there will likely be less snowpack. Since we don't get much of our precipitation in the summer, if this trend continues we are likely to have drier soils during the growing months of summer. This could drastically alter our upper Roaring Fork Valley life zones and species composition, and it's consistent with the U.S. National Assessment finding that Rocky Mountain alpine meadows are 'highly vulnerable' and are 'likely to disappear entirely in some areas.'"

Glaciers like the one below Pyramid Peak serve as sensitive gauges to significant changes in climate. As the miners of a century ago heeded the canary in the coal mine, it would be prudent to heed the glacier's warning in our own backyard.❖

The exposed ice face in the Pyramid Peak rock glacier reveals annual growth rings.

Fossils in the Maroon Formation discovered by a hiker in 2001, near the Maroon Bells, indicate that about 290 million years ago reptile-like creatures about the size of pigs roamed the area. This four-legged creature, with the head of a turtle and the body of a lizard, is named Diadectes. It existed 70 million years before the dinosaurs, when the Aspen region was part of the supercontinent Pangea.

2 Geology

"This is a grand illustration of an eruptive range, and appears also to be an example of a sudden violent or catastrophic action. The immense faults, complete overturning of thousands of feet of strata, and the great number of peaks, all composed of eruptive rocks, indicate, perhaps, periodical and violent action…"

—FERDINAND HAYDEN

on the Elk Mountain Range

1874

THE GEOLOGICAL STORY of the Elk Mountains was first revealed by the Hayden Survey of 1873-74. Ferdinand Hayden, an agent of the U.S. Geological and Geographical Survey of the Territories, led his legendary "Rover Boys" into the Maroon and Castle Creek Valleys, naming many of the peaks, including one for their leader—Mt. Hayden. The survey team members were among the first white men ever to see the Roaring Fork Valley.

Hayden had no core samples by which to determine the composition of the Elk Mountains and no preceding geological studies to compare. Hayden and his team studied the configuration of mountain peaks, examined rock types, and made the dramatic conclusions that helped to usher in the silver mining boom of the 1880s.

Accompanying Hayden was the renowned photographer William Henry Jackson, whose photographic record of Colorado stands as an artistic and historical milestone. Hayden's chief map maker was Henry Gannett, for whom the tallest peak in Wyoming is named. His geographer was the celebrated James Terry Gardner.

The maps these men produced later attracted hoards of silver miners and brought fame and fortune to Aspen. Hayden's contribution to expansive settlement in the West was considerable and prompted one contemporary to exclaim: "I look upon your survey as an institution of the country."

Understanding the scope and scale of geological events requires an active imagination and practiced visualization. The mind must stretch to comprehend the drama of mountain building, erosion and glacial carving, all of which occurred over hundreds of millions of years. By grasping the early beginnings of the Elk Range, we gain a new perspective on the enormous continuum of time required to form and shape the landscape we see today.

Ferdinand Hayden and his "Rover Boys" at a campsite in the 1870s

COLORADO HISTORICAL SOCIETY

7

THE BIRTH OF THE ELK MOUNTAINS

THE GREATEST INFLUENCE on the geology of the Elk Mountains is plate tectonics—the shifting, pushing, buckling, and clashing of huge, elastic rock masses that together form the crust of the earth. These enormous plates undulate with the earth's deepest forces. All surface features—every river, mountain range, desert, earthquake, volcano—are the result of impulses far below the earth's surface.

The earliest known geologic activity affecting the Aspen area occurred about 1.8 billion years ago when crustal plates collided, one riding over the other, in what is called a "subduction zone."

When these plates ground against one another, they created incredible friction and heat. Rocks were pulled down to depth and melted by contact with hot magma and intense pressure. This forged metamorphic granite, basalt, and gneiss, the foundation rocks of the Elk Range.

Following what geologists call an "unconformity," a mysterious break in the geological timeline of 900 million years, the geological record of the Aspen area resumes about 520 million years ago. Erosion from wind and water had worn down the landscape into low hills and broad valleys. Tectonic activity subsided and the land sunk, allowing a shallow sea to form. The inflow and outflow of the sea over tens of millions of years established deep marine sediments.

About 315 million years ago another collision between two continental plates caused the land to rise in two mountain ranges near Aspen—the Ancestral Front Range to the east and the Ancestral Uncompahgre Range to the southwest. The Aspen area was nestled  between these ranges in a cleft called the Central Colorado Trough, which became a catch basin for eroded sediments washed down from the two ranges.

The Maroon Formation is made up of this eroded material, which was deposited in some places over two miles thick. These sediments contain hematite, an iron-bearing mineral, which is susceptible to rust and turns red, or "maroon," from oxidation. This gives the Maroon Bells their color.

Powerful winds then scoured the region and deposited layers of loess (wind-deposited silt), which form intervals within the Maroon Formation. Sand dunes were formed, which hardened under pressure to become Entrada Sandstone, yellowish or pinkish-gray layers up to 150 feet thick with. Entrada Sandstone is seen at Gold Butte along the Rio Grande Trail, west of Cemetery Lane, and on the ridge of Tiehack, across from Aspen Highlands.

Slow-moving streams began meandering through the Aspen region, laying down deposits that formed bands of varicolored sediments. Layers included gray-purple shales of the Morrison Formation, deep red State Bridge and light red Chinle Formations, seen today as stripes on Red Butte and on the ridge of Tiehack.

During the Cretaceous Period 103 million years ago the Aspen area was covered by an inland sea—the Cretaceous Seaway—which spanned the continent from southern Alaska to the Gulf of Mexico for 30 million years. Buff-colored Dakota Sandstone from this period can be seen on Red Butte and Tiehack Ridge. Clay and silt were compressed into dark gray Mancos Shale, seen at Shale Bluffs on Highway 82 and along the Rio Grande Trail west of Gold Butte.

Between 65 and 70 million years ago, the subduction of the Pacific Plate beneath

the North American Plate accelerated significantly. The resulting crustal stress set the stage for today's Rocky Mountain Range in what geologists label the "Laramide Orogeny." Orogeny, or mountain building, generated large magma intrusions called batholiths. These mushroom-like domes formed deep underground and pushed toward the surface.

The Laramide Orogeny is termed a "revolution" by geologists because it was so dramatic. The floor of the Cretaceous Seaway began to rise at the dizzying speed of five inches per century and it rose at this rate for five million years, draining off the water and gradually exposing thick layers of sedimentary rock. Born in this uplift were the early beginnings of the Sangre de Cristo, Wet Mountain, Sawatch, Gore, Park, Front, and Mosquito Ranges.

A batholith heaved up beneath a thick blanket of sedimentary rock overlaying today's Sawatch Range, east of Aspen, which includes the tallest mountains in Colorado. Thick sedimentary layers buckled, cracked, and then broke loose in a colossal slab of rock—a gravity thrust sheet—that slid west toward Aspen over a bed of shale.

There is nothing in our human experience to compare with the monumental force of the gravity thrust sheet. Over 21,000 feet thick, 50 miles long, and 30 miles wide, this tremendous slab plowed into the nascent Elk Range, overturning rock beds and creating what Ferdinand Hayden called a "geologic jumble".

Faulting and tremendous heat created a subterranean pressure cooker in which super-heated ground water dissolved trace metals and permeated the fault zones with solutions of lead, zinc, copper, gold, and silver. This mineral-laden water was cooled by contact with rock whose chemical properties caused the metals to precipitate into concentrated veins. The Colorado Mineral Belt was established, as was Aspen's rich mining potential.

Renewed tectonic activity produced swells of igneous magma that burst from enormous volcanic vents. Magma beneath the Aspen region rose in bulb-shaped forms called "plutons." Two prominent plutons—the Snowmass Pluton and the White Rock Pluton—elevated thick beds of the Maroon Formation and gave birth to the Elk Mountains 35 million years ago.

Plutons were formed of granodiorite, the raw material for many peaks in the region: Taylor, Star, Keefe, Capitol, and Mt. Sopris. Other mountains, Castle Peak, Mt. Hayden, Hunter Peak, and the lowest visible layers of the Maroon Bells—reveal hornfels, a layer of the Maroon Formation that was baked and hardened to a light gray color by the heat of the igneous plutons.

About three million years later, another magma intrusion injected the region with porphyritic granodiorite, so-called because of its larger crystals (an inch or more across) of feldspar and other minerals. This molten rock invaded fractures in

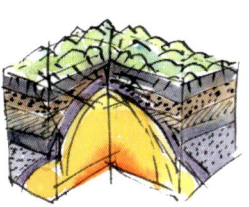

the Maroon Formation, where it is visible as a vertical white stripe, or "dike," on the north ridge of North Maroon Peak and as horizontal stripes, or "sills," along bedding planes on Sievers Mountain above Maroon Lake to the north.

About 32 to 35 million years ago, regional uplifting further elevated the Elk Mountains as subterranean heat

- 200 million years ago in the Aspen area, palm-like trees and huge ferns grew in forest lands inhabited by large reptiles. During this period, the first birds and mammals appeared.

- 70 to 103 million years ago the climate in Aspen was warm and humid, with coastal swamps, sandy beaches, lagoons and estuaries. Dinosaurs roamed the swamplands. Ammonites, extinct cousins of the early nautilus, inhabited the Seaway. Vegetation included pines, ferns and early flowering plants.

- 70 million years ago dinosaurs become extinct after 150 million years of dominance. There was a simultaneous extinction of ammonites, which had existed far longer than the dinosaurs. Geologists surmise that a huge meteorite struck the Earth and created a cloud of dust and ash that blotted out the sun and radically altered the global ecosystem.

conveyed more minerals via superheated water.

The most famous vein from this era is the Montezuma in Montezuma Basin of upper Castle Creek. There were also low-grade deposits of molybdenum and pyrite (iron sulfide) injected in massive deposits throughout the region. The Pitkin Iron Mine deposits above Ashcroft were established at this time.

About 8 to 11 million years ago, further uplifting created extensive drainage patterns that led to the formation of the Colorado River system. Up until now, the region had been semi-arid, with little rainfall. As elevation increased, so did precipitation. River courses became charged with high flows. The Colorado River began carving the Grand Canyon and flowed all the way to the Gulf of Mexico.

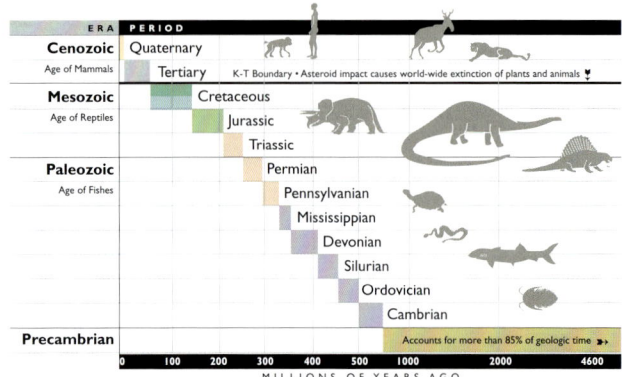

ERA	PERIOD		
Cenozoic Age of Mammals	Quaternary		
	Tertiary	K-T Boundary • Asteroid impact causes world-wide extinction of plants and animals	
Mesozoic Age of Reptiles	Cretaceous		
	Jurassic		
	Triassic		
Paleozoic Age of Fishes	Permian		
	Pennsylvanian		
	Mississippian		
	Devonian		
	Silurian		
	Ordovician		
	Cambrian		
Precambrian		Accounts for more than 85% of geologic time ▶▶	

0   100   200   300   400   500   1000   2000   4600
MILLIONS OF YEARS AGO

A S THE LAND ROSE HIGHER, temperatures cooled and permanent snow-fields grew into glaciers. At least four different periods of glaciation sculpted the landscape around Aspen—carving the arêtes, horns, and cirques that give the Elk Range its rugged beauty. Glacial outwash formed long, flat terraces in the lower valleys while erratic boulders were deposited on some of today's mountaintops by rivers of ice thousands of feet thick.

The City of Aspen occupies a recessional moraine from the Third Valley glaciation, which left erratic boulders on top of Red Mountain. The fourth and last glacial epoch melted off about 10,000 years ago at the end of the Wisconsin Ice Age.

Today, the forces of erosion—gravity, water, wind, and frost-shattering—are active agents constantly working to shape the mountains. Rock fall is common on the steep slopes of U-shaped glacial valleys, streams continue to cut through glacial moraines to form new alluvial deposits, and the freeze-thaw cycle continues to chip away at the strata.

Occasional earthquakes in the Aspen area remind us that tectonic influences are far from over. Rapid river cutting in the Roaring Fork Valley indicates that the mountains around Aspen are still rising and that the mountains we marvel at today will one day be reduced to gravel, sand, and dust, only to be used for building future mountains in some faraway time and place.

Rivers of Ice

GLACIERS CARVE THE LAND

0   2   4   6
SCALE IN MILES

Snowmass Village

Aspen

Hunter Creek Glacier

SMUGGLER MOUNTAIN

▲ Baldy Mtn. 13,155'

Roaring Fork Glacier

Aspen Mountain 11,372'

▲ Buckskin 13 370'

Maroon Creek Glacier

Highland Peak 12,382'

Conundrum Creek Glacier

Castle Creek Glacier

RICHMOND RIDGE

North Maroon Peak 14,014'

▲ Pyramid Peak 14,018'

▲ Hayden Peak 13,561'

New York Peak ▲

South Maroon Peak 14,156'

Cathedral Peak 13,943'

Ashcroft Mountain 12,381'

East River Glacier

Precarious Peak 13,360'

Castle Peak ▲ 14,265'

Taylor River Glacier

White Rock Mountain 13,318'

Pearl Mountain 13,362'

▲ Star Peak 13,521'

• 32 million years ago the climate of the Aspen area changed to cooler and dryer conditions that caused the extinction of many sub-tropical plant species, while heartier species like the ponderosa pine, became dominant.

• 30 million years ago the climate of the Aspen region was that of a semi-arid steppe that supported oak-juniper forests and grasslands. Fauna included horse, camel, rhinoceros and antelope. The region was 3000 to 5000 feet in elevation.

• 10,000 to 12,000 years ago Early Man entered the Roaring Fork Valley after the retreat of the glaciers, as did other plant and animal species.

Water is responsible for carving many of the dramatic topographical features of the Castle and Maroon Creek Valleys, whose water quality and quantity is one of our richest and most sustainable natural resources Aspen enjoys. It is gravity fed, naturally purified, and recharged annually by winter snows. The water flowing in Castle and Maroon Creeks comes largely from snowmelt held in the glacial rock, gravel, sand and silt of subalpine aquifers. When snow melts or rain falls, it trickles through the ground and is filtered by the variegated sediments deposited by glaciers. As the water percolates through these sediments, it pools in aquifers and is gradually discharged to maintain steady streamflows. Even on the coldest months of winter, the aquifers flow.

The waterfall from Minnehaha Gulch (near the Crater Lake campsites) runs full and loud in early summer.

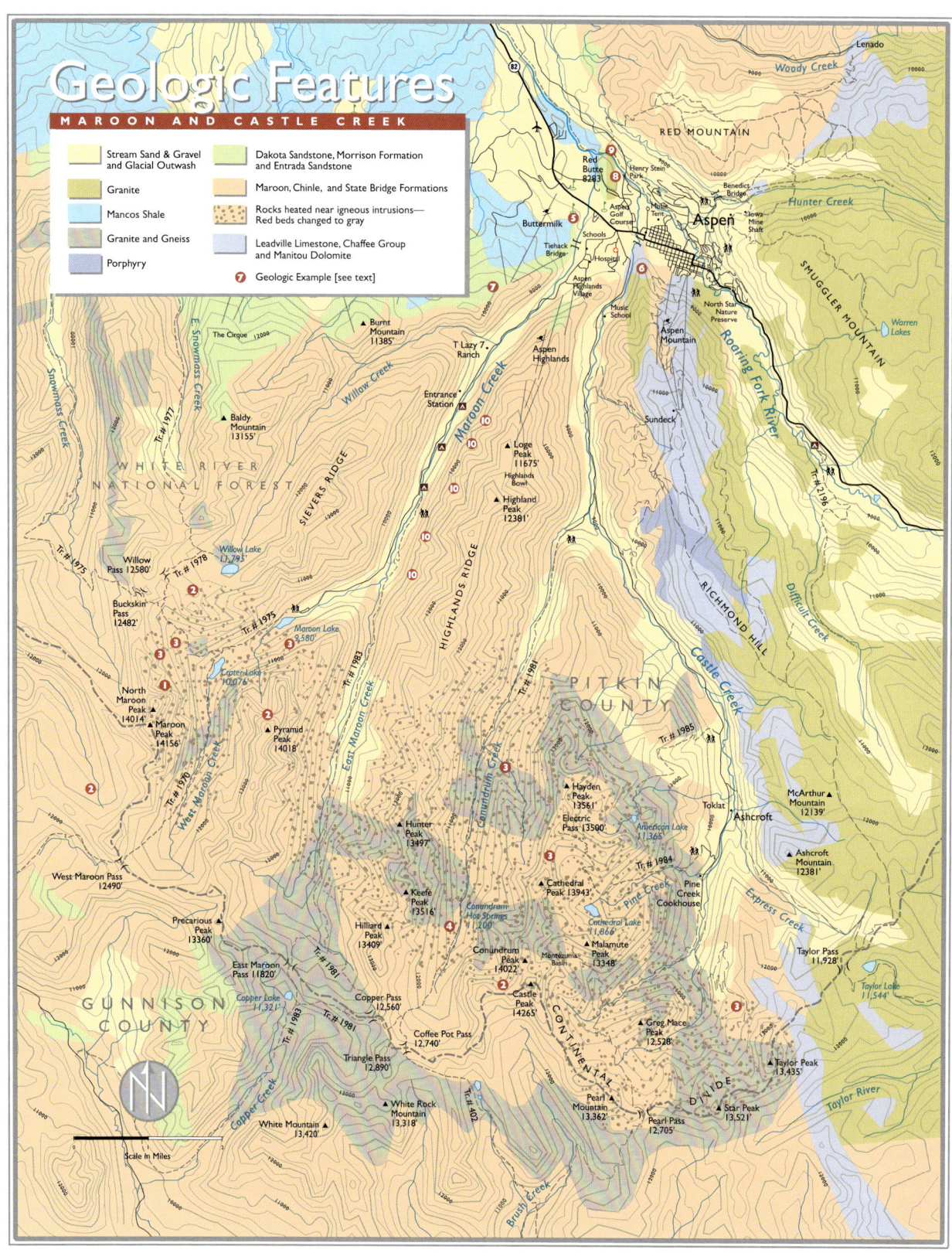

Geologic Features

MAROON AND CASTLE CREEK

Legend:

- Stream Sand & Gravel and Glacial Outwash
- Granite
- Mancos Shale
- Granite and Gneiss
- Porphyry
- Dakota Sandstone, Morrison Formation and Entrada Sandstone
- Maroon, Chinle, and State Bridge Formations
- Rocks heated near igneous intrusions— Red beds changed to gray
- Leadville Limestone, Chaffee Group and Manitou Dolomite
- ⑦ Geologic Example [see text]

Lenado

Woody Creek

82

RED MOUNTAIN

Red Butte 8283' ⑨ ⑧ Henry Stein Park

Benedict Bridge

Hunter Creek

Buttermilk

Aspen Golf Course ⑤ Moth Tent

Aspen ⑥

Schools Hospital

Slowa Mine Shaft

SMUGGLER MOUNTAIN

Warren Lakes

Aspen Highlands Village

Tiehack Bridge

Aspen Highlands

Music School

North Star Nature Preserve

Aspen Mountain

Roaring Fork River

Sundeck

Burnt Mountain 11385'

The Cirque 12400'

T Lazy 7 Ranch

Willow Creek

E Snowmass Creek

Baldy Mountain 13155'

Snowmass Creek

Tr.# 1977

Entrance Station

Maroon Creek

⑩

Loge Peak 11675'

Highlands Bowl

Highland Peak 12381'

WHITE RIVER NATIONAL FOREST

SILVERS RIDGE

⑩ ⑩ ⑩

⑩

⑩

HIGHLANDS RIDGE

Tr.# 1978

Willow Lake 11795'

Willow Pass 12580'

Tr.# 1975

Tr.# 1975

Buckskin Pass 12482'

③ ③

③

Maroon Lake 9580'

RICHMOND HILL

Castle Creek

Difficult Creek

PITKIN COUNTY

Tr.# 1983

North Maroon Peak 14014'

① ②

Crater Lake 10076'

Maroon Peak 14156'

Pyramid Peak 14018'

West Maroon Creek

Tr.# 1970

②

Tr.# 1981

Conundrum Creek

Tr.# 1985

Hayden Peak 13561'

McArthur Mountain 12139'

Toklat

Ashcroft

West Maroon Pass 12490'

Hunter Peak 13497'

③

Electric Pass 13500'

American Lake 11365'

Ashcroft Mountain 12381'

Precarious Peak 13360'

Keefe Peak 13516'

Cathedral Peak 13943'

Pine Creek Cookhouse

Tr.# 1984

Pine Creek

Express Creek

East Maroon Pass 11820'

Hilliard Peak 13409'

Conundrum Hot Springs 11200'

Cathedral Lake 11866'

Malamute Peak 13348'

Taylor Pass 11928'

Copper Lake 11321'

④

Copper Pass 12560'

Conundrum Peak 14022'

Montezuma Basin

Taylor Lake 11544'

GUNNISON COUNTY

②

Castle Peak 14265'

Coffee Pot Pass 12740'

CONTINENTAL DIVIDE

Greg Mace Peak 12528'

③

Taylor Peak 13435'

Copper Creek

Tr.# 1983

Tr.# 1981

Triangle Pass 12890'

Tr.# 402

Pearl Mountain 13362'

Pearl Pass 12705'

Star Peak 13521'

Taylor River

White Rock Mountain 13318'

White Mountain 13420'

N

Scale in Miles

Brush Creek

South Maroon 14,156'
Dike
North Maroon 14,014'
THE SLEEPING SEXTON
Red Rock Maroon Formation
Dike
Gray Rock Maroon Hornfels
Talus
Rock Glacier
Talus
Rock Glacier

THE MAROON BELLS

THE MAROON BELLS, named by the Hayden Survey team (1873-74), are so-called because of their distinctive shape and color. The reddish hue of these twin peaks derives from the rusting of hematite, an iron-rich mineral within the Maroon Formation. Their inverted-bell shape is the result of erosion from weathering and glacial carving.

The grayish coloring of the lower Maroon beds occurred 35 million years ago when intense heat from deep igneous intrusions created hornfels, a metamorphic rock. Higher on the peaks, lighter-colored beds are comprised of coarse-grained sandstone and conglomerates, while dark red beds are made of fine-grained sandstone and siltstone. These varicolored strata give the Bells a layered texture. A thin, vertical, light-colored dike of porphyritic granodiorite cuts through the Maroon beds near the summit of North Maroon Peak. This dike intruded in molten form 29 million years ago.

The Maroon Formation is a sedimentary formation of mud and rock thousands of feet thick that was deposited by powerful rivers that flowed from the Ancestral Rocky Mountains 280 to 310 million years ago. North Maroon Peak stands 14,014 feet above sea level; South Maroon 14,156 feet.

GLACIAL VALLEYS AND SCULPTED RIDGES ❷

GLACIATION of the Aspen area began about two million years ago and ended about 10,000 years ago at the end of the Wisconsin Ice Age. Glaciers carved most of the high mountain scenery in the Maroon and Castle Creek Valleys, sculpting the high peaks and sharp ridges and gouging the U-shape of the Maroon Creek and

HANGING VALLEYS

Hanging valleys were formed by small tributary glaciers. These valleys are seen 1,000 to 1,500 feet above the valley floors and are often marked by steep drops with rushing streams or waterfalls. Hunter Creek Valley is a prominent local example of a hanging valley. ❖

upper Castle Creek Valleys. When glaciers met at a ridgeline from three or more directions, they shaped triangular peaks or "matterhorns" such as Pyramid Peak, Castle Peak, Sievers Mountain, and the Maroon Bells.

ROBERT LEWIS

ROCK GLACIERS

ROCK GLACIERS are remnants of glaciers from the last ice age (10,000 years ago) covered by thick layers of rockfall. There are more than fifty rock glaciers within the upper reaches of the Maroon and Castle Creek Valleys, mostly between 10,800 and 12,000 feet. Rock glaciers are active, moving as fast as eight feet a year. The rock glacier in this picture is viewed from the Pitkin Iron Mine Road above Ashcroft in Cooper Basin at about 11,500 feet.

CONUNDRUM HOT SPRINGS

BECAUSE THE CRUST of the earth in the Rocky Mountain West is warmer at depth than in the eastern and central U.S., there are many hot springs. The heat is produced by igneous rock associated with tectonic friction from 70 million years ago.

Conundrum Hot Spring is the Aspen area's most prominent and popular geothermal feature.

CONUNDRUM HOT SPRINGS	YAMPA HOT SPRINGS GLENWOOD SPRINGS
Volume 38 gallons/min. (54,720 gal./day)	Volume 2,430 gallons/min. (3,500,000 gal./day)
Temperature 93° Fahrenheit	Temperature 122° Fahrenheit
Total dissolved solids 1,910 ppm (parts/million)	Total dissolved solids 20,000 ppm (parts/million)

MORAINES

AS GLACIERS MOVED down the valleys, they brought with them enormous loads of rock that formed moraines. Some of the oldest glacial moraines are now high above the valley floors, indicative of river cutting over the past 10,000 years. Terminal moraines mark the foot of past glaciers and lateral moraines mark their sides. Glaciers also produced stream outwash, which filled valleys with rock, sand and gravel and spread into large plains. The City of Aspen is built on a glacial outwash plain.

SHADOW MOUNTAIN/WEST ASPEN MOUNTAIN

WEST ASPEN MOUNTAIN was originally named by geologist J. E. Spurr in 1898. Fashioned by the Sawatch Uplift and the Castle Creek Fault, and later eroded by weathering and stream cutting, this highly faulted ridge is today known as Shadow Mountain for the shade it casts over Aspen. Two major faults intersect across Shadow Mountain: one bisects the mountain vertically between two exposed rock ridges; the other, the Pride Fault, cuts laterally across the north face.

THE EDGE OF TIEHACK: 190 MILLION YEARS OF GEOLOGY

BEST VIEWED from Aspen Highlands, the exposed rock on the south face of Tiehack displays a cross-section of part of the geological sequence of the Mesozoic Era. At the top of the ridge, yellow Dakota Sandstone caps the gray shale of the Morrison Formation, followed by a golden band of Entrada Sandstone and finally the red layers of the State Bridge Formation.

RED BUTTE

RED BUTTE stands out from a glacial outwash plain just north of Aspen along the Roaring Fork River. A geological anomaly, it is known as an "overturned fold" and was formed 65 million years ago when deep subterranean forces overturned the layered beds. The older formations lie above the younger strata.

From the top of the ridge, the inverted layers are State Bridge Formation, Chinle Formation, Entrada Sandstone, Morrison Formation, Dakota Sandstone, and Mancos Shale.

GOLD BUTTE

GOLD BUTTE, on the north side of the Roaring Fork River across from Red Butte, reveals yellow-tinted Dakota Sandstone, which was deposited as sediment from the Cretaceous Seaway 100 to 103 million years ago. The Rio Grande Trail passes directly beneath Gold Butte, which is frequented by rock climbers.

AVALANCHE is one of the most lethal natural hazards in the Maroon and Castle Creek Valleys. Devastatingly powerful avalanches roar down mountainsides during most winters, wiping out swaths of mature forest and sweeping across roads. In Colorado, during an average winter, more than a dozen deaths are reported due to avalanches, mostly involving backcountry users.

The Maroon Creek Valley is a gauntlet of steep chutes and broad basins that spawn deadly avalanches during major snow cycles. Upvalley from T-Lazy-7 Ranch, avalanche chutes pour down from the left, off Highlands Ridge. The most active avalanche chutes are marked by a lack of trees and the scattered remains of broken tree trunks and branches which have been scoured from the mountainside. Some slides have swept across the valley floor and covered the Maroon Creek Road with many feet of snow.

Large slide zones in the Castle Creek Valley begin just above Pine Creek and occur at regular intervals on the Pearl Pass Road. The Express Creek Road is also crossed by major slides, as is the Conundrum Creek Valley, which is practically impassable during the winter because of avalanche risk.

Avalanches are caused by the build-up of snow on steep slopes where the weight of the snow conspires with variations in temperature to alter the structure of the ice crystals within the snowpack, causing stresses and weaknesses. When snow layers lose stability, usually as a result of added weight, the snowpack may crack in a fault line or shatter altogether, releasing tons of snow in a roaring cascade rushing down at speeds of over 100 mph. ❖

OPPOSITE PAGE TOP
The aftermath of a major avalanche in Maroon Bowl in 2003 revealed a long fracture line below the ridge and tumbled debris throughout the bowl.

OPPOSITE PAGE BELOW
Avalanche debris fills West Maroon Creek well into late summer below steep slopes on South Maroon Peak.

THIS PAGE In the mid-1990s, an avalanche roared down into the Castle Creek Valley above Pine Creek in the late 1980s and killed Lynn Dur, a cross-country skier. These dramatic images of a cataclysmic, naturally released avalanche were captured by a tourist riding to the Pine Creek Cookhouse on a horse-drawn sleigh. The slide ran across the valley, then continued upvalley into Cooper Creek.

COURTESY JOHN WILCOX

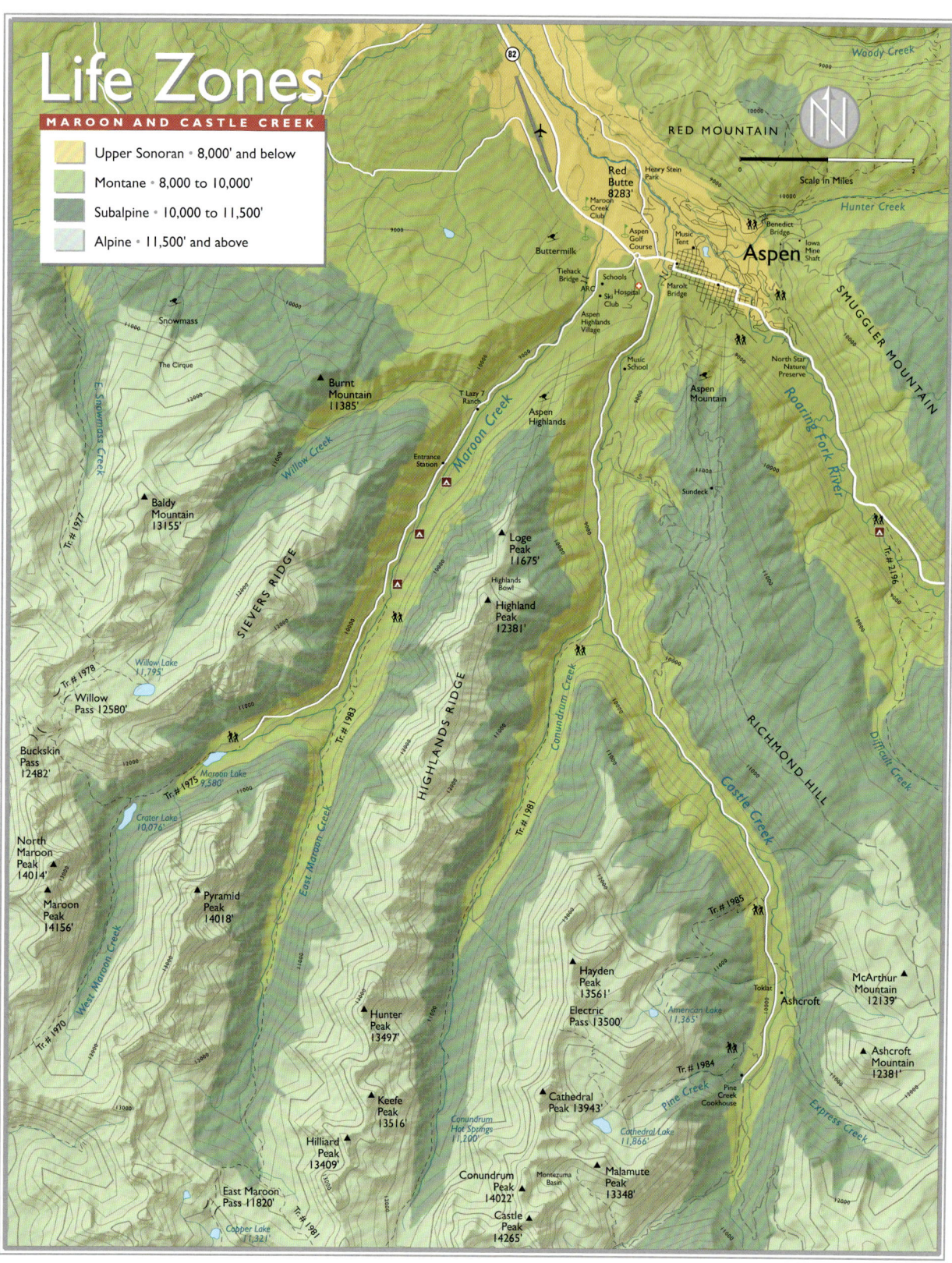

Life Zones

MAROON AND CASTLE CREEK

- Upper Sonoran • 8,000' and below
- Montane • 8,000 to 10,000'
- Subalpine • 10,000 to 11,500'
- Alpine • 11,500' and above

Scale in Miles

RED MOUNTAIN

Woody Creek

Hunter Creek

Red Butte 8283'

Henry Stein Park

Maroon Creek Club

Aspen Golf Course

Music Tent

Aspen

Benedict Bridge

Iowa Mine Shaft

Buttermilk

Tiehack Bridge

ARC

Schools

Ski Club

Hospital

Marolt Bridge

SMUGGLER MOUNTAIN

Aspen Highlands Village

Music School

North Star Nature Preserve

Aspen Mountain

Roaring Fork River

Snowmass

The Cirque

Burnt Mountain 11385'

T Lazy 7 Ranch

Aspen Highlands

Entrance Station

Maroon Creek

Sundeck

Baldy Mountain 13155'

Willow Creek

Loge Peak 11675'

Highlands Bowl

Highland Peak 12381'

SIEVERS RIDGE

Tr. # 1977

Willow Lake 11,795'

HIGHLANDS RIDGE

Conundrum Creek

Tr. # 1978

Willow Pass 12580'

Tr. # 1983

RICHMOND HILL

Difficult Creek

Buckskin Pass 12482'

Maroon Lake 9,580'

Tr. # 1975

Castle Creek

Tr. # 2196

North Maroon Peak 14014'

Crater Lake 10,076'

East Maroon Creek

Tr. # 1985

Maroon Peak 14156'

Pyramid Peak 14018'

Hayden Peak 13561'

American Lake 11,365'

Toklat

Ashcroft

McArthur Mountain 12139'

West Maroon Creek

Electric Pass 13500'

Tr. # 1970

Hunter Peak 13497'

Express Creek

Ashcroft Mountain 12381'

Tr. # 1984

Pine Creek Cookhouse

Keefe Peak 13516'

Pine Creek

Cathedral Peak 13943'

Conundrum Hot Springs 11,200'

Cathedral Lake 11,866'

Hilliard Peak 13409'

Montezuma Basin

Malamute Peak 13348'

East Maroon Pass 11820'

Conundrum Peak 14022'

Tr. # 1981

Castle Peak 14265'

Copper Lake 11,321'

3 Life Zones and Ecosystems

N THE CASTLE AND MAROON Creek Valleys there are four life zones and seven ecosystems, each of which is defined by vegetation types and elevation. Each life zone and ecosystem harbors life forms that are adapted to particular niches.

UPPER SONORAN LIFE ZONE (8,000 feet and below)

THE UPPER SONORAN LIFE ZONE encompasses the vicinity of the Highway 82 roundabout and includes the Moore Open Space parcel, the Marolt Barn historic site, Meadowood subdivision and the lower slopes of Tiehack. Named for the Sonoran Desert of northwestern Mexico, this zone is arid and produces desert-like grasslands and shrublands proliferating with sagebrush, cactus, Gambel oak, chokecherry, serviceberry and dryland grasses.

MONTANE LIFE ZONE (8,000–10,000 feet)

THE MOIST, COOL, UPLAND SLOPES of the Montane life zone are often characterized by narrowleaf cottonwood, willow, alder and lush aspen groves. Common Montane flowers are columbine, meadow rue, aster, Indian paintbrush, monkshood, and cow parsnip. Shrubs include kinnikinnick, raspberry, thimbleberry, mountain ash, mountain maple, and several willow species. The City of Aspen is located at the lower edge of the Montane Life Zone.

SUBALPINE LIFE ZONE (10,000–11,500 feet)

THE SUBALPINE LIFE ZONE reaches from the Upper Montane boundary to timberline, encompassing steep mountainsides, open meadows, stands of spruce-fir climax forest and aspen groves. Deep snows common to this life zone provides critical water storage for year-round stream flows in aquifers that hold and gradually release water purified by percolation through glacial deposits.

ALPINE LIFE ZONE (11,500 feet and above)

THE ALPINE LIFE ZONE is a treeless, high altitude landscape of rock and tundra. Numerous hiking trails in both valleys climb into the Alpine zone, as do the Pearl Pass and Taylor Pass roads. The Alpine life zone is the most severe of the life zones. Bare rock and thin soil support low-lying plants with specially-adaptive qualities. More than 100 alpine tundra plants grow where trees cannot survive.

THE GRASSLAND ECOSYSTEM (8,000 feet and below)

Mountain Bluebird

THE GRASSLAND ECOSYSTEM of the Upper Sonoran life zone is defined by patches of wild grasses, sagebrush, serviceberry, chokecherry, and Gambel oak. These species identify an ecosystem that is desert-like and arid.

The Moore Open Space parcel, located along the north side of the Maroon Creek Road between the Highway 82 roundabout and Iselin Park, is a prime example of a pristine Grassland ecosystem of the Upper Sonoran life zone. It provides habitat to coyotes, foxes, mule deer, weasels, and numerous small mammals.

About three miles up the Maroon Creek Road from the Highway 82 roundabout, just after the road crosses the creek, a large meadow appears on the right. This Grassland ecosystem contains blue flax, yarrow, scarlet paint-brush, and shrubby cinquefoil. In the spring-time, this meadow, which is part of the T-Lazy-7 Ranch, is a carpet of dandelions (see pages 88-89).

Mountain Cottontail

Beyond the T-Lazy-7 Ranch, grasslands are seen in avalanche run-out zones where trees have been repeatedly scoured away. Further up the Maroon Creek Valley another grassland lies near the confluence of East and West Maroon Creeks in the shadow of Pyramid Peak. Most of these grasslands are former cattle and sheep pastures that are slowly regaining native plant populations.

A large grassland is found in upper Castle Creek Valley, stretching from Toklat to the end of the paved road at Pine Creek. This grassland includes the town site of Ashcroft. Mammals of the Ashcroft grassland include the Wyoming ground squirrel, meadow vole, striped ground squirrel, pocket gopher, meadow mouse, deer mouse, red fox, bobcat and coyote. Raptors include red-tailed hawk, sparrow hawk, and great horned owl.

American Kestrel

yarrow

Western Meadowlark

Serviceberry

Blue Flax

Gambel Oak bark

Gambel Oak leaf

Black-billed Magpie

Raven

ROBIN HENRY

Scrub Jay

Deer Mouse

Scarlet Gila

Ponderosa pine cone

Ponderosa pine needles

Shrubby Cinquefoil

Meadow Vole

Ponderosa pine bark

Chokecherry

American Robin

Wyoming Ground Squirrel

Coyote

Pasqueflower

Scarlet Paintbrush

Sego Lily or Mariposa Lily

THE ASPEN FOREST ECOSYSTEM (8,000–11,000 feet)

ASPEN TREES are the most common deciduous tree in the Montane and Subalpine life zones. Aspen trees are regarded as secondary successional species because they grow in areas that have been cleared by fires or avalanches.

Light is able to reach the ground through the quaking aspen canopy and the soils are richer due to the annual falling of aspen leaves and branches, which decompose into a thick, composted soil layer.

Long-tail Weasel

Common flowers are Colorado columbine (the state flower), meadow rue, asters, Indian paintbrush, monkshood, and lupine. In the Subalpine life zones, aspen forests contain scarlet paintbrush, fireweed, larkspur, green gentian, and wild geranium.

An aspen forest is composed of one or more stands, made up of clones. A "mother" tree sends out runners from which individual trees sprout. These clones are all related and are of the same sex. This accounts for variegated fall foliage as clones often turn different colors at different times. One clone may be yellow, while the next is orange or red, all within the same forest.

Because these clones originated from a single tree and one original seed, they share the same DNA. The cells of each tree are therefore genetically identical. Typically, all of the trees in a particular aspen clone are part of one single organism. A particularly large aspen clone in Utah covers hundreds of acres and is said to be the world's single largest known living organism.

Because young aspens are flexible and resilient, avalanches roll over them without destroying young trees. With age, however, the trees become less flexible and more prone to avalanche damage. Aspen trees are a source of food for elk, which strip the bark to eat the green under layer. Beavers cut down aspens for their dams and store aspen branches for winter food in the mud at the bottom of their ponds.

Bobcat

Rufous Hummingbird

Geranium

Parry's Gentian

Fritillary

Red Fox

ANNADAY HISER

Aspen bark

Great Horned Owl

ROBIN HENRY

Aspen leaf

Fireweed

Harebell

Cow Parsnip

Common Flicker

RICHARD HOLMES

LODGEPOLE PINE FOREST
(9,000 feet and lower)

T YPICALLY, lodgepole pines inhabit the dry slopes of the Montane life zone and can sometimes be found growing side by side with spruce and fir. Because of its tall, straight trunk, the lodgepole pine was frequently used by Native Americans for teepees or lodges, hence the name.

Because sunlight does not easily penetrate to the ground in a lodgepole pine forest, this ecosystem rarely supports an understory of flowering plants, but is instead carpeted with pine needles and cones. The cones of the lodgepole are tightly compressed and often require the heat of a forest fire to open and release their seeds. The lodgepole pine is successful in colonizing burned-over areas. ❖

Lodgepole pine
bark, needles, and cone

Black Bear in an Aspen yard

CATHERINE GARLAND

Mule Deer

Black-capped Chickadee

THE RIPARIAN ECOSYSTEM (8,000–11,500 feet)

Spotted Sand Piper

THE RIPARIAN ECOSYSTEM occupies moist valley bottoms, where the forest meets the river and water-loving vegetation thrives. When vegetation decays it contributes organic matter to the entire aquatic food chain.

The Montane riparian ecosystem supports kinnikinnick, raspberry, thimbleberry, mountain ash, mountain maple, several willow species, narrowleaf cottonwood, blue spruce and alder. In the higher life zones, Engelmann spruce and subalpine fir are interspersed with willows and alders. Riparian flowers include Parry's primrose, Indian paintbrush, monkeyflower, marsh marigold, Queen's crown, and bog orchid.

At about 11,200 feet, in the lower Krummholz Ecosystem, the bog birch joins the willow in becoming the dominant riparian species. The edges of mid-elevation subalpine pools support sedges and rushes.

Muskrat

Alder leaf

Montane riparian ecosystems are rich in wildlife due to the abundance of water, flowering plants, and fruit-bearing shrubs. Beavers, muskrats, mule deer, raccoons, water shrews, and meadow voles are common. Birds include ducks, geese, the American dipper, flycatchers, and the belted kingfisher.

Beavers work in the Castle and Maroon Creek Valleys damming the creeks and inhibiting the free flow of water. When the water is slowed, sediments settle and gradually form benches or steps in the Riparian Ecosystem, which are colonized by other species. Beaver ponds become habitat for fish, frogs, western garter snakes, muskrats, water shrews, herons, sand-pipers, and ducks. The American dipper, or water ouzel, prefers rapids and cascades for feeding; it nests under overhanging cliffs above the river or beneath bridges.

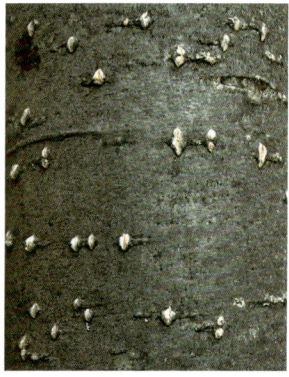
Alder bark

Although riparian ecosystems compose only a fraction of the land area, the majority of all the mammalian inhabitants of the Maroon and Castle Creek valleys depend on them. This makes their preservation essential and their study fascinating.

Western Tiger Swallowtail

Alder cones

False Hellebore

Mallard Duck (male)

Stonefly larva

Brook Trout

Redwing Blackbird

Caddisfly larvae

Belted Kingfisher

Queens Crown

Narrow-leaf Cottonwood bark

Parry's Primrose

Dragonfly

Marsh Marigold

Narrow-leaf Cottonwood leaf

American Dipper

Colorado Columbine

Racoon

Beaver

Monkeyflower

THE CONIFEROUS FOREST ECOSYSTEM (8,000–11,500 feet)

Pine Siskin

TWO SPECIES OF CONIFERS form the major part of this ecosystem— Engelmann spruce and subalpine fir. The trees look similar at a distance, but on closer inspection reveal distinguishing characteristics.

The needles of the Engelmann spruce are sharp and stiff, while the needles of the subalpine fir are blunt and soft. The bark of the spruce is grayish brown and scaly. The bark of the fir is solid gray and perforated with pitch blisters.

Subalpine Fir needles

The cones of the Engelmann spruce are about two inches long and hang down from the branches. They fall to the ground and are found in piles beneath the trees. The pine squirrel harvests spruce cones for their seeds by snipping the cones with their sharp teeth. The falling cone scales often accumulate in piles, or middens, beneath trees.

Subalpine Fir bark

The cones of the subalpine fir are about two inches long and 1.5 inches in diameter. They are green at first and turn brown when they mature. Unlike spruce cones, they point upward. In the fall, their cone scales fall to the ground as seeds are released and carried by the wind. This leaves the bare axis of the cone pointing straight up from the branch.

Spruce/fir forests can be seen on either side of the Castle and Maroon Creek Roads where they cloak the mountainsides in thick, dark greenery. Sit quietly in a spruce/fir forest and you may hear the chatter of a pine squirrel or hear the cones dropping to the forest floor as the squirrels harvest them. Animal life includes yellow-bellied marmot, least chipmunk, golden mantled ground squirrel, and black bear, all of which hibernate in the winter months.

Gray Jay

Coralroot Orchid

Cone Midden

Yellow-bellied Marmot

Engelmann Spruce bark

Mountain Chickadee

Golden Mantle Ground Squirrel

Subalpine Arnica

Engelmann Spruce cone

Pine Squirrel

Thimbleberry

Porcupine

Engelmann Spruce needles

Clark's Nutcracker

Red Columbine

Mountain Lion

Scarlet Paintbrush

Elk

Calypso Orchid

Blue Grouse

THE TUNDRA ECOSYSTEM (11,500 feet and up)

Globeflower

THE WORD TUNDRA has ancient origins and is closest to the Lapp word *tundar*, meaning "hill." Tundra defines subarctic regions that exist in far northern latitudes and which are mirrored in the high Rocky Mountains.

Here extreme winter conditions—low temperatures, high winds, and low humidity—create a harsh environment. Tundra is without frost for only six weeks a year. Winds can exceed 100 mph and most precipitation is in the form of snow. Tundra is delicate and easily marred by human activity: scars last for decades.

White-crowned Sparrow

Adaptability in the tundra dictates that plants hug the ground, so most flowering plants are stunted. Many species are "cushion plants" less than one inch tall. One species of hearty willow reaches only an inch high. Other shrubby willows grow in watercourses and on the lee sides of exposed, open ridges, where deep snow protects their buds.

Hall's Penstemon

Brilliantly colored but usually minute flowers live in tundra meadows with sedges and grasses. Colorful lichens and green mosses cover rocks. Nearly all tundra plant species are perennials, which grow from the same rootstock every year. Starting from seed is practically impossible in the harsh climate and short growing season.

The flowers of tundra plants are usually small, as are their leaves, which are often covered with wax or hairs to prevent dehydration in high winds. Tundra plants reproduce on a rapidly accelerated schedule compared to plants at lower altitude, because they must compensate for a brief growing season.

Stonecrop

Tundra wetlands are dominated by colonies of marsh marigolds and globeflowers. Widespread alpine flowers on drier ground include alpine forget-me-nots, alpine lilies, moss campion, alpine sunflower, sky pilot, snowball saxifrage, and alpine avens. Only four species of birds nest in the tundra: rosy finch, pipit, horned lark, and ptarmigan. ❖

Pika

Bistort

Alpine Sunflower

Mountain Goat

Moss Campion

Alpine Lily

Alpine Willow

Spotted Saxifrage

Horned Lark

CHARLES MELTON

KRUMMHOLZ ECOSYSTEM
(11,200 - 11,500 feet)

THE NAME KRUMMHOLZ is derived from the German "crooked wood," which aptly describes the stunted, irregular trees in this region. Trees of the Krummholz are easily recognized "flagged trees" whose windward branches are heavily pruned by prevailing winds and whose leeward branches are thickly feathered and resemble flags. The Krummholz ecosystem is the interface between the Subalpine and Alpine life zones, and defines an approximately 300-vertical-foot swath at the edge of timberline.

The only trees in the Krummholz ecosystem are Engelmann spruce and subalpine fir. Engelmann spruce, which normally grow tall and conical, are either whipped into flagged trees or beaten into dense, crawling mats called "cushion trees." Subalpine fir are stunted, but with no change to their conical, symmetrical shape. ❖

Willow

Mountain Sheep

Sky Pilot

Ptarmigan

Conundrum Hot Springs first attracted the Utes and later a growing legion of hikers and horseback riders. This small log cabin was built as a shelter. Forest Ranger Len Shoemaker (standing on left) took this photo in the mid-1920s. Shoemaker maintained trails that made the hot springs accessible to visitors.

4 Into the Land of the Utes

CROSSING THE HIGH PASSES

COLORADO HISTORICAL SOCIETY

Ute Indian chief Ouray and wife Chipeta

THE CASTLE AND MAROON CREEK Valleys were a summer home to White River Ute Indians, one of seven Ute sub-groups. The Utes derived from the Fremont people, who are thought to have come from Archaic nomads. Their distant ancestors, the Paleo-Indians, crossed the Bering Straights 10,000 to 12,000 years ago. Bands of Utes hunted and gathered in the Roaring Fork Valley during summer. They wintered at lower elevations at the edge of the Colorado Plateau near present day Montrose.

By the mid-1800s, land-grabbing treaties had pushed the Utes into ever smaller corners of the state. The Utes had few rights and no way to fight the onslaught of settlement. With little recourse, they saw their sacred lands confiscated. This was the Cain and Abel story told against the backdrop of Manifest Destiny, where the hunter-gatherer was systematically eradicated by the farmer, the townsite planner, the railroad builder, and the mining speculator.

Under the Brunot Treaty of 1868, the Utes lost legal rights to the upper Roaring Fork Valley. Soon prospectors cast eager eyes west of the Continental Divide from Leadville and over the Elk Range from the "Gunnison Country." Exploration was permitted by the U.S. government, but townsites and mining claims were prohibited until an official survey was completed. Ferdinand Hayden performed that survey in 1873-74.

The Castle and Maroon Creek Valleys played a central role in the early settlement of Aspen. The earliest explorers and prospectors came to the upper Roaring Fork Valley over high passes in both valleys. Even before Ferdinand Hayden's survey party had entered the region, men had traveled into the area looking for gold and silver. Hayden's party discovered a coffeepot on top of Coffeepot Pass, which indicated an earlier crossing and gave the pass its name.

The high passes—Taylor, Coffeepot, Triangle, East Maroon, West Maroon, and Independence—were used by early pioneers because, until 1881, the lower Roaring Fork Valley west of the 107th meridian belonged to the Ute Indians, some of whom were hostile. A further deterrent to access via the lower Roaring Fork Valley was the nearly impassable gorge of Glenwood Canyon. The headwaters of the upper Roaring Fork and its tributaries provided the safest access, difficult though it was, to the silver riches of Aspen.

By the mid-1870s, the Leadville silver boom had run its course. Since Aspen was only one mountain range further west, incursions were made. Billy Belden ventured west from Leadville over Hunter's Pass, for which Hunter Creek is named, and prospected the Great Divide. On July 4, 1879, he found a gold strike and named his claim Independence (the namesake of Independence Pass). Soon thereafter, another party of Leadville prospectors—Charles Bennett, Almon Fellows,

Walter S. Clark, and S. E. Hopkins—followed Belden, pushed past his claim and struggled down the Roaring Fork Valley.

A week before Belden filed his claim yet another party of prospectors—Phillip Pratt, Smith Steele, and William Hopkins—crossed over Triangle Pass into the Conundrum Creek Valley from the Gunnison Country. Simultaneously, Edward Fuller and Con Albright crossed over East Maroon Pass from the mining town of Gothic at about the same time. Fuller and Albright became trapped in a forest fire that destroyed most of their gear and from which they barely escaped with their lives. Bereft of supplies, they met up with Pratt, Steele, and Hopkins, who re-supplied them somewhere in the Maroon Creek Valley drainages.

This illustration from the 'Ashcroft Journal' in the late 1800s showed the mood of settlers toward the soon-to-be displaced natives.

I N JULY 1879, the three parties convened by chance near Ute Spring at the base of Aspen Mountain, near today's Gant Condominiums on Ute Avenue. Gathered around a campfire, the prospectors agreed to protect each other and their unproved mining claims. This tacit agreement was perhaps the first political exercise in Aspen.

The Utes were still present, but to the miners they represented just another natural obstacle to be overcome. There was no sympathy for the Utes once the ore carts were rolling, the smelters were producing, and the inertia of industry was set into motion. The entitlements of the white man were interpreted as divine providence, where the white man's God granted a stronger race dominion over a weaker one.

Ethics aside, the pioneers of Aspen were heroic. Their decisive actions and risk-laden adventures forged communities in the wilderness. They stopped at nothing—neither privation nor personal risk—to seek their fortunes on the American frontier. The inertia of settlement in Aspen was halted only briefly by the Meeker Massacre of 1879, a violent Ute uprising.

The fury of the whites was piqued by the massacre, prompting Governor Frederick Pitkin to decree: "The Utes Must Go!" He announced: "My idea is that, unless removed by the government, they [the Ute Indians] must necessarily be exterminated. The state would be willing to settle the Indian trouble at its own expense. The advantages that would be accrued from the throwing open of 12 million acres of land to miners and settlers would more than compensate all expenses incurred."

By 1880, the early pioneers of Aspen called their settlement "Ute City" in ironic deference to those they had displaced. These hearty, opportunistic emigrants pitched tents and built log cabins. They asserted the authority of the "Great White Father" and justified their claim to the land.

Pitkin's decree became policy in 1881, when the Utes were marched under military escort onto three separate reservations. The Ute nation was forever divided. The last Indian nation to offer armed resistance in the lower 48 states was banished from their homeland.

With the Utes out of the way, the momentum grew rapidly. Soon, Aspen and environs was crawling with prospectors. The town was platted in 1881, when Ute City was officially changed to Aspen. ❖

CROSSING TAYLOR PASS IN 1880

ASPEN HISTORICAL SOCIETY

David R. C. Brown

TAYLOR PASS, at the head of Express Creek, a tributary to Castle Creek, was the first major thoroughfare into Aspen for wagons. Independence Pass was the most direct route from the Arkansas Valley, but it was not suitable for wagons until late 1881. The first emigrant wagons crested the 11,929-foot divide over Taylor Pass in the summer of 1880.

A first-person account of crossing Taylor Pass, written by David R. C. Brown, describes the rigors of mountain travel in Aspen's earliest days. Brown, whose children, grandchildren, and great-grandchildren live in the Roaring Fork Valley today, pioneered the crossing with Henry P. "Grandpap" Cowenhoven, his wife Margaret, and their daughter Katherine, who later became Brown's wife (in July 1880). As with most pioneers of that time, the Brown/Cowenhoven party had already come a long way before venturing over the Elk Range into the Roaring Fork Valley.

Cowenhoven had emigrated from East Prussia and Brown came to the U.S. in 1877 from New Castle, New Brunswick, Canada. Their journey to Aspen began after Cowenhoven sold his general store in the mining town of Black Hawk, Colorado, where Brown had served as his clerk. Looking for new opportunities once the fortunes of Blackhawk had begun to decline, these venture capitalists entrusted their collective future to rumors of vast silver riches in an unknown valley.

In order to reach Taylor Pass, they drove wagons through South Park to Fairplay, crossed 13,000-foot Mosquito Pass to Leadville, then crossed Cottonwood Pass into Taylor Park. The following is an excerpt from Brown's handwritten manuscript, "My Trip from Blackhawk to Aspen."

WE MADE THE FOOT of the range and found a road camp of eight or ten men working on a road. They said we couldn't make the top with our wagons and we might as well camp, but, nothing daunted, we continued and in a day and a half made the top and then our troubles began.

We had to keep to the tip of the ridge above timberline where we could see the tracks of McFarlane's wagon, and at the head of the south fork of Castle Creek [Express Creek] we took down an awfully steep strip, but the ground being soft we made it. Just at timberline the head wagon with Mr. Cowenhoven and his family drove into a bog and we had quite a time getting the mules out. We made camp and next morning took everything out and made the wagon as light as possible, but after working half a day we were just in the same fix as when we started. I finally said, "I can get it out by using a Spanish windlass," and they never had heard of such a thing. We got the ropes up and we got them in shape, put a rope on the end of the tongue and put the mules to it and in an hour, with the help of Price and the windlass, had the front wheels up on the sod. The mules then pulled the wagon out. The other wagon we took around the bog and after that I drove the lead wagon.

In the morning we loaded up and started again. In about a mile, or less, we came to a drop of about 40 feet–practically a straight bluff. We unloaded the wagons, packed the stuff around and got it all down. We then lowered the wagons by ropes and got everything down in good shape. We continued for several days in much the same manner, unloading the wagons and lowering them when we came to impassable places. This made our progress very slow, in fact it took us two weeks to go ten miles. Finally we came to a very sidling side hill, but by slow and careful driving we made slow progress and, at last, I saw tents and people in Ashcroft, but where we camped we were at least 1,000 feet above the valley.

Next morning I went down to Ashcroft and hired two men and they came up with axes and a chain for rough rocks. They cut down trees, that is they cut down the trees at the roots and used them by attaching the tree to the axle and the roots dug into the soil. I drove and the two men, with ropes, kept the wagon from tipping over and we made the valley about 3 p.m. All the talk was about Ashcroft as they thought they had the greatest mines in Colorado, but we left for Aspen next morning and it took us all that day to make eight miles, which brought us within four miles of Aspen. In the morning we broke camp about 10 o'clock and at 2:30 p.m., in July 1880, we had our first view of the Roaring Fork Valley and, to me, it was the most wonderful sight I ever beheld.

We drove up to what they called Ute [City] where there was a big spring and where most everyone was camped. About 4 p.m. our old fiend [sic], Bill Blodgett, put in appearance and the next morning he sold Mr. Cowenhoven a lot for $75.00 on which a few days after he (Mr. Cowenhoven) commenced a log building for a store and also a building for a home. [These were the first wooden structures built in Aspen.] ❖

The ghost town of Ashcroft stands humbly before peaks of the Elk Range above Cooper Basin.

In recent years, the Elk Mountain Lodge in Ashcroft has hosted corporate events and elaborate weddings, reflecting the most recent "boom" in upscale tourism. The lodge is now a private residence.

5 Ashcroft

THE HISTORY OF A GHOST TOWN

It was word of mouth that attracted silver-crazed miners, prospectors, speculators, freighters, whores, hoteliers, sawyers, and every brand of frontier opportunist to Ashcroft.

VISITORS TO ASHCROFT see only a dim shadow of its former glory. Scattered cabins and two rows of dark, weathered log buildings stand in a somber duel of survival, as if to see which one can longer stand the ravages of time and climate at 9,000 feet. Windows are sagging and elliptical. Fascia has been stripped off by winter gales. Grass and wildflowers grow high on Main Street. Other forgotten structures have succumbed to gravity and decay and lay as wreckage strewn over wildflower meadows or crushed beneath heavy snowfall.

The only constant in Ashcroft is the towering Elk Range, which has withstood the advances of those who once sought their riches, those whose bones now enrich the soil. Where are their robust voices and their grand dreams? They are heard in the wind, in the ceaseless rush of the creek. They are remembered among the dilapidated structures that creak and rattle in a storm.

Ashcroft once eclipsed Aspen as the "Silver City" of the Elk Mountains. During seven years of fevered activity, from 1881 to 1887, Ashcroft was a boomer's paradise. A stroll through the vacant, weed-grown streets and decrepit buildings today shows the finality of a boom gone bust.

ASHCROFT GOT ITS START in 1879 when a group of prospectors ventured over the "Taylor Range" from the Gunnison Country and explored the headwaters of Castle Creek. Two of these men, Amos Kindt and Charles Culver, remained behind that autumn. Little is known about Culver, but Kindt was reputed to have been a buffalo hunter on the Texas plains and was known as "Panhandle" Kindt. He and Culver survived the long, cold winter and were joined in the spring of 1880 by fellow adventurer William Coxhead, who came from Leadville. Coxhead formed a partnership with Culver and together they decided to make a permanent camp at the confluence of Express Creek and Castle Creek. They called the town "Chloride," and later, "Castle Forks."

Kindt fell out of the partnership, so Culver began acquiring titles to land while Coxhead walked back to Leadville for supplies. Culver, a fierce booster, accosted miners on their way over Pearl and Taylor Passes. Culver was so adamant about promoting Ashcroft that he earned the nickname "Crazy Culver." Crazy or not, Culver had nearly twenty-three men in camp by the time Coxhead returned.

On June 17, 1880, the prospectors of Ashcroft formed the "Miner's Protective Association" and elected Culver president. A townsite was soon organized and surveyed by Harry Wilkes, who divided the broad meadow along Castle Creek into 840 lots, six streets and six avenues. T. E. Ashcraft, a prominent miner and town builder who had earlier founded the nearby town of Highland, came to the camp and apparently made an impression on the Association. The town was renamed Ashcroft, either for him or for the English interpretation of the aspen tree as "ash" and the open meadow as "croft."

By 1881, the two primary streets, Castle and Main, were lined with stores and saloons, some framed with false fronts, others housed in tents. Soon there were

ABOVE **The early days of Ashcroft show a booming town. The denuded slopes of Mt. Hayden were cut for lumber, and the forests we see today have grown up since the town was largely abandoned in the late 1890s.**

RIGHT **Fourth of July, 1894, was celebrated by the hearty residents of Ashcroft.**

36 ASPEN'S RUGGED SPLENDOR

hotels—the Ferrell, the Riverside, and the Fifth Avenue. Lawbreakers were incarcerated in a crude jail. There was no cemetery, so grave sites were scattered in the wilderness where inscriptions, if any, intoned the plight of long forgotten adventurers: "HERE LIES DICK REYNOLDS. DIED ONLY GOD KNOWS HOW."

As Ashcroft grew, Culver built a boarding house and began working four mining claims—Captain Kidd, Eureka, Miner's Delight, and Water Lily. Dozens of other prospectors filed claims in record numbers. In 1881, Culver made the biggest change to Ashcroft by bringing his wife, Mary, to the town. She ran the boarding house and became the town's maternal figure, softening the all-male image of the camp and symbolizing Ashcroft's civilized future.

In an article she wrote for the *Ashcroft Journal*, Mary encouraged ladies of the mining camps to "work patiently and courageously toward the standard of true womanhood." She advocated improving one's character through a "genuine commitment to the welfare of others," and she warned against "the pitfalls of gossip, gaudy displays of wealth, and pondering and sighing over what might have been." By the summer of 1882, the female population of Ashcroft doubled with the arrival of Mrs. Flynn, a merchant's wife.

Meanwhile, the male population clamored for greater feminine influence and the stability it provided, hoping to bolster Ashcroft's rustic image and attract reputable stakeholders. Following the town's first election, the *Journal* ran an advertisement on behalf of Ashcroft's most eligible bachelors: "Here is a [town] council composed of six members and everyone a matrimonial prize. Not a blank in the lot. Girls, do you hear that?"

NEWSPAPERS PLAYED A ROLE in promotion, but it was mainly word of mouth that attracted silver-crazed miners, prospectors, speculators, freighters, whores, hoteliers, sawyers, and every brand of frontier opportunist to Ashcroft. The promoters did their job and the new town saw a swell of population, at least during the summer. The first school opened in 1881 with crude desks made of rough wooden slabs and old wooden boxes

ASPEN HISTORICAL SOCIETY

for seats. A telegraph line was strung over the spine of the Elk Mountains south to Crested Butte that year, "subscription rates being one pole per customer," the *Ashcroft Journal* reported.

According to *Crofutt's Gripsack Guide*, a field guide for Colorado pioneers of the 1880s, Ashcroft, which was still part of Gunnison County, was hardly viable by 1881. "Ashcroft—Gunnison County, is a small mining camp and shows some rich 'prospects', but no developments," listed Crofutt.

In the summer of 1881, the population of Ashcroft grew to 500, and daily mail-stage service was available to and from Aspen, Independence, and Leadville. Ashcroft was incorporated that year and a July Fourth jubilee was held, complete with patriotic speeches, sporting events, and fireworks. Another winter passed in near seclusion for the few who stayed. Spring brought renewal, and on June 5, 1882, the *Rocky Mountain News* reported that Ashcroft was booming: "Ashcroft:

Fifteen men at work clearing and grading the streets. Hotels fast nearing completion. Boom has arrived. Snow fast disappearing, roads improved."

That summer, Ashcroft's rising property values and ore production provided the town a surge of growth. Lots that had once sold for five dollars went for $150 to $400. The Pearl Mining Company shipped ore to Leadville assaying at over 12,000 ounces of silver per ton. The town boasted three new hotels—the Elma, St. Cloud, and St. James. There was a baseball team, fourteen saloons, a meat market, two grocery stores, a boot and stationary store, and a smelter under construction that would be operational the following year.

Rich silver ore had been found in Pine and Express Creeks along with reports of pockets of gold on Michigan Ridge above Cathedral Lake, then called "Blue Lake." These finds sparked outside interest in Ashcroft and a trail was built from Ashcroft up to Michigan Ridge, which was traveled daily by pack trains of burros laden with ore and supplies. That trail was dubbed the "Panorama Trail" and is known today as Electric Pass.

The discoveries that really put Ashcroft on the map—the Montezuma and Tam O'Shanter mines— were located in 1881 by the Fitzgerald Brothers and Jake Sands on claims they leased in Montezuma Basin. After having found silver, they tried to extend their lease, but the owner refused. They hired additional men and feverishly mined $196,000 worth of silver ore before the lease expired.

IN THE FALL OF 1882, Horace Tabor and Joel Smith of Leadville took over the Tam O'Shanter and Montezuma claims for $100,000. With an infusion of capital from Tabor, the mines produced a record amount of ore. The area below Montezuma Basin was called "Jacktown" for the hundreds of burros stabled there. Burros hauled ore and their braying could be heard all the way to Ashcroft. Jacktown was later named Kellogg after a man who in 1882 built a mill there to reduce silver ore. The Castle Creek Smelter was built at roughly the same time by Brooks & Bethusen, near what today in known as the Mace Hut, and served the mines in Montezuma Basin.

A road was built over Pearl Pass in 1882, connecting Ashcroft to the Rio Grande railhead in Crested Butte, but to reach Ashcroft in the early days, most travelers crossed Taylor Pass. By 1883, the

HORROR'S DEN

In an incident headlined Horror's Den in the Leadville Daily News *on August 13, 1880, Henry Kavanagh of Ashcroft described a grisly scene. The following are his words:*

THAT REGION lying beyond the camp of Ashcroft is reported by venturesome prospectors as one abounding in deep caverns, mountain lakes and narrow passes through walls of granite…wholly impassable except to savages and wild beasts. I penetrated a deep gully into a rocky valley through which ran a silvery brook.

In the shelter of a hanging rock was the ruins of a cabin, out of whose clay chimney came thin blue smoke and the sound of a woman's voice babbling irrelevancies alternating with moans and cries. Upon investigating, I saw a gray-haired woman, fantastically clad, and smelled the decaying bodies of two men lying in the cabin, whom she had evidently killed with an ax.

PHOTO ILLUSTRATION BY DAVID HISER

After concluding the bodies were those of her husband and son, I returned to camp for help. Three men returned to take the maniac to Buena Vista. They thought it might be safer in the morning and it was; she had killed herself in the night. They buried her and what was left of the other two and took away the only clue, a letter from Kansas City reading:

'Dear Abe: I hear you are going to the Gunnison Country, and have got tired of Leadville. Write us the prospects. Your old friend, Harvey Bennett." ❖

ASPEN HISTORICAL SOCIETY

Dan McArthur, Pete Larson, and George Crawford standing in front of Dan's Saloon, the last place of business in Ashcroft.

Colorado State Business Directory survey reported Ashcroft's seasonal population: "Summer, 1,000; winter, uncertain." The town had doubled in two years, but was deserted during winter. Despite the promise of rich ore and working mills, the costs and uncertainties of mining in this remote backwater began to cripple the local economy. The Castle Creek Smelter could not process ore at a reasonable price, in part, because the ore became complex and difficult to smelt. Tabor and his partners began shipping ore to Crested Butte over Pearl Pass, which raised costs and lowered profits.

The smaller miners could not afford to pay the toll over Pearl, so their ore collected in piles. In the summer of 1883, an arsonist set fire to the St. James and Elma hotels. George Bethune, half owner of the Castle Creek Smelter, mortgaged his share and left town. That winter, avalanches killed five miners near Ashcroft, and the town was scandalized when the bookkeeper of the Tam O'Shanter Mine fled town after embezzling $400.

Hope springs eternal for mining towns, and Ashcroft rebounded in 1884 and 1885 when the town reached the peak of its boom. The population was estimated at 2,500, with another 1,000 transient prospectors in the outlying area. The town had six hotels, dozens of stores offering general merchandise, and seventeen saloons. The Tam O'Shanter and Montezuma mines were producing and the Castle Creek Smelter was operating. The Hunley Addition became Ashcroft's only suburb, which was inspired by a rich silver strike at the nearby Wichita Mine.

Ashcroft gained a modicum of notoriety when it was rumored that Jesse James spent a winter hiding out there when things were too hot for him in the outside world. He was described as "a polished gentleman, a nifty dresser, a good poker hand." Legend has it that he called himself "Mr. Howard" or "Mr. Sears." It was said that his cousin had married the owner of the best hotel in Ashcroft and had invited the famous outlaw to visit.

JUST WHEN IT LOOKED like the town had reached critical mass, events conspired against it. Workers at the Tam O'Shanter Mine moved to a boarding house closer to the mine and abandoned Ashcroft. The rich strikes in Aspen siphoned off Ashcroft's work force, and gradually the population of the town drifted downvalley. Many former residents dismantled and moved their homes to Aspen. By 1886, the town reported only $5.60 in its treasury at year's-end. When the railroads reached Aspen in 1887-88, Ashcroft lost its shipping traffic as the high passes—Taylor and Pearl—fell into disuse.

Soon "MOVED TO ASPEN" notices filled the once boosterish *Ashcroft Journal*. In 1887, the Pitkin County Treasurer sold 60 town lots for $140 in back taxes. Gradually, a new group of miners and prospectors moved into Ashcroft, taking advantage of falling prices. These were older, single men who formed a rough community based on low expectations and a fraternal loyalty that centered on Dan McArthur's saloon, one of the only viable businesses left.

By 1888, the social fabric of the town began to unravel, evidenced by Mary Culver, the town's first female resident, filing for divorce, citing abandonment. Charles Culver, her husband and the town's co-founder, had moved out of their home and into a mining cabin with his partner B. F. Wilson. Soon after the divorce papers were filed, Culver and Wilson vanished from the area. The *Journal* speculated that they died in their mine somewhere above Ashcroft.

Mining remained Ashcroft's chief industry as prospectors drilled and hammered on every hillside in a last ditch effort to find the motherlode. The town desperately lobbied for a railroad, but the railroad building days were over. Still, in 1888, the Fourth of July was celebrated in frontier fashion as reported by the *Aspen Evening Chronicle*:

"The day was ushered in amid the roar of giant powder that continued until nightfall, at which time ladies and gentlemen of the locality repaired to the City Hall that had been appropriately festooned, and to the melody of rich music, discoursed by the Thistle String Band, began to trip the light fantastic that was continued until early morn. Joe Vannah observed the national festival by pulling the plug from two lusty kegs of Zang around which his friends collected. A case of three-star brandy was added to this and the walls of his hospitable cabin were lashed with eloquence that would have done credit to the swell clubs of the east."

IN 1889, a group of Ashcroft men formed the Pecos Mining & Milling Company to develop the Pecos and other claims near Pearl Pass. The venture failed due to a lack of promising ore. New hopes for a railroad raised spirits when there was talk of a Midland Railroad branch line built to Ashcroft and beyond, but the grade never got beyond the Newman Tunnel in the

PROPAGANDA IN THE *ASHCROFT JOURNAL*

ASPEN HISTORICAL SOCIETY

The *Ashcroft Journal* was published by Davis H. Waite, who had an ownership interest in the *Aspen Times* and was later elected the first Populist Party governor of Colorado. In his inaugural editorial in 1882, Waite described the mission of the Journal: "…We shall aim to make our paper a representative of the business interests of Ashcroft. Its columns will mainly be devoted to a full and fit representation of the mines and mining prospects of this portion of Pitkin County and such a complete advertisement of their products, advances and capabilities as shall seem best calculated to invite capital and labor to their development."

The *Journal* was an organ of promotion for Ashcroft, whose residents were urged to further their own interests by sending the *Journal* to their friends and families. Only with outside investors and a growing population could the town become a sustainable community. The more investors, the better the prospects for those already invested there. Through bluster and propaganda, the Journal promoted a pyramid scheme for marginal Ashcroft.

One of the hallmarks of respectability was a population of upstanding women, so the *Journal* promoted women and marriage. Victorian values were broadcast to depict the town as a safe place. The *Journal* also painted a picture of great prosperity in Ashcroft, hoping to lure wealthy investors. Like the false fronts on Castle Avenue, hyperbole in print added to the stature of Ashcroft.

Its pages filled with boosterism, politics, and social commentary, the *Ashcroft Journal* became the voice of the town and a barometer of its fleeting success. The existence of a newspaper was as important to the town as the minerals underground and the buildings on the streets. It spoke of culture, community and business opportunities.

Once the fortunes of Ashcroft turned for the worse in the mid-1880s, the *Ashcroft Journal* was one of the first businesses to leave town. The frontier newspaper proved only as viable as the community it publicized. ❖

Summer visitors at Dan McArthur's Saloon in the early 1900s

lower Castle Creek Valley.

The operators of the Montezuma Mine—Horace Tabor and Joel Smith—tried to breathe new life into their claims by building an aerial tram from the mine to the Castle Creek Mill, but the project failed to make a profit. Silver lost most of its value when it was demonitized by the U.S. Treasury in 1893, leaving Ashcroft a ghost town and plunging Aspen into forty years of economic decline.

By 1895, Ashcroft had only a post office and Dan's Saloon facing each other across a deserted street. In 1912, the post office closed and in 1916, the population of the town was down to nine men. Dan McArthur, the bar owner, ran a weather observation station for the U.S. Weather Bureau in Ashcroft until his death in 1923, a job he held for twenty-two years.

Ashcroft was a summer-only community, but McArthur, who came to Aspen in 1886, stayed open year round. In 1892, at the height of Aspen's boom, Dan's Saloon reported gross receipts of $2,059.05. His off-season revenue that year, between December and April, was $188. In 1893, after the repeal of the Sherman Silver Act, Dan's Saloon grossed $1,000. In 1894, his revenues fell to $449.65. Over the next decade, Dan's was the only business left in town that could claim a steady clientele, for whom drinking became a mainstay.

McArthur, for whom McArthur Peak is named, was a warm, hospitable man who welcomed visitors. For entertainment, he had an old phonograph and more than 1,000 cylindrical records. Historian Len Shoemaker described an evening spent with Dan McArthur in 1921 when they sat talking until 2 a.m. They listened to more than 200 records and Dan described the early days of wagon travel into the valley. "The next day," wrote Shoemaker, "we climbed the mountain and he pointed out the trees that had been used to rope down the wagons and the ruts made by the wagon wheels."

Following the Silver Crash of 1893, wrote Jon Coleman in *The Skeletal Shell Game: A History of a Colorado Ghost Town, 1880-Present,* "the town's population was mostly older, single, socially-marginal men whose meager incomes were supplemented by fishing, hunting, and trapping. Most were poor drunks without pasts or futures."

Jack Leahy was the last resident of Ashcroft. A former prospector and miner, Leahy called himself the "Mayor of Ashcroft." He wrote poetry and could, according to accounts, "deliver an oration on any subject at any time." The high basin at the head of Pine Creek is known as "Leahy Basin" because of a cabin Jack used there for many years. Jack Leahy was Ashcroft's quintessential rustic philosopher and literary scion. He studied law and read the classics. He was able to quote Shakespeare, Plato, Voltaire, and Plutarch. He once reportedly prevented a mining strike in Aspen by reciting a passage from *Candide*.

Jack Leahy was Ashcroft's quintessential rustic philosopher and literary scion

In 1939, when he died in Glenwood Springs a few years after nearly dying of starvation in Ashcroft from starvation, Leahy's obituary in the *Aspen Times* referred to his poems as "the finest pieces of descriptive literature in existence today." The article said

ASPEN HISTORICAL SOCIETY

Leahy was regarded as "one of the most highly educated men in the Rockies" whose "wit and brilliance of mind amazed all with whom he came into contact." The article claimed that Leahy's cabin "housed what is probably the finest personal library in existence in Colorado today, containing volumes and articles on every conceivable subject that ever appeared in print."

LEAHY WAS A MAN whose eccentric life fashioned a legend for Ashcroft. He is remembered for his poetic renditions at Dan's Saloon and for his contribution to the written history of Ashcroft with his acclaimed and spirited poem: *How We Built a Church in Ashcroft*. The poem describes a despicable cast of characters, from debauched town trustees to a flock of flagrant prostitutes, all debating the merits of a church.

Following is another Leahy poem published as a tribute to Ashcroft in the *Aspen Times*:

> *When our grub pile's slim and scanty*
> *Not a dollar in the shanty*
> *And our threadbare garments letting in daylight*
>
> *The pay-streak still eluding*
> *And barren dikes intruding*
> *And we are chased by harsh collectors, day and night*
>
> *When our efforts lose their footing*
> *Our pard's insults sure cutting*
> *And misfortune's cruel jeers and sneers are keen*
>
> *From Ashcroft habitation*
> *We behold bleak desolation*
> *When sear Autumn's gold's transformed to silver sheen.*

Summer visitors explore Ashcroft ghost town.

After Leahy's passing, Ashcroft became a true ghost town. The Kellogg Camp, where twenty buildings once stood, and the Montezuma Mill and its boarding house all disintegrated over time and were gradually scavenged for building materials. By 1916, only the crumbling foundations were visible. Ashcroft had succumbed to forces far greater than natural decay and weathering, namely the financial vagaries of a mercurial boom and bust mining economy. ❖

This painting of Baby Doe Tabor, by C. Waldo Love, displays the comely beauty that stole Horace Tabor's heart, and whose visit to Ashcroft during the height of the mining boom prompted a town-wide celebration with open bars for all comers.

THE "SILVER KING" OF ASHCROFT

HE WAS KNOWN as the "Silver King of Leadville." In Ashcroft he was a patriarch who brought investor wealth and opulent revelry to the frontier. Ashcroft served the Silver King's purposes perfectly. Not only did he invest in Ashcroft's mining and smelting, he conducted an illicit affair in Ashcroft that had tainted his reputation and political career in Leadville and Denver.

Horace A. W. Tabor was a storekeeper from Maine before he came to Colorado with his wife Augusta during the 1858 gold rush. Tabor arrived in Leadville in 1860 and acquired dozens of mining claims, including his Matchless Mine, which was fabulously rich in silver. His fortune was legend in Denver where he built the "Tabor Block" and the five-story brick Tabor Grand Opera House and combined office building.

In Leadville, Tabor built a second Tabor Opera House, the Leadville Bank, and the Tabor Grand Hotel. He owned two lumber companies, a water company, a gaslight company, a horse-car company, a real estate company, and the Leadville Stock and Mining Company. When he learned of Ashcroft's promise, he bought the Montezuma and Tam O'Shanter Mines in Montezuma Basin, bought a smelting operation in Ashcroft, and incorporated a street-railway system in Aspen.

During his Ashcroft venture Tabor was smitten by the young and beautiful Elizabeth McCourt Doe, who had become known by Central City miners as "Baby Doe." She divorced her first husband when he failed to strike it rich and set out to snare Leadville's famed Silver King. She moved to Leadville, met Tabor, and seduced him.

Tabor scandalously divorced his wife Augusta in 1883 and married Baby Doe in Washington, D.C., where Tabor filled a brief appointment in the U.S. Senate. The divorce crippled his political career because it symbolized a breakdown in moral values. The couple was shunned from prominent social circles in Denver in which Augusta had been active.

After his purchase of the Montezuma and Tam O'Shanter mines above Ashcroft, Tabor made frequent trips across the Continental Divide to inspect his properties. When he arrived in Ashcroft in 1883 with his young new wife, a major celebration was held. The entire town was treated by Tabor to a 24-hour banquet and ball; all thirteen of the town's saloons opened their bars. One can only imagine the booming mining camp in a drunken revelry as miners flocked from the hills.

The Tam O'Shanter and Montezuma claims held great promise and initially produced rich silver ore at $20,000 a month. The deeper the mine went, however, the more complex became its ore, which was invaded by veins of undesirable zinc. One large shipment of Tam O'Shanter ore sent to the Philadelphia smelter at Pueblo, Colorado, was so tainted with zinc that the entire shipment was dumped into the Arkansas River.

Tabor's speculating, his ostentatious lifestyle, and the Silver Crash of 1893 conspired to wipe out his once great fortune. He died in Denver in 1899. Baby Doe lived in Leadville until 1935 when, at eighty, she died a pauper. Dressed in rags, she was found frozen to death in a crude mining shack near the famed Matchless Mine that had furnished Tabor his once great fortune. "Never let go of the Matchless," Tabor had instructed Baby Doe. "It has a future." ❖

PRESERVING A GHOST TOWN

The ghost town of Ashcroft was in an advanced state of decay by the early 1970s. The U.S. Forest Service and the Aspen Historical Society, urged on by Stuart Mace and Ramona Markalunas, began restoring Ashcroft in 1974 with construction of a boardwalk leading from the parking area through the town. A "shingling bee" was held, and five of the eight cabins got new roofs.

In 1975, the old hotel was rebuilt after it had fallen down beneath heavy winter snows. In 1976, a floor was installed in a miner's cabin to provide housing for resident "ghosts," or docents, volunteers who give tours and safeguard the ghost town. In 1978, the Blue Mirror Saloon received a new floor, rebuilt walls, and a blue mirror. A "chinking bee" was held to patch up the decrepit log walls. In 1982, the cabin of Jack Leahy was restored. A "liar's bench" was added to the porch where he had spun tales and recited poems. The gooseberry bushes planted by Leahy are still growing at the site.

The ghost town is open for self-guided walking tours in the summer and ski tours in the winter. ❖

6 The Mines of Castle Creek

N THE SUMMER OF 2002, an Aspen photographer was hiking in a nearby wilderness valley when he spotted a mine tunnel perched on a steep mountainside. The climbing was difficult to reach the tunnel, but the rewards were ample. Inside the hand-hewn cave was a collection of mining equipment from over century ago. "It was like they had dropped their picks and shovels and walked away, never to return," he said.

Evidence of mining is prevalent in the Aspen area, and highly evident in Castle Creek Valley, where old mill sites, enormous tailings piles and decrepit tunnels and shafts give evidence of the legacy of silver mining. Historic mine sites describe the greatest distinction between the varied histories of Castle and Maroon Creeks. Hundreds of old mines and prospects are scattered throughout the Castle Creek Valley while the Maroon Creek Valley has only a few.

The reason lies in the diverse geology of the two valleys. Where dramatic faulting of particular formations allowed precious metals to flow as super-heated mineral solutions into subterranean fissures in Castle Creek, there were different rock types and conditions in Maroon Creek. The mines of Castle Creek were not the richest in Aspen, but two of the Castle Creek mines operated longer than most of the Aspen mines. The Midnight Mine produced silver, lead and zinc through the 1960s and the Pitkin Iron Mine produced iron ore through the early 1980s.

Many of Castle Creek's mining ventures are still visible, even from the Castle Creek Road, though most require some exploration to reveal old tunnels and shafts. Caution: old mine tunnels are rife with dangers, including carbon monoxide poisoning, cave-ins, and open shafts. Careless exploration could prove fatal.

The following histories are not in chronological order. Instead, they follow Castle Creek from the roundabout upvalley to its headwaters.

LEFT **Work stoppage: an old mine apparently undisturbed, hidden not far from a popular hiking trail in the Castle Creek Valley.**

RIGHT **An Aspen miner with a hammer, hand drill and pickax displays the tools of early silver mining.**

THE NEWMAN TUNNEL

N 1888, George F. Newman founded the Newman Mine with partner Percy LaSalle a mile and a half from Aspen on the east side of Castle Creek. The company owned 2,700 feet of a mineral vein that ran from a point near the Sundeck Restaurant at the top of Aspen Mountain down to Castle Creek. The Newman Tunnel is marked by a large mound of tailings above the Aspen Music School and Aspen Country Day School parking lot.

Newman was of English descent and was born on the East Coast. According to early accounts, he dressed well and "took on airs" in Aspen. He was more of a stock investor than a miner, so his visits to Aspen were brief. He often stayed at the Hotel Jerome, a favorite haunt of roving, well-heeled bachelors.

Newman developed the mine site to make it look like an English country estate. The property included stables and a large bungalow. The mine administration building was outfitted with pool tables for the miners in what is today the Aspen Music School student lounge. The Student Services office contains the original vault that held the mine payroll.

Newman exerted considerable financial influence in Aspen and successfully convinced the Colorado Midland Railroad to run a spur to his mine. He built a hydroelectric plant that was considered one of the finest at the time. Located where the present Music Hall stands, the plant generated electricity from a head of water produced by a dam two miles upstream on Castle Creek. The water was channeled down a wooden flume on the east side of Castle Creek, powered generators at the mine, then emptied into one of the ponds on the music campus. The flume alignment can be seen today.

In an effort to follow the silver vein through Aspen Mountain, two tunnels were driven 2,500 feet upward toward the Sundeck. The tunnels ran side-by-side at a 45-degree incline. Loaded ore carts were lowered to the mine portal by gravity. They were attached to a cable that ran through a large pulley at the top of the tunnels. As the loaded carts came down, the unloaded carts went up through the adjacent tunnel.

The present Percussion Building is located on the site of a former ice house once filled with blocks cut from the ponds during the winter. The ice blocks lasted all summer and were sold to local businesses and homeowners in Aspen.

Newman reportedly entertained guests lavishly by chartering passenger trains from the Midland Railroad and opening his grounds to large gatherings. At one party he surprised his guests with special gifts he had collected during his world travels.

Even after the Silver Crash of 1893, Newman kept the mine operating with thirty-eight men. The mine eventually closed in the early 1900s, and was aban-

ABOVE **The Newman Tunnel and mine, as seen from Castle Creek Road in late 1890s, shows the Tudor-style mining headquarters. The mine tunnel was located in Keno Gulch on Aspen Mountain, where bare slopes indicate prior logging. The railroad is the Colorado Midland, which ran a spur up Castle Creek to the mine.**

RIGHT **The grounds for the Newman Tunnel now serve as a campus for the Aspen Music School and Aspen Country Day School.**

doned and stripped of all valuable equipment by freelance miners. The Newman property was deserted during Aspen's "Quiet Years," except when Aspen youth threw secret parties in the bungalow. During the 1940s and '50s, various Aspen families lived at the Newman bungalow.

The Four Seasons resort and the Copper Kettle restaurant were located on the site from the 1950s to the '70s. The Four Seasons featured tennis courts and a swimming pool. The tennis courts were located in the grassy area across the road from the Administration Building and the "pool" was the smallest of the ponds. The property was purchased by Robert O. Anderson in 1964. He later donated it to the Aspen Music Festival and School. Before then, music classes were held throughout town in private homes and available buildings. Music administration offices were in the Wheeler Opera House. Additions were made to the campus over time, designed by Fritz Benedict in conjunction with Curtis Besinger, professor of architecture at the University of Kansas at Lawrence.

Today, the Tudor campus is used jointly by the Music School and Aspen Country Day School. Tours are available through the Music Festival and School.

THE CASTLE CREEK RAILROAD

DESPITE the mortal blow the Aspen Mining District was dealt by the Silver Crash of 1893, the city buzzed with the prospect of a third railroad serving its outlying mining interests. Plans were made for construction of a rail line to serve the Castle Creek Valley, with the hope of establishing a rail link across the Elk Range.

The proposed Castle Creek Railroad was described by the *Aspen Times*, January 1902:

"Hope springs eternal in the breast of man and the new railroad has caused the people of this city to look forward to great improvements and development in that part of the country through which the new road is to run. Ashcroft, Difficult Gulch, Lincoln Gulch and the districts near the city have all made substantial progress since the building of the railroad has practically been assured.

"The plan is to follow Castle Creek from Aspen to Ashcroft. This will take in the Montezuma Mine of former greatness and the other groups of mines in that region. The road will then go southwest to the Elk Mountain Range. The grade is steep and a tunnel will be made which will probably be half a mile in length."

Despite claims that the Castle Creek Railroad would rejuvenate Aspen's mining outlook, the scheme never materialized. Aspen entered the "Quiet Years" without a third railroad and the Castle Creek Valley remained a rural route to the ghost town of Ashcroft.

Mines and Ranches

OF MAROON AND CASTLE CREEK

Mine Portal
Ranch
4WD Road/Trail
Paved Road

RED MOUNTAIN

Red Butte 8283'

Hunter Creek

Holden Lixiviation Works

Moore Ranch

Aspen 7907'

Marolt Ranch

SMUGGLER MOUNTAIN

Warren Lakes

ASPEN DISTRICT

Roaring Fork River

82

Newman Tunnel

Burnt Mountain 11385'

T-Lazy-7 Ranch

Charcoal Kilns

Sheridan's Camp

Queens Gulch

Midnight Tunnel

John Wayne Tunnel

Willow Creek

Maroon Creek

Baldy Mountain 13155'

Loge Peak 11675'

Richmond Hill District

Little Annie

Highland Tunnel

Midnight Mine Shaft

Highland Peak 12381'

Little Annie Mine

SIEVERS RIDGE

East Snowmass Creek

Willow Lake 11,795'

Highland

Hope Tunnel

HIGHLANDS RIDGE

Maroon Lake 9,580'

Castle Creek

RICHMOND HILL

Difficult Creek

North Maroon Peak 14014'

Crater Lake 10,076'

West Maroon Creek

Pyramid Peak 14018'

East Maroon Creek

Conundrum Creek

PITKIN COUNTY

Maroon Peak 14156'

Hayden Peak 13561'

Devaney Creek

Toklat

McArthur Mountain 12139'

Ashcroft

Express Creek

American Lake 11,365'

Precarious Peak 13360'

Hunter Peak 13497'

Carey's Camp

Ashcroft Mountain 12381'

Keefe Peak 13516'

Conundrum Hot Springs 11,200'

Cathedral Peak 13943'

Pine Creek

Taylor Pass 11928'

Hilliard Peak 13409'

Cathedral Lake 11,866'

Taylor Lake 11,544'

Conundrum Peak 14022'

Montezuma Mine

East Maroon Pass 11820'

Montezuma Basin

Malamute Peak 13348'

Copper Lake 11,321'

Triangle Pass 12890'

Castle Peak 14265'

CONTINENTAL

Greg Mace Peak 12,528'

Pitkin Iron Mine

Taylor Peak 13,435'

Copper Pass 12560'

Coffee Pot Pass 12560'

GUNNISON COUNTY

DIVIDE

Star Peak 13,521'

Taylor River

Copper Creek

White Rock Mountain 13,318'

Twin Lakes 11,770'

Brush Creek

Pearl Mountain 13,362'

Pearl Pass 12705'

White Mountain 13,420'

Scale in Miles

THE MIDNIGHT MINE

ASPEN HISTORICAL SOCIETY

A miner operates an air drill in Midnight Mine before World War II.

A heightened demand for lead and zinc after World War I enlivened the mine until the early 1930s, when the mining industry in Aspen hit bottom at the start of the Great Depression. Still, the Midnight Mine persevered, operating on a steady production basis from 1929 to 1953.

THE MIDNIGHT MINE was one of Aspen's longest working mines. It was first patented as a mining claim in 1883, just two years after the City of Aspen was incorporated, and was active for over seventy years. The original Midnight shaft was located in Little Annie Basin, just below Richmond Ridge. The Midnight eventually amassed seventy claims encompassing 600 acres along Richmond Ridge.

By 1885, the Midnight Mine had a shaft 40 feet deep that intersected a silver ore-bearing vein twenty feet thick. Mine owners Judge Deane, Dr. Slagle, Fred Bassinger and George Pesser—all Aspen pioneers— followed the vein until the falling price of silver made mining uneconomical in the early 1890s.

The mine languished for almost twenty years before B. Clark Wheeler, another Aspen pioneer, formed the Midnight Mining Company in 1919. Rather than drive the original shaft deeper, Wheeler opened a tunnel about 1,000 feet below Little Annie Basin in Queen's Gulch on what today is known as Midnight Mine Road. The Midnight Mine Tunnel was surveyed to intercept the original shaft and drain water from the mine workings. As with many Aspen mines, the Midnight changed hands frequently. Wheeler worked the mine for a short time, then sold his consolidated interests to Golden Grover, owner of the Mesa Store in Aspen.

In 1923, Fred Willoughby came to Aspen from Paonia and became president and general manager of the Midnight Mine. The Midnight Tunnel was completed in 1929 under his leadership and mine production began in earnest. A flotation mill was built at the tunnel portal in Queen's Gulch, remnants of which can be seen today. The mill concentrated silver ore and separated lead and zinc at a capacity of 75 tons per day. A boarding house and shop were also erected at the portal.

A heightened demand for lead and zinc after World War I enlivened the mine until the early 1930s, when the mining industry in Aspen hit bottom at the start of the Great Depression. Still, the Midnight Mine persevered, operating on a steady production basis from 1929 to 1953. An estimated $1.5 million in silver ore was produced over the life of the mine, and that was at exceedingly low silver prices. The Midnight Mine was one of the principal sources of employment for Aspen during the "Quiet Years" of the 1930s and '40s.

Fred Willoughby died in 1943 and Lloyd Russell, a director of the company and long-time resident of Aspen, took over. He served as manager until 1946, when Frank J. Willoughby, one of the sons of the original manager, took over. The other son, Fred T. Willoughby, served as co-superintendent.

Falling metal prices and rising operating costs conspired to close the mine in 1953, but the property was held intact until it was sold to the Richmond Hill Exploration Company in 1962. This new enterprise extended the Midnight Tunnel to 6,000 feet beneath Little Annie Basin in an attempt to contact the orebody at greater depth. The tunnel never hit its target and the mine closed.

Many of the Midnight Mine properties were later incorporated into the proposed Little Annie Ski Area (see pg. 102).

JOE POPISH: MEMORIES OF A MIDNIGHT MINER

JOE POPISH reflects on the mining days in Castle Creek with genuine fondness. In the garage of his Carbondale home he displays a plum-sized, 99 percent pure silver nugget in callused hands that evince the life of a working man. A collection of mining memorabilia hangs on a wall, including headlamps of all shapes and size, some of them worn by Popish himself during a career that left an indelible impression upon him.

Born in Aspen on July 11, 1924, Joe is the son of Primosh Popish, who immigrated to Aspen from Yugoslavia in 1905. Joe's mother, Jennie Vedic, was born in Aspen that same year. As a young woman, Jennie worked for Primosh, caring for his mother and Joe's half brother, Bernie, who was born to Primosh in a first marriage to Mary Zupancis. Mary died six months after Bernie was born and Primosh later married Jennie, who later gave birth to Joe. Jennie Popish lived to ninety-five.

Raised in Aspen during the "Quiet Years," Joe worked for Snowmass rancher Jens Christiansen during his high school years in the late 1930s. He picked potatoes at the Christiansen ranch and earned two dollars a day, plus room and board. Joe shared meals with the family in their home and slept in the barn. After high school Joe worked for Strong Brothers, cutting timber props for coal mines. His pay remained steady at two dollars a day.

Joe remembers early winters on the unplowed streets of Aspen where groceries were delivered by a sleigh that dragged a heavy chain to pack down the snow. Ruts in the springtime snowpack were two or three feet deep, he recalls, and the streets were practically impassable. The population of Aspen was about 400.

Joe's father, Primosh, worked for forty years in Aspen silver mines. As a young man, he leased the Smuggler Mine, made a sizable strike, and worked it for three years with a crew of eight miners. Lessees paid a percentage to the mine owners, and often there were several lessees in one mine, each working a "block." Joe went into the Smuggler to work with his father at age fourteen. His father taught him mine safety, and Joe came to appreciate the hard work and excitement of exploring underground.

"Any mine is as safe as you want to make it," said Joe. "It's up to the individual. You've got to know the ground. When you were prospecting, you drove tunnels into new formations and wondered if there was going to be a strike. There's still plenty of silver under there, but it's low grade and it would take millions of dollars to get it out."

When he came of age, Joe signed up for a stint in the Navy. When he returned to Aspen after World War II, he worked at the Midnight Mine with a starting wage of $5.50 a day. In a scrapbook, Joe saved a State of Colorado Information Report for 1949 that reported his total wages for that year of $2,866.62. He worked in the mine through 1951.

"That was the only work available that paid any money," explained Joe. "We worked eight hours a day, which included travel time to and from the mine, which meant six hours underground. The Midnight Mine was the last mine to produce anything in that country —silver, lead, and zinc. It was all hard rock mining."

Stockholders owned the Midnight Mine and mine manager Fred Willoughby, Sr., controlled the majority of the stock. Joe worked under Willoughby's sons, Frank and Fred, and recalls when young Fred once climbed the huge smokestack at the Holden Lixiviation plant and did a handstand at the top.

"We hit an underground lake and it was like tapping into a water main with 200 pounds of pressure. When we tapped into it, we took the drilling machine off the steel shaft, and it shot the steel down the tunnel about 50 feet. It was like a fire hose. My partner said: 'What do you want to do?' and I said, 'I don't know what you want to do, but I'm going to the top deck,' and I was out of there."

—JOE POPISH

Joe and Barbara Popish grew up in Aspen and now reside in Carbondale.

Joe described the Midnight Mine as a good prospect because of a strong indication of rich silver ore that was tied into the Little Annie vein. The main tunnel of the Midnight Mine drove horizontally under Annie Basin, where it met the shaft, which provided air circulation. The workings of the Midnight Mine tunnel went down 1,800 feet below Little Annie Basin.

When he started at the mine in 1946, Joe operated an electric motor car pulling a train of ore cars from the depths of the mine to the crusher at the mill site in Queen's Gulch. In 1947, Joe changed jobs and timbered the tunnel, "square-setting" with ten-by-ten timbers, which were logged from the top of Richmond Ridge. Joe's next job was running an air-powered drilling machine and setting off charges deep underground.

"We would drill holes six-foot deep, load powder, shoot them, and shovel out the next morning," explained Joe, "then drill another six foot. When the powder was set, you would move off about 100 feet, go around a corner, and wait for the blast. We would count the rounds going off to make sure there were no live caps or dynamite. Smoke cleared overnight, and in the morning we would load the cars with shovels. It was just like everyday work," Joe said, "except that it's dark and you've got a light to work with. Pumps kept the water out twenty-four hours a day."

WATER was one of the most difficult technical challenges in the Midnight Mine, which pumped fifty to 100 gallons per minute to keep the tunnels from flooding.

"I was down on the 1400-foot level one time with my partner and we were drilling," said Joe. "We hit an underground lake and it was like tapping into a water main with 200 pounds of pressure. When we tapped into it, we took the drilling machine off the steel shaft, and it shot the steel down the tunnel about fifty feet. It was like a fire hose. My partner said: 'What do you want to do?' and I said, 'I don't know what you want to do, but I'm going to the top deck,' and I was out of there. It took three weeks to drain that lake and we were probably pumping 300 gallons per minute. Later, we shot the holes with dynamite, and there was a big hole in there, a big water pocket."

Saturated with ground water, absorbant layers of rock became fluid and made it difficult to keep the Midnight Tunnel open. "The ground was so heavy it kept pushing all the time," explained Joe. "It would squeeze and we would pull timbers, widen it, and put new timbers in. In the lower workings, we would set 10x10 timbers in the morning and by afternoon, they were bent. There was constant pressure."

Working the mine during winter, the miners had a continual battle with deep snow. The Midnight Mine Road was plowed to the main portal, but plowing up to the shaft on Richmond Ridge was another matter.

"Toward the end," said Joe, "they didn't want to keep the road plowed from the mine to the shaft in Little Annie Basin, and that's where we had all our timber and dynamite. So I would follow the tunnel to the shaft and climb ladders 550 feet inside the mine to the top of the shaft every morning. I would lower the timber and dynamite, and in the afternoon I would climb back down. Then they got the idea that I could go up to the top of Ajax on a ski lift first thing in the morning, then I could ski down Little Annie Basin and lower all that stuff down for them. Then I could put on my skis in the afternoon and ski down the basin to the mine tunnel and catch the crew bus back to town. I did that for one winter."

One summer Joe and another man re-timbered the entire Midnight shaft. They climbed into a big ore bucket and lowered themselves down, re-timbering as they went. "It took us all summer," he recalled.

At peak operation in the mid-1940s the Midnight Mine employed a crew of sixty and produced 100 tons of ore a day. The ore was "trammed" out of the tunnel on a motorized train, run through a crusher, then through a mill to separate the silver from the zinc and lead. Miners worked in three shifts; the mill men worked in two shifts.

"The train was still coming into Aspen then," explained Joe, "so they would truck the ore down and ship it by rail to the Leadville smelter. But then the Leadville smelter wouldn't take the zinc so they had to ship it to El Paso, Texas. In the summertime, the Midnight used trucks to take the ore over Independence Pass and save the rail freight. They had high grade ore, but the price of silver was 80 to 90 cents an ounce, so when they got to the low-grade, it didn't pay to mine it, and that's when they shut down."

T HOUGH ASPEN was just beginning as a ski resort then, skiing was nothing new to Joe. He had skied as a boy and described an early crossing of Pearl Pass during a cross-country ski race.

"I used to ski a lot before there were any lifts or trails. We skied down the old miners' trails on skis we made ourselves. We used rubber bands to hold on our skis and there were a bunch of us kids skiing. When they put the lifts in, I got to skiing pretty well.

"One winter Fred Willoughby called me up and asked if I wanted to cross-country ski to Crested Butte. The Chambers of Commerce in Aspen and Gunnison had a wager to see which was faster, skis or snowshoes, so we had a race. On March 9, 1951, four of us skied over Pearl Pass to Crested Butte, while a group from Crested Butte hiked over on snowshoes. I was in good shape from climbing those ladders in the mine and skiing Annie Basin, and we skiers won the bet."

The Willoughby boys were strong advocates of skiing, so the Midnight Mine loaned the Aspen Ski Corporation heavy machinery to install the first ski lifts. "They were skiing on Aspen Mountain when I first started working the mine in '46," said Joe, "but they didn't have any lifts, so the skiers rode up in our bus from town to the Midnight Mine. They would hike up from the mine and ski into town from the top.

"Aspen was a lot of fun then. Everybody knew each other and there wasn't a locked door in town. If you needed something from somebody, you just walked in and left a note. You could buy houses for fifteen dollars. After the mine closed down I worked on the mountain loading ski lifts, but I just couldn't see any future in loading skiers, so I apprenticed as a plumber and eventually worked up to master plumber."

In 1951, Joe began a thirty-three-year-long career in plumbing with Grant & Co. That same year he married Barbara Hauth, who had spent part of her childhood on the family ranch at Woody Creek where gonzo journalist Hunter Thompson later resided. The couple has two sons, Edward and Tony.

Barbara and Joe Popish have lived in Carbondale since Joe's retirement in 1984. His thoughts often return to his younger days when Aspen was a sleepy town and the Midnight Mine produced silver. "I liked being underground," he said. "There was no public to contend with, like there was with plumbing. I went in, did my job and nobody ever bothered me."

"Aspen was a lot of fun then. Everybody knew each other and there wasn't a locked door in town. If you needed something from somebody, you just walked in and left a note. You could buy houses for fifteen dollars."

—JOE POPISH

THE CHARCOAL KILNS OF CASTLE CREEK

BEFORE COAL became widely available as a source for smelting ore in Aspen, charcoal was widely used. Charcoal kilns on Castle Creek at Sheridan's Camp met this demand along with kilns in Basalt and in the upper Frying Pan Valley. Sheridan's Camp was established three miles south of Aspen on the west side of Castle Creek where three brick charcoal kilns were built in the early 1880s. The camp was named for A. G. Sheridan, who cut and hauled wood for the kilns.

ASPEN HISTORICAL SOCIETY

The kilns are impressive beehive-shaped structures that consumed enormous volumes of wood that was burned in a controlled, oxygen-deprived atmosphere, which converted the wood to charcoal. The kilns were constructed of native stone and unfired brick bonded with mortar. Their exteriors were coated for protection from the elements and there were openings at the top and bottom to control combustion. On cold winter days the kilns steamed like geysers and melted a circle of snow with their radiant heat.

Wagons delivered freshly cut firewood to the kilns, then reloaded with charcoal, which was utilized in blacksmithing and heat-treating mining drills. The smelting process also required this concentrated form of carbon to heat the ore to the melting point. The main function of a charcoal kiln was concentrating carbon for the smelters.

Charcoal kilns were made obsolete by the arrival of the railroads, the ready availability of coal, and the establishment of coking ovens in Cardiff, near Glenwood Springs, and in Redstone. Coke is a higher-quality smelting carbon, which replaced charcoal and saved some of the remaining forests from the ax. After they became obsolete, the kilns at Sheridan's Camp were used as barns to shelter livestock for a homesteader in the late 1890s. Two of the kilns remain standing on a private road in the Castle Creek Valley amid a tall aspen forest.

RIGHT **Charcoal kilns consumed vast quantities of timber. The men who worked them hated the heat in the summer, but loved it in the winter.**

BELOW **These kilns are located on private land in Castle Creek valley.**

Flywheels, pistons and boilers mark the remains of the old Montezuma Mill in Castle Creek Valley.

THE LITTLE ANNIE MINE

ONFLICTING LEGENDS account for the name of the Little Annie Mine and Little Annie Basin. One story claims they were named for a little girl, the daughter of a miner, who picked flowers around the shaft while her father went below. Another account, sent to the Aspen Historical Society in 2000 on a handwritten note from "Annie's" granddaughter, offers greater detail.

Annie Stancil was born in Frederick, Maryland. Her brother, Charles Keyser, a geologist and prospector, went west to explore for silver. He found what he was looking for on Richmond Ridge and named the discovery for his little sister—the Little Annie Mine. Keyser mysteriously disappeared and Annie's father took the family west looking for him. They made it only as far as Kansas where the father became ill and could travel no further. Annie eventually became a school teacher in Baltimore and, according to the granddaughter, later married the school principal.

The shaft of the Little Annie Mine was started in the early 1880s at 11,300 feet on Richmond Ridge. Working from the top of the ridge, miners followed a silver vein 200 feet down. The mine property consisted of a small boarding house and mill. B. Clark Wheeler, who drew up the original plat for the City of Aspen, expanded the Little Annie Mine in 1886.

Though the vein was rich, flooding by groundwater was a recurring problem and required constant pumping. After the Silver Crash of 1893, working a mine at high elevation and with a constant flow of water proved too great for investors, so the mine closed. Several efforts to tap into the Little Annie orebody were undertaken in later years through the Highland Tunnel, Hope Tunnel, and Midnight Mine.

THE MONTEZUMA MINE

HE MONTEZUMA MINE opened in the early 1880s with a portal located at about 12,500 feet in Montezuma Basin. A mill was built 2,000 feet below the mine on Castle Creek where silver ore was delivered, first by burros, then by a mining tram. A predecessor of the modern chairlift, the tram utilized large ore buckets suspended on a cable supported by wooden towers.

Remnants of the mine and mill are visible today in the rocky basin beneath the north face of Castle Peak where rusted cables and tailings piles lay in disarray. The ruins of the mill, complete with boilers and water-powered turbines, provide testimony to the rigors of the freighters who shipped huge pieces of heavy machinery by wagons and mule teams into the Castle Creek Valley.

THE JOHN WAYNE TUNNEL

NEIGHBORING TUNNEL to the Midnight Mine in Queen's Gulch came to be known as the John Wayne Tunnel. John Wayne, the movie star, may have put up some money for the project, but he reportedly had little personal involvement with his namesake mine. The John Wayne Tunnel was started in the 1950s by Russell Holmes and was driven only a short distance—perhaps fifty feet—beneath the Midnight Mine Tunnel. Since the property was owned by the Midnight Mine Company, the John Wayne Tunnel was probably worked on a lease agreement after the Midnight closed in 1953.

PITKIN IRON MINE: OF MOUNTAIN TRUCKS AND STEEL MILLS

THE PITKIN IRON MINE was Aspen's last large scale mining venture. The story begins in 1880 when claims were staked above "Cooper's Camp" in the Cooper Creek Valley above Ashcroft where iron ore deposits on Taylor Peak were obvious by their bright orange hue. In 1886, claims were acquired there by the Colorado Fuel & Iron Company (CF&I), but little development occurred.

In 1953, long after the mining excitement had died away in Pitkin County, L. S. Wood, an entrepreneur, engaged the services of a young Glenwood Springs attorney, Robert Delaney, in opening a coal mine in Coal Basin west of Redstone; this later became Mid-Continent Resources. As an adjunct to that development, Delaney and Wood began exploring for other mining opportunities that might fit with the steel industry. They came upon an old U.S. Geological Survey Report pertaining to a vast iron deposit in Cooper Basin.

"We learned that there had been a wagon road built up to the deposit during the early mining days when the smelter was operating in Aspen and a small quantity of iron ore was hauled down to be used as a kind of flux at the smelter," explained Delaney.

Delaney and Wood studied the literature, which revealed a high magnetite content in the basin. "The report indicated that because of mining difficulties, it was not likely to be mined," said Delaney. "However, the equipment that was then available and the techniques then in use shed a different light on it."

Delaney and Wood developed a market with CF&I, the huge steel maker in Pueblo, and performed exploration and feasibility studies for financing an iron mine in Cooper Basin. "I rode on horseback up to look at it with a man associated with the coal industry," said Delaney, "and we found it quite rugged, extending from 10,000 to 13,000 feet. We learned that the iron outcrop is adjacent to a Leadville limestone deposit."

The coal mining operation that Wood had started west of Redstone was going apace of the iron mine development, so Wood and Delaney hired Morrison Knudsen Company of Boise, Idaho, to work both mines. Pitkin Iron Company was incorporated in 1960 and entered a joint venture agreement with Morrison Knudsen. The mining company would handle the contract mining in Cooper Basin, and Delaney and Wood would market and process the ore.

"It worked out quite well and the prospects looked pretty good," explained Delaney, "so we worked out a deal with the Pitkin County Commissioners whereby we would develop and pave the road above Ashcroft to the base of Cooper Basin. We also worked out a deal to get electricity to the same location. The road was built without any tax outlay by the county, and we received credits for the work we did."

The road on the mountain face accessing the open pit mine was improved to handle specially designed "mountain trucks" that were capable of bearing heavy loads of iron ore on steep grades at high elevation. These large dump trucks were customized with torque retarders (engine brakes) and were operated by fearless drivers who contended with multiple hazards.

Ron Arbaney, a third generation Aspenite, drove one of the mountain trucks and gained considerable respect for the iron mine roads. "That was a pretty spooky hill road," said Arbaney. "The top part was pretty steep; we called it 'The Steep.'

Rich with iron, Taylor Peak was home to the Pitkin Iron Mine for twenty years, from 1961-81. The steep switchbacks of the mine road proved a constant challenge to truck drivers, many of whom worked as ski patrollers and ski instructors during the winter.

It's probably a 17 percent grade. The trucks were off-road Mac Trucks equipped with jake brakes and hydraulic retarders and we came down fairly slow. We were going to the very top of those mountains."

"That iron ore looked just like cast iron. It was very heavy and the deposit was at the very top of the mountain. It didn't take much of that iron ore to make up a load. On the highway trucks, you could hardly even see they had a load; it was so small and heavy. And they had crews up there drilling and blasting all the time."

"It was impressive to see a D-9 cat hanging over the edge up there," said Delaney. "The 'dozers would push the ore down, bench-by-bench, until they could load it into the mountain trucks. The mountain trucks hugged the inside of the road, so if they lost their brakes they could turn into the mountain and stop."

THE MOUNTAIN TRUCKS hauled the iron ore to the base of the mountain where it was run through a crusher. The crushed ore was then loaded onto highway trucks for the 11-mile run down the Castle Creek road to the shipping depot at Woody Creek. From a dumping site alongside Highway 82, the ore was loaded onto a conveyor belt and moved across the Roaring Fork River where it was loaded onto Rio Grande railroad cars for shipment to the CF&I steel mills in Pueblo.

"The mine provided summertime employment for ski people," explained Delaney, "and it was welcome at that time. It paid well and many people remember working there, with some degree of nostalgia."

For Arbaney, who worked at the mine from 1971 to '73 and spent winters working for the Aspen Skiing Company, memories include terrifying electrical storms. "When a storm came in, the iron ore made that mountain into a huge lightning rod. Electric Peak is named because it gets a lot of lightning strikes, and there's still a lot of iron ore up in those mountains."

While the mountain trucks were specially equipped for steep grades, they were still prone to occasional runaways, as Arbaney described.

"We had quite a few runaway trucks. That was before maxi-brakes, where if you lose your air, the brakes come on. Those trucks didn't have that. If you broke the retarder hose, you'd lose your air really quick. So we had a few runaways and the thing was, you had to put the truck in the bank right away. And that iron ore was so heavy it would break loose the hinges on the dump box and slide up onto the cab sometimes. That hill run was definitely the harder of the two truck runs, especially when it rained. It got really slick up there."

The mine had a fleet of six to eight mountain trucks and twelve highway trucks during the height of operations in the late '60s. Several hundred thousand tons of ore were mined over the life of the mine, which produced through 1981. In addition to the technical difficulties of hauling iron ore from a sheer mountainside on a rough, rocky road well above timberline, the quality of the ore caused the eventual downfall of the mine, which was a summer-only operation.

"The problem with the iron ore was that it had a high sulfur content," explained Delaney. "We experimented with removing sulfur and agglomerating the fine particles. We built a test plant at Woody Creek for that purpose, but it was not successful, so we abandoned it. We also had a great quantity of 'fines' that were too small for the blast furnace in Pueblo because it plugged the air flow. They solved that problem through an agglomeration process, but when they shut down that process, the mine shut down, too. We eventually sold the 'fines' to cement companies on the Eastern Slope and used some for a process of washing and screening out the coal at Coal Basin."

A large metal building constructed by Pitkin Iron at Woody Creek was eventually moved to the Pitkin County Landfill. The eighty acres at Woody Creek used for storing ore and as the site of a secondary crusher was designated for development with a mix of "affordable" and "free market" housing in the late 1990s.

BELOW The Hope Mine on Castle Creek was launched by optimistic Aspenites in 1910 as a last hope for Aspen's mining economy.

RIGHT Mechanized mining, as shown by this tramway, was pioneered in Aspen area mines.

THE HOPE TUNNEL

I N 1910, ALMOST twenty years after the Silver Crash of 1893, a group of Aspen investors formed a cooperative company with the hope of reviving the town's silver economy. Stock was sold and the enterprise was underwritten mostly with local funds. Some shareholders agreed to work on the tunnel in exchange for a share of the earnings. All goods and materials for the mining operation were purchased in Aspen in a commitment to support the local economy.

The Hope Tunnel was an extension of the old Highland Tunnel, which had been driven into the mountainside from the Castle Creek Valley a decade before. The plan was to continue the tunnel underneath Little Annie Basin, de-water the workings of the Little Annie Mine, and access the silver vein.

A mill site was located just above Castle Creek across from the Conundrum Creek Road, where a shop and boarding house were built. An air compressor was brought in from another mine, and work on the Hope Tunnel was started in 1911. Six miners lived on-site along Castle Creek where the wife of one of the miners served as cook.

Acid mine runoff was so strong in the tunnel that it corroded the metal rails and pipes. Layers of white gypsum, a weak rock layer through which the tunnel passed, were also eroded by the mine water and caused instability. This plagued operations and made progress slow and costly.

The *Aspen Times* reported in August 1915 that Ted Cooper, Arthur Demaris and two girls went into the Hope Tunnel on a lark, exploring the deep passageway. The children were overcome by carbon monoxide. When they were found, Demaris was dead, Cooper was in serious condition, and both girls were unconscious.

Another incident regarding the Hope Mine was described by the late Aspen native Matt O'Block. It involved an Aspen man named Ben Kobey who was elected mine president by shareholders in the early 1920s. Kobey was Jewish and some of the shareholders resented his appointment. O'Block described the conflict:

"It was the time when the Ku Klux Klan was at its zenith in Colorado, and Rifle was supposedly the location of a kleagle (chapter) of the Klan. One night, these lower valley klansmen, who were stockholders in the Hope Mine, brought up a cross and set it on fire on Kobey's front lawn, fired some rifle shots into the air, and hurriedly fled down the valley as cowards are wont to do. Kobey's next door neighbor, Mr. John Elder, came out of his house in his pajamas, picked up the fiery cross and threw it out into the street."

Kobey retained the presidency and the Hope Tunnel eventually reached over a mile beneath Little Annie Basin. Ore was found, but it was not rich enough to balance the books, and the enterprise was scaled back. In 1922, the Hope Mining and Leasing Company reported a cash balance of $131.13.

By the mid-1920s, the mine appeared on the verge of resurgence as a new mill was constructed. The Hope Mine was ill-fated, however, as revealed in a report from a technical mining paper dated 1929:

"Fire completely destroyed the new mill and practically all the surface property. The new mill had not been in operation over two hours when fire, thought to be caused by defective wiring, put a complete end to work of the company. Loss, estimated at $100,000, was not covered by insurance. Rebuilding unlikely at present."

From an anonymous poem titled *The Hope*, the following stanza reflects the miners' commitment to saving mining in Aspen:

They called it their Hope, did this mountain band,
In their mine the hope of the county lay,
And never wavered their faith, although
The seasons changed from spring to snow;
While the grey earth flew
And the tunnel grew,
Nor storm nor snowdrift, the work might stay. ❖

ABOVE **Miners developed a strong sense of community as they struggled to make their enterprise earn a profit.**

RIGHT **This small hydroelectric plant on Maroon Creek supplies all the electricity needs of T-Lazy-7 Ranch.**

WATER POWER

FROM HYDRANTS TO HYDROELECTRIC

I N A CITY BUILT OF WOOD, fire was a recurring nightmare. Without a ready supply of water, Aspenites lived under the threat of a catastrophic blaze. There was plenty of water in the rivers, but transporting it into the city was a costly engineering feat. The challenge of building a citywide water system fell to two of the town's most innovative entrepreneurs, H. P. Cowenhoven and DRC Brown. They established a water company and built a flume from Castle Creek in the fall and winter of 1885-86 to supply the town's hydrants.

Once the hydrants were charged, Aspen realized another boon from its water-power. On May 25, 1885, Aspen became one of the first municipalities in the United States to harness hydroelectric power for lighting homes, businesses, and streets. Power was generated by a hydroelectric plant at the Aspen Smelter.

In 1886, the Consumer's Light and Power Company was formed with DRC Brown as president. The company generated hydroelectric power with Pelton wheels and dynamos at the site of today's Aspen Art Museum, which was the city's first municipal power plant. In 1887, another technological milestone was reached when engineers Frank Sprague and J. H. Devereux contracted to electrify the

Veteran Mine with a street-car motor outfitted as a hoist. This was the first known application of hydroelectricity to mining equipment in North America.

In 1892, the Aspen Electric Light and Power Company built a large power plant at the west end of Cooper Avenue on Castle Creek. This historic brick and stone structure, seen today beneath the Castle Creek Bridge on Highway 82, was one of the largest brick and stone structures from Aspen's early days. Waterpower came from Castle and Maroon Creeks via wooden flumes and iron pipes. In 1947, when Lift 1, Aspen's first chairlift, opened on Aspen Mountain, it was run by hydroelectric power from the Castle Creek plant.

In 1958, the rising costs of maintaining the power plant and the falling price of electricity caused the closure of the Castle Creek plant, which was then converted into city shops. Aspen, which had been energy independent for over seventy years, became a customer of the Bureau of Reclamation.

Today, the City of Aspen continues to generate a substantial portion of its electrical power from hydroelectric sources. A hydroelectric plant at the Ruedi Dam in the Frying Pan Valley produces 31.5% percent of the city's electrical needs, and a small hydroelectric plant on Maroon Creek produces 5.4% of the city's power. The remainder of Aspen's power needs is met by wind power, coal, natural gas and large scale hydro plants on the Gunnison and Colorado River systems. ❖

7 "It Sure is a Conundrum."

THE VALLEY OF MINES AND HOT SPRINGS

LONG BEFORE the Conundrum Hot Springs became a backpackers' paradise, the Conundrum Creek Valley was known as a mining region. Conundrum Creek enters Castle Creek about five miles south of Aspen and was one of the earliest routes into the Roaring Fork Valley. The earliest known settler in the Conundrum Creek Valley was Abe Lee, who built a cabin about eight miles up the valley from Highland near Conundrum Hot Springs and grazed a small flock of sheep in the high basins above the springs.

When the first miners found "gold float" in the sandbars of what was first known as West Castle Creek, they searched high and low for the motherlode, but never found it. "It shore is a conundrum!" said one of the miners, and the name "Conundrum" stuck.

In the summer of 1879, a group of town promoters led by T. E. Ashcraft (pronounced Ashcroft) ventured into the Conundrum Creek Valley from the Gunnison Country and laid out a townsite at the confluence of Conundrum and Castle Creeks. They called the town Highland in honor of Ferdinand Hayden's "Highland Triangulation Station" on Highlands Ridge near Triangle Pass. The town was surveyed by Charles Armstrong, who lived in Highland and remained a Castle Creek Valley resident for many years. Armstrong's diaries are one of the few personal historical records of the region from that period. They describe Highland as the first surveyed mining town in the Roaring Fork Valley, predating Aspen and Ashcroft.

In the early 1880s, Highland was a fast-growing camp that briefly outpaced Aspen because of the promotional prowess of Ashcraft, who would later abandon Highland to promote the town of Ashcroft. Mining claims like Mountain Elk, Iron, Little Russell, Opher, Hercules, Richmond, Ajax, Florence, Sheridan, Pittsburg [sic] and Silver King were staked east of Highland on Carbonate and Copper hills.

Risks were part of life in this region, just as they are now, and in 1880 two men—William Reading and George Perry—met with fatal accidents. According to newspaper accounts, Perry was killed in an avalanche in Conundrum Gulch and Reading drowned after falling into Castle Creek.

In the summer of 1882, an entrepreneur known as Captain Carey located claims and started a mining camp about seven miles upstream from Highland where a dozen cabins were built and a half dozen men mined silver. A small store was opened that year and a post office was established in August 1882 in what became "Carey's Camp." A wagon road was graded up the Conundrum Creek Valley as far as Carey's Camp in 1883 and was later extended to Lee's cabin near the hot springs.

In the spring of 1884, disaster struck Carey's Camp when an avalanche roared into the narrow valley and buried the cabins. There were five men sitting around Jim Thorn's cabin when the slide hit. They were buried and suffocated. A rescue party reached the camp several days later where they discovered the corpses and took them by sled into Aspen. Three weeks later, when the victims' families asked rescuers to retrieve the personal belongings of the victims, a party returned to the

Three weeks later, when the victims' families asked rescuers to retrieve the personal belongings of the victims, a party returned to the avalanche site. As they were digging through the debris, they heard a scuffling sound under one of the bunks. They dug the snow and ice away and found Thorn's dog, "Bruiser," on the verge of death, but miraculously alive. They took the dog to Aspen, cared for it, and nursed it back to health. A collection was taken to buy the dog a silver collar engraved as a memorial to the disaster.

In 1884, Jim Thorp's dog Bruiser became a local celebrity after being buried in a Conundrum Creek Valley avalanche for three weeks.

avalanche site. As they were digging through the debris, they heard a scuffling sound under one of the bunks. They dug the snow and ice away and found Thorn's dog, "Bruiser," on the verge of death, but miraculously alive. They took the dog to Aspen, cared for it, and nursed it back to health. A collection was taken to buy the dog a silver collar engraved as a memorial to the disaster. The dog was sent to Thorn's next of kin in New York State.

The largest mining claim in the Conundrum Valley was the Cummings claim, located a half mile downstream from Carey's Camp. The miners who worked the claim and the wood-cutters who provided fuel wood to the boilers lived at the camp. The mine was at the bottom of a steep mountainside and the mine machinery was stored in an underground room excavated to protect it from avalanches. In 1921, Forest Ranger Len Shoemaker visited the mine and discovered the room, with everything intact since the closing of the mine. The large steam engines were packed with stiff white grease.

Other claims in the Conundrum Creek Valley included the Southern Home, St. Elmo, Silver Chief, Iron Cross and Pride of the West. In 1885, a black marble quarry was established two miles up Conundrum Creek from Castle Creek, where several cabins were built for workers. The quarry was acquired almost a century later by Stefan Albouy, who removed samples in 1991 (see pg. 67).

In 1886, as the fortunes of Highland diminished because of competition from Aspen and Ashcroft, Highland lost most of its population. The *Colorado State Business Directory* that year listed Highland as: "A small camp in Pitkin County; Population 10; Post Office at Aspen."

In 1912, a group of Aspen citizens and the U.S. Forest Service excavated a small pool at the Conundrum Hot Springs and constructed a bathhouse over it. A small cabin was built near the hot springs by the Forest Service and was made available to all visitors, making it the first wilderness hut in the Elk Mountains open to the public.

Len Shoemaker, in his book *Roaring Fork Valley*, described replacing in 1929, the 64-foot, 2-inch iron pipe that channeled hot water from the hot springs to the pool: "I remember it as the most difficult packing job I ever tackled," said the veteran horse packer and trail builder. "I had the pipe cut into eight-foot lengths and after four hours of trial and error I found a hitch that would hold it in the proper position on my two pack-horses. I arrived at the hot springs at 8:30 p.m. after thirteen hours of strenuous labor, tired but happy." Shoemaker recalls a later visit to the hot springs in 1938. The bathhouse had been torn down because of rot and a tent had been set up over the pool.

Today, the hot spring fills two rock-lined pools in Conundrum Basin. This geothermal destination has become a mecca for backpackers who soothe weary muscles in 93-degree water after hiking deep into the Maroon Bells-Snowmass Wilderness.

AVALANCHE IN CONUNDRUM GULCH

DEVON MEYERS, ASPEN TIMES

EDITOR'S NOTE: *The following story appears in Mary Eshbaugh Hayes' book* The Story of Aspen. *It originally ran in a February 1893 issue of the* Aspen Times.

A T ABOUT 8 O'CLOCK last night a weary band of 20 men came slowly into Aspen dragging a wounded comrade upon a rudely constructed hand sled. They had come from a point about 14 miles distant from Aspen in Conundrum Gulch, where they had experienced the force of an awful snow slide of more than 2,000 feet in width and fully 20 to 60 feet in depth. The story of their adventures, as given by Charles H. Munn, is about as follows:

There were 20 men in the camp and they were engaged in driving a tunnel for Mr. O'Brien. On last Wednesday morning, the snow was so deep about their camp, which was situated on the mountain's side, and the danger of snow slides so imminent, that the men did not dare venture more than a few feet from the door of their rude but substantial log cabins.

About 10 o'clock, one of the men named Pete Anderson took a shovel and started to make a pathway from the bunkhouse to the cook shanty, but a few feet away, when suddenly there came dashing down the mountainside a terrible avalanche of snow. So swift was its flight that the startled man had time to take but a step or two in the direction of safety before it overtook him, carrying him in its course for a distance of over 400 feet where he struck a tree that prevented his going further.

His startled companions in the bunkhouse immediately rushed out expecting to find the man buried far beneath the surface. They commenced shoveling snow from about the place where Anderson had last been seen, when suddenly one of the party raised the cry: "There's Pete," pointing down the side of the mountain.

All eyes were immediately turned in the direction indicated, and one glance satisfied the men that their companion was badly injured. Hurrying to his aid, they found him a pitiable sight indeed. The front half of his scalp was torn and hanging down over his eyes, while a great open wound reached clear across one side of his face.

The men bore the poor fellow to their camp and one of their number drew the scalp back in place and sewed up both wounds as best he could. Poor Anderson suffered greatly, but bore his pain with fortitude, while the men did everything in their power to alleviate his sufferings, and waited in fear and trembling for the second avalanche, which they believed was certain to fall, and so it did.

Late Wednesday night Thomas Lavin was selected to watch over the wounded man while the others retired to their bunks to rest. The long night was fast drawing to a close when about 4:15 o'clock Thursday morning the men were suddenly awakened to Lavin's cry of "Boys, she's coming." Realizing that there was no safety in flight, the brave men held their breath, waiting for the awful concussion, which the roaring sound told them was upon them.

Mr. Munn, in relating the experience and suspense of that moment, says that an old boyhood friend was sleeping with him, and put his arms about him as a mother would her child. When the great force struck the strong log cabin it swayed for a moment, but, to the great joy of the men, resisted the shock.

As soon as the men could get out next morning, they quickly saw to what they owed their preservation. Directly below the cabin was piled about 400 cords of wood kept in place by guy ropes of steel. When the slide struck this wood the ropes broke, allowing the wood to go down the mountainside, but the resistance afforded by the wood had been sufficient to check the snow in some degree and to this occurrence the men attributed their escape.

Yesterday morning at 6 o'clock the men placed their wounded companion upon the sled and started for Aspen. At about 5 o'clock in the afternoon they arrived at the Famous Ranch about six miles out, and George Bell, employed by Mr. Wheeler at the ranch, brought the men on into town, arriving here at 8 o'clock. The wounded man was taken to the hospital where he will receive the best attention. ❖

STEFAN ALBOUY'S BLACK MARBLE QUARRY

A DEPOSIT OF BLACK MARBLE was discovered in lower Conundrum Creek in 1885, and samples indicated a potentially lucrative resource. It wasn't until a century later, however, that the quarry saw much activity.

Stefan Albouy, an Aspen native, took an interest in mining as a young man. In the early 1960s, he began exploring many of the old workings around Aspen. Over time, Albouy acquired a number of abandoned patented mining claims for back taxes and established himself as one of a new generation of Aspen miners.

Albouy and his parents, Robey and Margaret, had visited the long abandoned marble quarry through the 1960s and '70s for family picnics. Later, Albouy researched the claim and, with his partner and mentor Ed Smart, gained ownership rights in the mid-1980s. Albouy then decided to develop the quarry and actively market the black marble. In 1991, he applied to the US Forest Service to remove marble samples to test their quality and assess a value for the claim. However, the quarry was by then encompassed by the Maroon Bells-Snowmass Wilderness and was technically off limits to motorized uses.

In defiance of the environmental community, Stefan Albouy, Ed Smart and a coterie of local miners removed from Conundrum Creek a sample of black marble. A flatbed pickup truck was used for later shipments, but the initial load was hauled by a horse-drawn ore wagon because the access road was too rough for motor vehicles.

Since the mining claim preceded the wilderness restrictions, Albouy was within legal rights to access the claim by motor vehicle. Mining is given traditional, preemptive rights to public land as a stipulation of the 1872 Mining Law, so once a mine owner proves that a claim is economically viable, he is granted the "right to mine."

Albouy knew the law was on his side, even if Pitkin County was not. He exercised his rights and was granted special permission by the Forest Service to remove marble blocks that had been quarried in the 1880s. Albouy would be allowed to drive into the wilderness, but only by making a compromise with the Forest Service that included no new mining at the quarry and a stipulation that he would only be allowed to haul off what he could load onto a flatbed truck.

Albouy's reactivation of a mining claim within wilderness—and his plans to drive to the site—proved controversial. Albouy said he received threats from environmental activists who vowed to try to stop him. Armed and ready for potential violence, Albouy, his mother Margaret, and a small group of friends and supporters drove to the site after cutting some trees to open the overgrown roadway.

Albouy hauled out his sample blocks of marble, but never reopened the quarry. An appraisal of the property eventually resulted in a purchase settlement. The federal government paid Albouy and his partner, Ed Smart, $4.2 million.

The settlement did little to appease the deep-seated frustration that plagued Albouy throughout his adult life. His numerous mining plans were derailed by constant opposition and bureaucratic regulations. Albouy felt ill-suited to the times in which he lived and his despair drove him to suicide in 1994. The black marble quarry has lain dormant ever since, having returned to the public domain with a protective wilderness designation.

SERIAL KILLER TED BUNDY HIDES OUT
IN CONUNDRUM CREEK

EDITOR'S NOTE: *The following episode may seem totally incongruous with the rest of the Conundrum Creek history, and it is. Serendipitous events occasionally shatter all past and future references. This is one of them.*

In February 1975, the nude and frozen body of Caryn Campbell, a young nurse from Michigan, was found along Owl Creek Road near Snowmass Ski Area. Campbell had been visiting Snowmass on a ski vacation with her fiancé. They were going out for dinner, and Caryn had apparently forgotten something in her room. She left her fiancé in the lobby of the Wildwood Inn to retrieve what she had forgotten and was not seen alive again.

Campbell became one of many victims of serial killer Theodore "Ted" Bundy, who became a household name in Aspen during a sensational trial in 1977. Bundy was little known at the time, but was later held responsible for the murders of twenty women and perhaps as many as sixty women over the course of a several-year rampage that made him one of the most notorious mass murderers in American history. In the national press, Bundy was described as a "monster" who had been jailed in Salt Lake City, Utah on a charge of aggravated kidnapping. He was then linked with the Snowmass murder and was extradited to Pitkin County to stand trial for Campbell's murder.

In June 1977, Bundy, 30, defended himself in the Pitkin County courtroom. A recess was called and Bundy, who had won the trust of his jailers, was left alone and unshackled. When no one was watching, he jumped 30 feet from a second story window and ran. As police swarmed Aspen, word spread of the suspected killer's escape. Local curiosity about Bundy immediately turned to terror. Children were taken out of schools. Doors and windows were locked. Roadblocks were established. For six frightful days, Bundy evaded capture.

After leaping from the courthouse window, Bundy, with an injured ankle, hobbled east to the Roaring Fork River where he shed a layer of clothing near "No Problem Bridge." (Bundy wore two sets of clothes to the courthouse that day in anticipation of an escape). Bundy sneaked through town, hiked up Aspen Mountain, then made his way down into Castle Creek, and eventually to Conundrum Creek, where he endured a cold, wet night in the rain, most likely huddled beneath a spruce tree. The next day, chilled and hungry, Bundy broke into a cabin at Conundrum and spent another

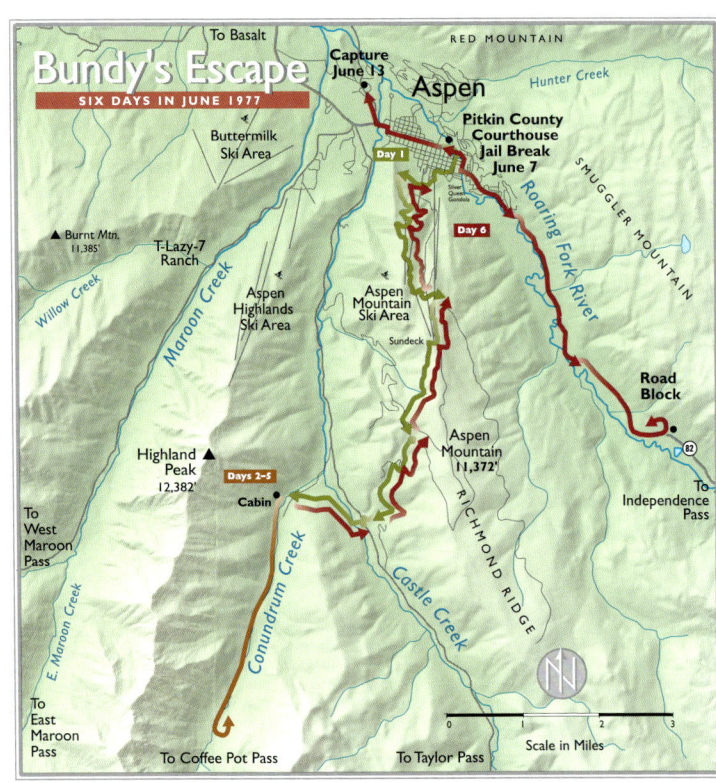

night recuperating from his chilly bivouac.

There was a rifle in the cabin, which Bundy stole, and on the third day of his escape, Bundy hiked up Conundrum Creek, armed and desperate. Using crude maps sketched by other inmates, Bundy headed south toward Coffeepot Pass, hoping to cross the Elk Range toward Crested Butte or Gunnison. High water, snow, and the vastness of the wilderness turned him back, however, and he returned to the cabin at Conundrum.

During Bundy's wilderness sojourn, a caretaker had noticed the cabin had been broken into and reported it to the police, who searched it for clues. Bundy returned to the cabin, realized that the police had been there, and spent another night outdoors. On the final day of his escape, Bundy retraced his footsteps up the backside of Aspen Mountain, hiked down the front of the mountain into Aspen, stole a car on Cemetery Lane—a Cadillac belonging to Paul Merihew that had keys in the ignition and the owner's wallet in the glove box—and tried to drive over Independence Pass. The pass was closed, however, due to a rock slide, so Bundy turned around and drove back toward Aspen. He made an errant swerve east of town, which caught the attention of police.

Bundy was pulled over as a suspected drunk driver by two sheriff's deputies, Gene Flatt and Maureen Higgins. Sergeant Don Davis was called for backup, and he carefully approached the car. Bundy, despite the loss of 20 pounds and a scratched and bearded face, was recognizable. "Hi, Ted," said Davis, who immediately drew his gun and made the arrest.

BUNDY WAS THEN TRANSFERRED to Garfield County Jail in Glenwood Springs, which was considered a safer jail. His trial reconvened and he was held another six months. One night in December 1977, he used a hacksaw blade to open a ventilation grate in his cell, wriggled through an air duct, dropped into the empty reception area, and walked out the front door. He stole a car, drove to Denver, boarded a flight to Chicago, then rode an Amtrak train east. By the time jailers discovered his disappearance Bundy was in Michigan en route to Florida. Within a matter of weeks he had killed two women in a sorority house at Florida State University. Two days later, Bundy's last victim, twelve-year-old Kimberly Leach, disappeared.

Bundy was captured in Florida on February 15, 1978, where he served eleven years on death row. At 7:06 a.m. on January 24, 1989, 42-year-old Ted Bundy was executed in the electric chair. On the eve of the execution, at least one Aspen bar held a "Ted Bundy Going Away Party."

Reviewing Bundy's escapade in the Elk Mountains, his sojourn describes the physical ordeal of a desperate man. Bundy had neither camping gear, rain protection, nor compass. He subsisted only on the food and water he could find in what is certainly one of the most bizarre wilderness odysseys in Aspen history.❖

8 Holden, Marolt, Mace, and Dean

PUTTING NAMES WITH THE PLACES

EDWARD ROYAL HOLDEN tied his fate to Aspen perhaps more than any other entrepreneur, and for that he paid the ultimate price. Unlike the lucky few who became millionaires, Holden took a fortune, sunk it into a bold enterprise on the banks of Castle Creek, and lost everything. A bold visionary, Holden had impeccably poor timing.

Born in New York City in 1855, Edward Royal Holden studied metallurgy before moving to Leadville, Colorado, in 1880. He arrived at the end of the Leadville mining boom and worked as a miner in Horace Tabor's Little Pittsburgh Mine. Later, he collaborated with assayers and chemists and formed a partnership, Chanute & Holden.

His sterling reputation as a metallurgist won him a court appointment as receiver for the Emma Mine in Aspen following an ownership squabble. The appointing judge regarded Holden as competent to "not only tell what a piece of ore was but to present intelligently its constituent parts." A newspaper noted that Holden "takes in everything going on about him … His opinion is worth something…He is a fighter from away [sic] back and will make a hard battle for his opinions."

Holden moved to Aspen and was soon working for the North Texas Smelter Company, which in 1882 had proposed building a large smelter on Castle Creek. The smelter was never started due to a lack of capital, so Holden determined to build his own smelter. He staked his money and reputation on the bet that Aspen would produce ores of sufficient quantity to warrant the investment his former employers could not justify.

Holden founded the Holden Smelting and Milling Company in 1890, and soon began developing the Holden Lixiviation Works in Aspen. By 1890, the mines of Aspen produced one-sixth of the silver in the U.S. By the time Holden opened his reduction plant in Aspen, the district's silver production was the highest in the state, annually producing 2 million ounces more than famous Leadville.

Aspen was then the third largest city in Colorado, behind only Leadville and Denver. In 1892, the population soared to a peak of 12,000 and seemed capable of further growth. Holden knew that much of the ore produced in Aspen was low-grade and in great quantity. He also knew that it was too expensive to ship crude ore to Leadville, Denver or Pueblo. Even with two railroads serving the city, Aspen mine operators were eager to avoid costly freight charges.

The Aspen Mine was a case in point. During three years of production in the late 1800s, it produced $5.8 million in silver but paid $628,000 in smelting fees and $806,000 to the railroads. A concentrating plant was needed in Aspen that could reduce ore haulage expenses, boost mining profits and bolster the local economy. Since Holden owned shares in several Aspen mines, his interest in a concentrating plant was two-fold: his mines could operate profitably and Holden could secure profits from both ventures.

Holden chose a 20-acre parcel on the west side of Aspen, on Castle Creek, part

The Holden Lixiviation Plant was Aspen's largest industrial structure when it was built on the west bank of Castle Creek in 1891-92. The plant, which was eventually torn down for salvage, was located on the west side of the Castle Creek pedestrian bridge. The Marolt Barn historical museum is one of the few remaining vestiges of this grandiose ore-processing plant.

of a 400-acre parcel through which the Colorado Midland Railroad passed as it entered Aspen. The site was convenient, reasoned Holden, because of the proximity of the railroad and the availability of water from Castle Creek for ore processing and hydroelectric power. However, the Midland refused to subdivide its 400-acre parcel, formerly known as Stitzer's Ranch, and only after protracted negotiations was Holden able to acquire a lease on the property.

The Holden Lixiviation Works was incorporated in 1890 with an assessed value of $500,000. It was to be the largest and most expensive industrial plant built in Aspen, built of huge timbers on a massive stone foundation. The 27,200-square-foot, post and beam, five-story structure was built by a crew of skilled German shipwrights. The site was to be connected by a bridge to the city, and a new town was planned adjacent to the site on what is known today as the Marolt Property.

I N SUPPORT of Holden's plans, and with the prospect of a new town at the site, the City of Aspen and Pitkin County agreed to jointly construct a bridge over Castle Creek that would serve both the town and the plant, with a streetcar line extended to the facility. Holden and partner Richard Cline put up a $25,000 good-faith bond for the bridge.

The King Iron Bridge and Manufacturing Company won the contract and had begun casting the structural girders when Pitkin County reneged on its agreement due to serious financial problems involving a default in construction bonds for the new Pitkin County Courthouse. The project was rescued by partial state funding, and the bridge was built in 1891 from the west end of Hallam Street across Castle Creek. The bridge was 510 feet long and seventy-five feet high. It was used until 1961, when it was replaced by the current State Highway 82 Castle Creek Bridge.

The Lixiviation Works was under construction from May to November 1891. The main structure required 10,000 cubic yards of excavation, 72,000 cubic feet of stone work, 1.2 million feet of lumber, and 700,000 bricks. Huge furnaces and dust chambers were constructed which vented into a great smokestack that stood 165 feet high and six feet square. About 200,000 bricks were used to build the furnace and dust chamber and another 225,000 bricks were used for the main stack, which was then the highest stack in Colorado and a major landmark in Aspen until the 1950s. The stack was adorned with the date—1891—under a crescent with the letter "H". This symbol was also used as Holden's brand and marked his 5,000 cattle at his 18,000-acre ranch in Wichita Falls, Texas.

The mill was powered by water from Castle Creek. Electricity was generated by two Pelton wheels. An eight-foot wheel produced mechanical power for the mill machinery via a system of overhead shafts, which turned wheels and belts. A three-foot wheel ran an "Edison 250-light dynamo" for generating electricity.

The plant performed "lixiviation," a chemical process for dissolving silver ore and separating its parts. The mill included a sampling facility, salt shed, crushers, boilers, waterwheels, an electric generator, numerous conveyors and an intricate system of chemical vats. The plant was by far Aspen's most ambitious mining facility and symbolized the city's dramatic rise as an industrial city.

The Holden Lixiviation Works opened on November 1891 operating at a rate of 125 tons a day. During the first two months, nearly 17,000 tons of ore were concentrated. By the beginning of 1892, the plant handled 100 tons a day, with some of the ore coming from as far away as Leadville. Projecting rapid growth, investors planned to expand the plant to several hundred "stamps," or crushers, and a work force of up to 300 men. The plant would usher in "a new era of prosperity" claimed the *Aspen Times*, and secure Aspen's place as a regional mining center.

The sampling building, known today as the Marolt Barn, served as the ore depot. Railroad cars delivered ore and a portion of each load was tested through a process called "quartering," in which the ore was mixed to provide a uniform sample. Ore was then run through a "Blake Crusher," which operated on the same principle as a nutcracker. Large chunks fell into a wide opening at the top and, as the jaws of the crusher hinged back and forth, the crushed pieces fell through a narrower orifice at the bottom. From there, rollers converted the graveled ore into fine powder. Conveyor belts mounted with buckets then lifted the ore on a pulley system to the sampling floor where it was bottled for testing. The owner of the ore received a bottle to ensure a fair sampling for a proper assay.

The plant performed "lixiviation," a chemical process for dissolving silver ore and separating its parts. The mill included a sampling facility, salt shed, crushers, boilers, waterwheels, an electric generator, numerous conveyors and an intricate system of chemical vats. The plant was by far Aspen's most ambitious mining facility and symbolized the city's dramatic rise as an industrial city.

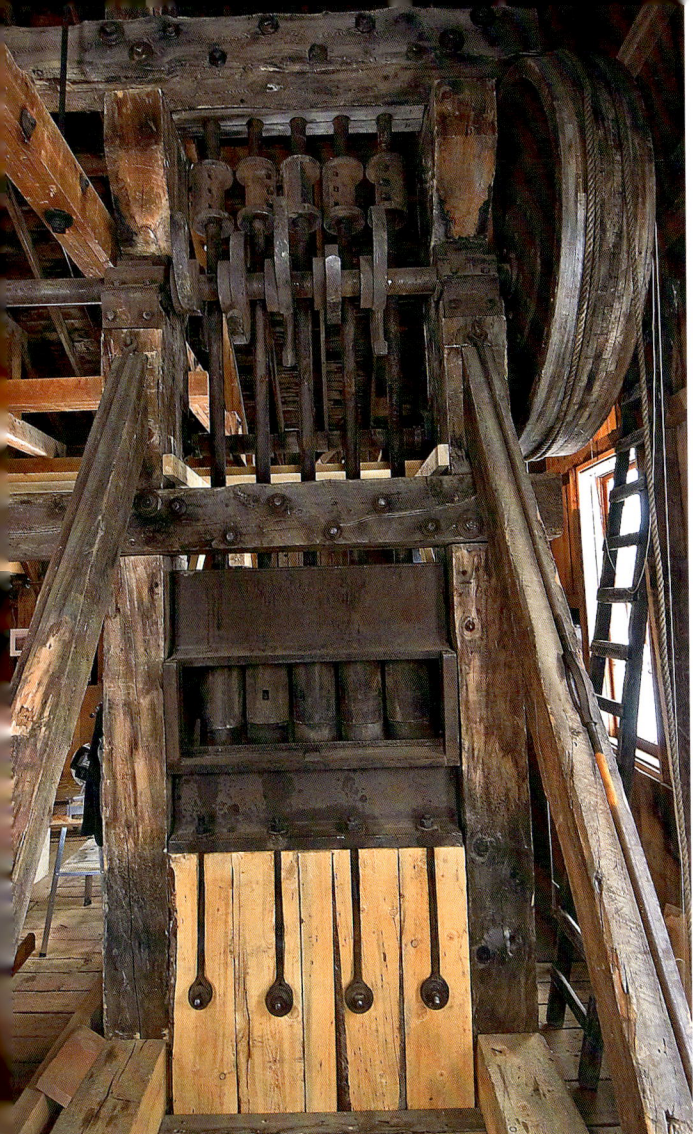

The five-stamp mill from Barr's Mill at the headwaters of Difficult Creek was disassembled and hauled to Aspen in 2002 by dedicated historians, Stoney Davis and Norbert Athes, who wanted to save the structure from gradual decay. The stamp mill is currently outfitted for demonstration at the Marolt Barn.

The crushing machines made a racket and shook violently. Hence, the need for a rock solid foundation, sections of which are visible today on a bench above the west bank of Castle Creek where the Marolt Pedestrian Bridge crosses from 7th Street to the Marolt Housing project.

Salt was a fundamental ingredient to the lixiviation process, and 300 to 500 barrels of salt were used monthly. The plant burned coal, which was shipped by Colorado Midland Railroad cars. The salt came by rail from Salt Lake City; the coal came from New Castle, west of Glenwood Springs.

Once a portion of the ore was sampled, the remainder of each shipment was dried on special drying shelves, then transported by tram to the stamp mill where thirty 850-pound stamps dropped ninety-two times a minute to crush the ore. Ten 650-pound stamps crushed the salt. The ore and salt were then lifted to the top of the 50-foot high Stetefeldt furnace where they were blended in a hopper and poured through the furnace where they became red hot and underwent the required chemical transformation. The dryers and the furnace were heated by coal gas made on-site at the rate of 1.5 million cubic feet of gas per day.

The fumes from the furnace rose into a large dust chamber 20 feet high, 12 feet wide and 50 feet long, then into an inclined flue, and finally to the base of the main stack. In an effort to trap silver in exhaust dust from the Stetefeldt furnace, the Holden Works installed a smoke condenser that ran furnace smoke through pipes immersed in cold water to induce condensation. It was projected that this process could collect $5,000 worth of silver per week, but the installation occurred just two weeks before the plant closed and the results were never known.

ONCE THE ORE came out of the furnace, it cooled on the concrete cooling floor and was then placed in huge leaching vats on the level below the cooling floor. Seven vats held 100 tons of ore. They were 17 feet in diameter and nine feet deep. Three liquids, one at a time, were introduced at the top of the vats and drained from the bottom. Water first removed the soluble salts and six additional solution applications removed the bulk of the silver.

Following the leaching treatments, the ore was moved into precipitation tanks one level below the leaching tanks where the silver sulfide was drawn off the tanks and taken to the sulfide room on yet another level. The precipitation tanks were 12 feet in diameter and eight or nine feet deep. Following precipitation of the ore, the tailings, or waste, was sluiced out of the tanks and dumped into Castle Creek, where it entered the watershed.

In the sulfide room, the material was filtered with a Johnson filter press operat-

ed by compressed air. A steam dryer was used for drying the sulfides. The end product, a soft, black material, contained over 3,000 ounces of silver per ton. This concentrated product was then shipped by rail to refineries. The chemical solutions were pumped back into their respective vats and reused. At peak efficiency, the lixiviation process netted a yield on raw ore of 85% silver.

Barely a year after the mill opened, when Holden's success seemed certain, the devastating Silver Crash of 1893 forced the plant to close. Despite its credentials as "the most complete Russell Lixiviation Plant in the country," the Holden Lixiviation Works was doomed to failure. The mill never expanded its capacity beyond 125 tons a day and it never employed more than 150 men.

I N THE WAKE of the Silver Crash, the Holden Works let go most of its work force. Holden issued a distress statement described by a newspaper as "the piercing cry of pain from a man whose fortune is locked up in silver mining and silver smelters, and who had suddenly thrust upon him the painful sight of his fortune melting into nothing." The Holden Lixiviation Works had operated for fourteen months and counted a profit of $5,343.

The plant went into receivership for its debts, and the collapse so plagued Holden that he claimed personal bankruptcy. It was reported that, years later, he

The Holden Lixiviation Plant looking south from the Castle Creek bridge toward Castle Creek Valley. The trestle of the Colorado Midland Railroad is in the background. The structures were later demolished and the site became the Marolt Cattle Ranch.

was seen selling newspapers at a cigar stand somewhere in the East. By 1917, Holden was reportedly living in Los Angeles and serving as president of the Holden Mining and Milling Company of Elko County, Nevada.

After the plant shut down, creditors filed numerous lawsuits to retrieve their losses. Among the creditors was the Jerome B. Wheeler Banking Company. In 1895, some creditors incorporated as the Aspen Union Smelting Company and reopened the mill, first as a sampling plant and then as a mill utilizing a new technique employing copper plates to collect pure silver. Two lessees, Captain George Thatcher, an Aspen pioneer and booster, and Edward R. Stark, struggled to keep the mill operational, but to no avail. The majority of the larger mines still operating in Aspen had their own mills and the quantity of ore was too small to keep the Thatcher and Stark mill operating profitably.

H. Hale of Manchester, New Hampshire owned the mill from 1901 to 1923. Title was then transferred to Marion C. Smyth of Hillsboro County, New Hampshire. In 1932, W. C. "Billy" Tagert bought the land. The mill had been closed and was in bad condition due to neglect.

The long-abandoned building was salvaged for wood and hardware, and by the time Tagert acquired the property, the mill was in ruins. Its various parts probably still adorn homes and ranches throughout the valley. In 1932, Tagert leased 20 acres of the site to Frank Jr., Rudolph, and Stephen Marolt for one dollar. They combined it with their purchase of the Midland Ranch to form what was later called the Marolt Ranch.

Before he sold the property, Tagert attempted to salvage bricks from one of the smaller smoke stacks, but he used too much dynamite and blew up most of the bricks along with the stack. The tall stack was dismantled over time, and most of the bricks were sold for scrap by the early 1950s.

In 1985, the Aspen Historical Society identified one remaining building—the sampling shed, which had been used as a barn on the Marolt Ranch—as the site for a mining and ranching museum. In 1989, the historical society negotiated a lease and renovated the building.

The Aspen Historical Society spent close to $300,000 stabilizing the sampling shed. The stone foundation was rebuilt, trusses were reinforced, and a new roof was added along with a cupola, which was designed from historic photographs. The renovators built a loft framed with locally cut spruce, repaired windows, installed a fire sprinkler system, and added bathrooms. The renovators strove to duplicate the techniques of the original builders by utilizing wooden pegs in the traditional mortise and tenon technique.

During renovation of the shed, workers discovered pieces of old ore-crushing equipment, remnants of rubberized canvas conveyor belts, a Pelton wheel with brass cups, a mummified pig, and piles of seed from the ranching days. One worker found the skeleton of a cat where it had curled up to die on one of the eaves among the ten-by-ten timber beams. The old salt storage shed was also renovated and is located just west of the Marolt Barn.

Today the site serves as a unique museum representing two of the primary industries of Aspen's early economy—mining and ranching.

EDITOR'S NOTE: *Documents from the archives of the Aspen Historical Society were relied upon for this history. Particular credit goes to Lysa Wegman-French and her Research Scholarship Project,* The Holden-Marolt Site.

THE MAROLT RANCH

PLANTING ROOTS IN ASPEN

AT ABOUT THE TIME Edward Royal Holden was raising capital for his lixiviation plant on the banks of Castle Creek, Frank and Francis Marolt were immigrating to Aspen from Yugoslavia. The couple first settled in Leadville, then followed the wave of town builders across the Continental Divide to Aspen where Frank operated a saloon. The Marolt family—with twelve children—lived above the saloon. Later, the family moved west of town to a ranch that encompassed part of today's Meadowood subdivision. Here the fourteen family members lived in a small, two-room ranch house near the present site of the Aspen Chapel. Because the house was too small for the large family, most of the children slept in the barn.

The Marolt family honored the traditions of the old country and maintained a pioneer way of life. Francis cooked the meals and sewed the clothing for the entire family, performing these duties despite a stroke that had paralyzed one of her arms. When sons Rudy, Frank Jr., Steve, and Bill grew up, they bought the adjacent Midland Ranch, formerly Stitzer's Ranch, and combined their ownership interests into a large family ranch. In 1929, Bill Marolt sold his share to his three brothers, and in 1932 the family ranch expanded onto the 20-acre Holden Lixiviation site. When the Holden site was acquired by the Marolts, five buildings remained from the original Holden Lixiviation Works: the office/assay building, the sampling works (the "Marolt Barn"), a salt warehouse, and two small outbuildings. The Marolt brothers promptly remodeled the old office/assay building, which was inhabited by Frank Marolt for a short time.

Following the death of Rudy Marolt in 1936, the ranch was inherited by Steve and Frank Marolt. They divided the holdings into two ranches; Steve owned the western half and Frank the eastern half, which included the Holden site. Two weeks after the division, Frank died. His wife, Elsie Helen Marolt, sold the eastern part of the ranch to another brother, Mike Marolt, in 1940.

The three remaining ranching brothers—Ted, Steve and Mike—ranched adjacent lands and remained a close-knit family. Their ranches spread from lower Castle Creek across the Aspen Municipal Golf Course to the Snowbunny subdivision, west beyond Buttermilk toward Snowmass, and south as far as Aspen Valley Hospital and Meadowood. The combined Marolt Ranch covered most of the western outskirts of Aspen.

Mike Marolt later married Opal Peterson, the daughter of Swedish immigrants who had first settled in Leadville and later Aspen. The couple lived in the old office/assay works of the Holden Lixiviation Works, which still contained the safe from the mill. The Holden sampling shed (the Marolt Barn) served as a granary, workshop, and hen house. It was partitioned by Mike Marolt to hold grain in bins where oats, barley, and wheat were delivered by an auger from the threshing machine. A hammer mill on the west porch, the former ore loading platform, ground grains instead of silver ore.

Mike built a shop near the south door of the barn, along the west wall, where he installed a work bench and forge. Here he shaped horseshoes, repaired plows

The 110-year-old Holden-Marolt Barn serves as the Aspen Historical Society's Ranching and Mining Museum.

and cultivators, and sharpened harvesting tools. Mike removed the original cupola, which may have housed an ore elevator during the milling days, from the rooftop to simplify his roof repairs. The building was altered many times for various uses as the Marolts' ranching needs changed. After Mike's death in 1967, Opal rented the barn to Don Westerlind, who used it as storage for his construction business. The cupola was rebuilt during the renovation of the building by the Aspen Historical Society in 1989.

DURING THE RANCHING DAYS, the salt warehouse from the lixiviation works was used as a horse barn and milking shed. The Marolts salvaged the east part of the shed to build a new barn shortly after World War II. They later added a corral built of lodgepole rails and oak posts from the Frying Pan Valley. In 1954, the Marolts sawed off the rotten lower sections of the shed and replaced the lower walls with cinder blocks on a new cement floor, converting the old salt shed into a milking barn where a hayloft was later added. The two smaller outbuildings were used for storage of tack and equipment, and Mike Marolt used the dust bin of the tall smoke stack as a locker for preserving beef and smoked sausage.

A salvager named Jake Lewis disassembled most of the big stack in the early 1950s while he lived on the Marolt Property in a shack he built along Castle Creek. Lewis knew not to blast the chimney, as Tagert had done, but instead built an elaborate chute inside the stack. He would climb the stack on iron rungs on the outside and dismantle the chimney one brick at a time, sending them down the chute. This technique still broke most of the bricks, so Lewis stacked a thick pile of straw at the bottom of the chimney and dropped the bricks onto the soft cushion. Lewis sold the bricks, which were used in local buildings. Later, Keith Marolt did the same to pay for his school expenses.

The doors of the granary bear the brand marks of Mike and Steve Marolt. Mike's brand was "XIII" or X-one-eleven. Steve's brand was U1/. During summer and fall, they grazed their herds in the Maroon Creek Valley above T-Lazy-7 Ranch and beyond Maroon Lake toward West Maroon Pass. The cattle were pastured at the Marolt Ranch during the winter and fed hay raised by the Marolts. The Marolts owned milk cows, from which they produced butter and enough cream to ship to creameries in Glenwood Springs and New Castle. Mike and Opal raised pigs and chickens.

COURTESY VICKY MAROLT

On irrigated land, the Marolts grew alfalfa, timothy, and brome grass for hay, from which they made two cuttings, one usually around July 4, the second in late September or early October. Potatoes, barley, and oats were also cultivated; the potatoes were shipped by rail to an agent in New Castle and then on to market. The grains were used to fatten cattle and pigs. Opal tended a summer vegetable garden in which she grew onions, lettuce, carrots, beets, string beans, corn, spinach, cauliflower, and cabbage. She made sauerkraut from the cabbage.

By the late 1950s, Mike's health began to deteriorate and gradually the children went off to college. Mike stopped raising cattle year-round and relied on summer-only cattle grazing, each of them attending the University of Colorado. The Forest Service reduced the grazing allotment for the Marolt herds and Mike began selling parcels of land, including the current sites of the Aspen Municipal Golf Course and Snowbunny subdivision. Mike died in 1967, and Opal moved to Boulder, Colorado, in 1986.

Several of the Marolt descendants became notable ski racers, and the children of Celia and Bill Marolt were particularly accomplished skiers. Celia and Bill, both of Yugoslavian descent, were married in 1929. Celia's parents, Lena and Joseph Tekoucich, were early Aspen residents. Joseph worked in the silver mines and Lena,

ABOVE **Cutting hay on the Marolt Ranch in the 1940s was part of the pastoral life during Aspen's Quiet Years.**

LEFT **In 1950, Vicky Marolt, Mike's daughter, sits beneath the partially demolished chimney of the Holden Lixiviation Works. The bricks were used in many Aspen homes built in the 1960's.**

RIGHT **Mike and Steve Marolt worked cattle in the lull between mining and recreation in the 1940s.**

COURTESY MAROLT FAMILY

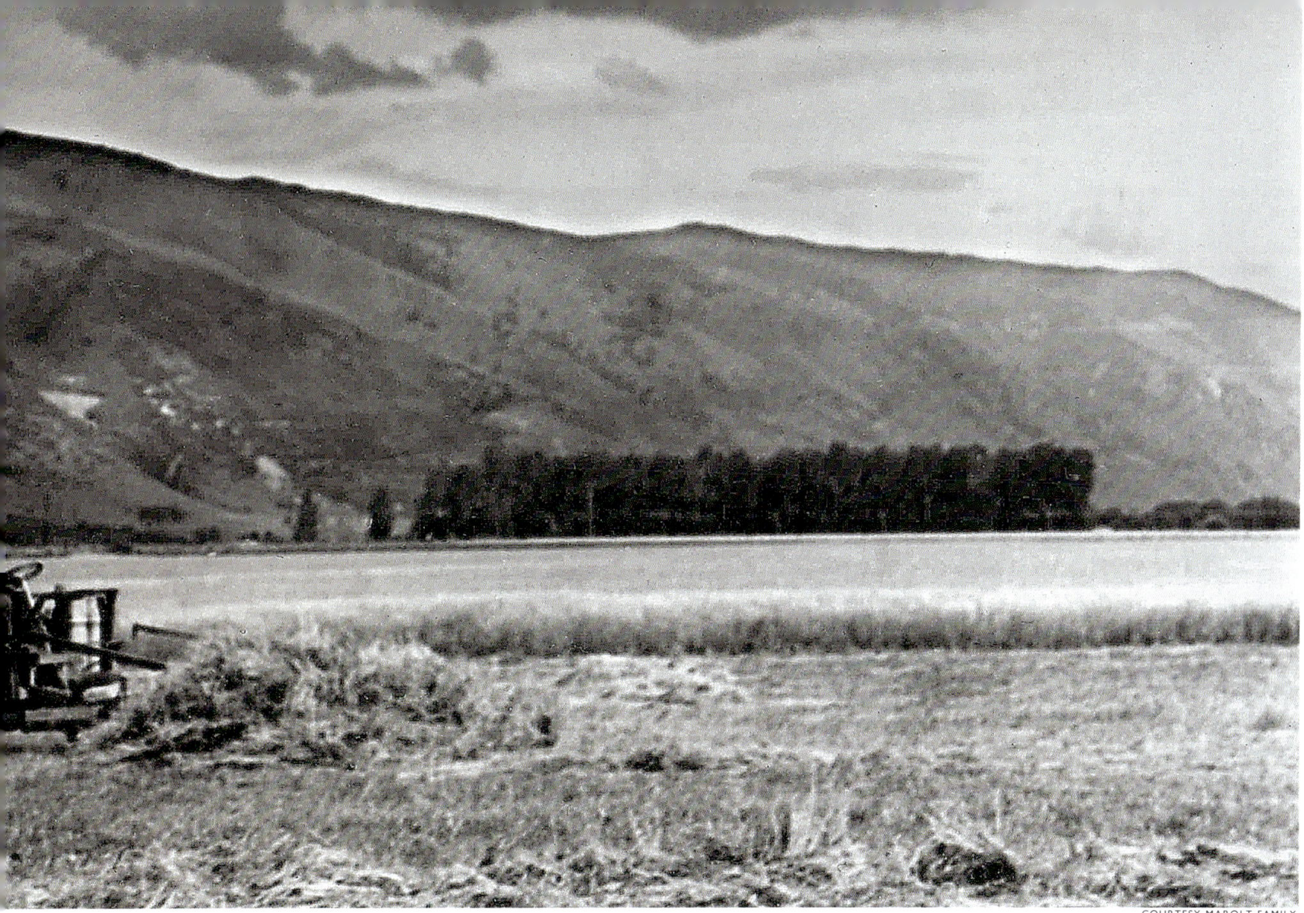

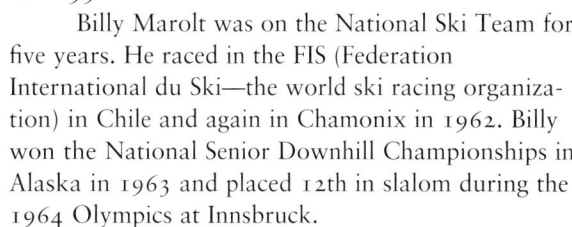

who was born in Leadville, settled with her parents on a homestead three miles up Castle Creek at "Sheridan's Camp," the site of three charcoal ovens, which they used as barns for livestock. After their marriage, Celia and Bill bought a house on Durant Avenue, which came with furniture and two lots for $35. Their children were Beverly (born in 1930), Bud (1932), Max (1936), and Billy (1943).

Bud Marolt won the National Downhill Junior Championship at Alta when he was seventeen. Max Marolt was on the U.S. National Ski team and was named an alternate to the 1952 Olympics. He was also on the FIS team in 1954 and raced in the 1960 Olympics at Squaw Valley. Max was elected to Aspen City council in the late 1990s.

COURTESY MAROLT FAMILY

Billy Marolt was on the National Ski Team for five years. He raced in the FIS (Federation International du Ski—the world ski racing organization) in Chile and again in Chamonix in 1962. Billy won the National Senior Downhill Championships in Alaska in 1963 and placed 12th in slalom during the 1964 Olympics at Innsbruck.

The Marolt Barn and the displays around it conjure the image of a historic working ranch. The grounds are open year-round and are best accessed by walking or biking across the pedestrian bridge from 7th Street to the Marolt Housing site. ❖

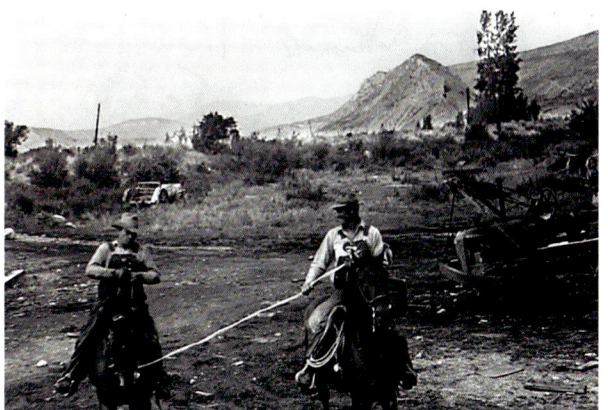

"STUARTSHIP"

STUART MACE MANIFESTS HIS VISION FOR HIS FAMILY AND ASHCROFT

The best use

of this valley

is its own use

as a high aquifer,

as a gene pool;

it is its own reason

for being and in so being,

it is useful to us.

—STUART MACE

LEFT **An aerial view of upper Castle Creek Valley shows Ashcroft ghost town on the left and Toklat Lodge on the right. Further up the valley Express Creek, in shadow, forks left to Taylor Pass and Castle Creek continues south to Cooper Basin and Star Peak, 13,521 feet.**

RIGHT **Stuart Mace**

T WASN'T SILVER, ranching, industry, or skiing that brought Stuart Mace to the Castle Creek Valley over half a century ago; it was philosophy. Armed with an unwavering personal code and an often contentious personality, Mace established himself as the ruling patriarch of the upper Castle Creek Valley from 1949 until his death in 1993. Mace became a powerful advocate for nature conservation and an uncompromising proponent for a life of activism, physical prowess and intimacy with what he revered as "the living world."

"Most legends become such after their deaths, but not Stuart Mace," wrote Mary Hayes in her book *The Aspen Story*. "He was a living legend who commanded a philosophy in such strongly and eloquently pronounced terms that his spirit spread beyond his persona and changed people's lives."

In his essay, *Painting With A Camera*, Mace defined his philosophy as a way of being that aligned him far more with the Ute Indians than with the miners and prospectors who preceded him in Ashcroft. "Life at Toklat has allowed us to mature and to raise a family in tune with the rhythms and responses that surround us in this glorious alpine valley we call home. We do not need to seek immortality. It is a gift we all receive. We only mark it as we can control our massive egos and reach a peace with the whole of our family. Our coming and going are only a part of our being one with the whole of reality. Real love and understanding never looks over its shoulder."

Isabel Mace, Stuart's devoted wife and partner, provided a quiet underlying strength to his forceful proclamations. Through arduous labor and selfless commitment, she furnished a foundation upon which they built their mutual vision of Ashcroft as a sanctuary. Isabel, who died January 30, 2006, at 87, was the nurturing energy from which Toklat Wilderness Lodge became a focal point for students of the wilderness ethic who came from far and wide to be tutored by Stuart and warmed by Isabel's home fires.

COURTESY MACE FAMILY

S TUART MACE WAS BORN in Denver in 1919. His father, who had immigrated from Scotland and worked as a photographer for the *Denver Post*, died when Stuart was four. As a teenager during the Great Depression, Stuart became a helper at a "roving boys' camp", which introduced him to camping and mountaineering. The campers climbed all of Colorado's fifty-four "Fourteeners" (peaks over 14,000 feet) in 1936 and '37, led by Stuart's mentor, Carl Melzer, from Denver. The ascent of Castle Peak first brought Mace to Ashcroft in 1937.

Mace graduated from Grinnell College in Grinnell, Iowa in 1940, where he met fellow student Isabel Pfrimmer Hays. Isabel was born September 13, 1918, in Corydon, Indiana. Her father was an attorney and a dairy farmer who read to her from great literature. Her mother was a college graduate, a musician, and an early practitioner of healthy living via natural, organic foods, a legacy Isabel embraced throughout her life.

The couple married in 1941 and soon moved to Boulder, Colorado, where Stuart had a job and they pursued their graduate degrees – his in botany, hers in sociology. Graduate school had barely begun when Stuart was drafted into the army and reported for service in Wyoming, where he was attached to a truck maintenance detail.

"Stuart didn't know the front end of a truck from the back end," quipped Isabel in an interview in 2001, "but that's the Army for you. He got transferred to Ft. Leonard Wood, Missouri as a typist, but he didn't know anything about typing, either, so I typed all his work for him. Then they put him in a medical detachment doing autopsies and that really turned him off."

Mace's next assignment was at Camp Chaffee, Arkansas, a new military installation. The Colonel in charge learned that Stuart was a botanist and they made a deal: "You handle landscaping for the camp and I'll see you get into officer training school." Stuart became a second lieutenant and was reassigned to the 10th Mountain Division at Camp Hale, Colorado, because of his mountain experience. Arctic survival became his specialty in the famed mountain troops.

Stuart and Isabel lived in Salida, Colorado, forty miles down the Arkansas River from Camp Hale, and Stuart would come home on weekends complaining of nothing to do. When the Army sent out a notice asking for a volunteer to take over the dog detachment, consisting of pack dogs, attack dogs, guard dogs, and sled dogs, in preparation for the Invasion of Norway, they had their man. Stuart took a liking to the dogs, particularly the sled dogs. The invasion was later called off and the sled teams were never employed.

Stuart Mace drives his dog sled in Ashcroft as a commercial venture in the mid-1960s.

After the war, explained Isabel, Stuart had a job in Boulder as a florist in a greenhouse where he hoped to pursue plant genetics, his greatest interest. "We had seven or eight dogs that he brought out of the Army because the Army was going to put them all to sleep. People were afraid of the sled dogs and the people in Boulder asked us to leave."

Walter Paepcke, who would usher in Aspen's renaissance as a cultural center in 1949, owned a ranch near Colorado Springs and wanted a mascot for the ranch. He had heard about Mace's dogs and came to see them in Boulder. Paepcke was so drawn to the dogs that he took one back to his ranch. He also took an interest in Mace, who explained that he was dissatisfied with his job "making bouquets." Paepcke suggested that Mace go to Aspen to run a sled dog operation there. Familiar with Aspen from his mountain climbing travels, Stuart was not hard to convince; he was looking for a natural setting in which to raise his family, and Isabel was game for a new start. With their first child, Greg, who was then just an infant, they drove in an open Jeep, with only a canvas top, over Loveland Pass in a snow storm. The trip took twelve hours. "We got into the hotel in Aspen at three in the morning," recalled Isabel.

The next day, Stuart announced his plans to relocate in Aspen to Ted Ryan, who had first met Stuart in 1937 when the Highland Bavarian Lodge was under construction and Stuart was climbing the Fourteeners. "Ted offered housing at the Highland Bavarian Lodge, and that sealed things," recounted Isabel. "We went back to Boulder and bundled everything up. We had about ten dollars at that time and had to freight the dogs over. We took residence at the Highland Bavarian Lodge on Castle Creek."

From Highland, Mace took his dogs into Aspen to give sled rides, but he spent more money boarding the dogs than he made on the sled rides. "Stuart began taking the dogs up the Castle Creek Valley to see what possibilities were up at Ashcroft," explained Isabel. "He got this idea of setting up a lodge and an eating place and taking people for sled rides on up to the high country."

The Maces were invited by Ted Ryan to build a lodge at Ashcroft on land he owned as part of the Highland Bavarian Corporation. Ryan offered the Maces a lifetime lease in return for their commitment to the stewardship of the upper valley. This agreement would define the rest of the Maces' lives as Stuart and Isabel put down deep roots on land that they would never own.

Stuart described this unusual approach in a 1974 interview with Bill Moyers: "I am trying to leave my children a heritage of inner strength and it's nothing that a wallet or the sale price of a home will buy. I am trying not to leave them anything in the form of money. Anything they are going to get from me they will get from me before I go." The Moyers documentary on Stuart Mace and his sled dogs was titled: *Living Free in the Rockies* and was introduced by Moyers as an example of "selfhood against mobism." The concept of self-hood was the kernel of the Mace's philosophy.

STUART AND ISABEL began construction in 1948, and the Toklat Wilderness Lodge opened for business for the first time in the summer of 1949. Stuart and Isabel Mace had found an end to their search for a permanent home for themselves, their two young children (Isabel was pregnant with a third), and twenty huskies. Toklat, an Eskimo word meaning "headwaters of a glacial mountain valley," evolved into a lodge, restaurant, home, ecology center, and art gallery. Toklat provided all that Stuart needed, especially its location in the midst of a vast mountain landscape that suited the scope of his vision quest.

Succinctly stating his utilitarian needs, Stuart explained his goal: "I am eager to find a way of life for myself and my family that is satisfying, independent in a personal way, and financially sound."

Mary Hayes, a close friend, described the Toklat experience, "Stuart and Isabel strove to make their home reflect a union with the environment and with Earth's native peoples. Its resident family would become the conscience of the Aspen community and, in particular, the upper Castle Creek Valley, provoking dialogue about man's impact on the Earth, locally and globally."

In the late '40s, Ashcroft was a remote backwater. The Castle Creek Road was left unplowed to the old ghost town and Stuart had to convince the Pitkin County Commissioners to keep the road open to Toklat. Once they were in residence, the county agreed. Over the next decade, Mace's dog pack grew from half a dozen to 130 dogs as he bred and trained his Malamutes and Siberian Huskies. The concrete floor of the original porch exhibited the names and paw-prints of the sled dogs. When visitors entered the lodge, they tread on these prints.

The dogs—Kiak, Chinook, Maux, Kluan, Yukon King, and others—pulled sleds around trails packed out with snowshoes by the Maces. Hollywood took note of Stuart's teams and the stunning scenery of Ashcroft and began movie and television work there in the mid-1950s. Stuart Mace, Ashcroft and the surrounding Elk Mountains were featured in the television series Sergeant Preston of the Royal Canadian Mounted Police and in a feature film, Three Redheads from Seattle. Four different dogs played the part of "King", Sergeant Preston's unflagging companion, and all were trained by Mace, who performed many of the stunts himself.

Toklat Wilderness Lodge was named from an Eskimo word meaning "headwaters of a mountain valley." Stuart and Isabel built the lodge and it served as a restaurant, art gallery and gathering place for Ashcroft for over fifty years. In 2005 it was acquired by Aspen Center for Environmental Studies.

D AY-TO-DAY LIVING in the mountains at 9,000 feet is demanding enough, but Mace wanted more. He endeavored to build a greenhouse for raising wild orchids, but it never got beyond the excavation. Toklat became the venue for famous fish fries with loads of trout Stuart acquired from a private fish hatchery on the Frying Pan River. Isabel recalled John Denver joining one fish fry and singing around the campfire. At Christmas, Stuart took his dogs to other communities and played Santa Claus on the dog sled. Stuart loved tea and he mixed his own blends with rose petals, local herbs, and other blends of tea from China. He sold them in handmade aspen wood boxes lined with foil that were branded with a hot iron "Toklat Teas." The Maces made trips to the Southwest and brought back Navajo rugs, pottery, sand paintings, and jewelry for the gallery.

When Toklat was first built, it was insulated with sawdust, which covered the floor. "We advertised that people could put their bedrolls down for the night, and a Canadian couple were the first customers we had," said Isabel. "Marsh Barnard came to Aspen and organized a group to climb and ski Mt. Hayden in the spring. I would make them an early breakfast and they would be up the peak by sunrise.

"Our first Christmas we had a lodge full from Texas. The county plow broke down and it took them a week to repair it. Then it snowed and the wind blew and drifted across the road and we couldn't get out. That was after we got the telephone and these businessmen called their bosses and said they couldn't make it … as if their bosses were going to believe them. We all built a big snowman out here that day and had a ball. You just struggled to make a living and you did what you could."

Isabel's passion was whole foods. She grew vegetable and grain gardens in a high-altitude environment and provided a menu based on sound nutritional values and wholesome comforts. Before a day of dog sledding with Stuart and his protégé, Dan MacEachen, guests were treated to a hearty breakfast of sourdough pancakes, teas specially blended by Stuart, and homemade jams and jellies made from mountain fruits and berries.

The sled rides followed the Pearl Pass Road above Ashcroft to Toklat Chalet, which was also known as the Mace Hut. Stuart built the chalet five miles beyond

Toklat in the upper Castle Creek Valley in 1950 and '51 with help from Bill Kirkwood. The original A-frame structure was made with wood salvaged from an old mule barn that served the valley during the mining days of the late 1800s. Following a typical dog sled outing, guests warmed themselves at a roaring fire in the lodge. Stuart mixed his famous "Dangerous Dan McGrew" cocktails and Isabel prepared Alaskan meatballs. Following dinner, Stuart would read from Robert W. Service, tell tales of the Arctic and his command of the Canine Corps in the 10th Mountain Division, or recount the history of Ashcroft and its many characters during the mining heyday.

The Toklat restaurant featured hanging tables suspended from the ceiling by steel rods. Stuart discovered this unusual table design in Alaska during World War II when he journeyed north as an emissary of the Canine Corps to buy dogs for the service. These tables became hallmarks of two other restaurant locations—the Hickory House and Chart House—which the Maces opened in Aspen as "Toklat in Aspen." At both restaurants, whole foods were the basis of the menu.

Stuart ended the Aspen franchises in 1969 and returned his attentions to Ashcroft, where Isabel had been managing the kennels and running Toklat. Dinners were so popular at Toklat that reservations were booked a year in advance. In 1978, the Maces converted Toklat into an art gallery where exhibits were on display and a pot of wild mushroom soup was kept hot on the wood-burning stove, served along with bread and tea.

With their mutual appreciation for art and their commitment to Toklat, the Maces lived somewhat detached from Aspen in the early days. "We never got down to any of the lectures or music," said Isabel. "We had to keep things going up here. But a lot of people would come visit, so we got to the point where we knew a group and they would come up—Lynn Harrell and Jim Levine—and they would give us a private concert and we would serve them dinner. We were fortunate to have this experience and I think the children would all say the same. Life was different for them. They did chores, worked in the kennels, and rode the bus to and from town."

The mountains cut man down to his proper size. They are a constant reminder of where I belong and where I fit into things.

—STUART MACE

L IVING IN REMOTE ASHCROFT provided many challenges for the young family. The eldest child, Greg, was home schooled the first few years until a bus was assigned to come up the valley and pick up Greg and his four siblings. Once, when Greg was seriously hurt, it took the Aspen community to save his life. "In 1950, when Greg was seven, he fell out of an Army cot and broke an artery," remembered Isabel. "The doctor came up to look at him and took him downtown, then told us we had to get him to Denver."

Sardy Field, the Aspen Airport, was only a grass strip, but Greg's condition required an emergency flight to Children's Hospital. Isabel recalled that a pilot flying his plane over Aspen, en route from Denver, was contacted by radio and asked to make an emergency landing in Aspen. He complied, but it was night by then and the airport had no lights. The Maces and their friends contacted everyone they knew with a car. The community responded by driving to the airstrip, lining up their cars side-by-side and training their headlights on the runway.

"When the pilot landed, they told him that Greg needed to get to a hospital in Denver," said Isabel, "so he said he would turn right around and take him there. They put Greg in the airplane and they took off for Denver where they whisked him off to Children's Hospital."

When the Maces first arrived in Ashcroft, cattle had the run of the valley. The valley floor was dust and the grass was mostly gone from overgrazing. "We moved in with the cows," explained Isabel. "I remember one morning watching a cow rubbing his face against the window at his own reflection. When Greg was young, he pushed them all down the valley without us knowing it. I looked around for Greg one day at lunch and couldn't find him. I went out and saw a Jeep coming up the road and asked if they had seen a little boy. They said they had and that he was down the valley driving the cows because that's what he'd seen us do."

Once the cattle were removed, the Maces worked hard to reintroduce native vegetation. The healthy grassland meadows seen today are the result of the Mace's commitment to restoring the valley to the way it was before the impacts of human settlement. Later, Stuart led many visitors and students on guided hikes, during which he discoursed on his "Philosophy of the Green World." His influence spread to Aspen where he was a founding trustee of the Aspen Center for Environmental Studies (ACES).

In 2002 Isabel Mace reflects on a half-century of life at Toklat. She passed away on January 30, 2006.

RIGHT American Lake at dawn. High above Ashcroft, the lake is the water-source for Toklat Lodge and a popular hiking destination.

IN AN EFFORT TO EXTEND his children's social interactions in remote Ashcroft, Stuart began an international exchange program. "We exchanged Greg with a boy from Switzerland through the head of the Swiss climbing school," said Isabel, "and, in exchange, we got a Swiss boy for a year. Greg came back very cosmopolitan at eighteen. He hadn't had much interest in school before then, but he came back gung-ho and graduated here with honors, then founded the Honors Society."

Stuart Mace furthered his environmental outreach when the family founded Malachite Farm in the 1980s in southern Colorado. Malachite was a unique, organic farm where children could learn about farming by working the land. Sustainable agriculture and crafts rounded out a hands-on curriculum run by Alan, Kent, and Bruce, three of the Mace children. Malachite remains in the family, but no longer operates as a children's school.

In 1974, Stuart decided to end his dog sledding career and gave Dan MacEachen, his chief musher and apprentice for four years, the entire Toklat kennels. Dan moved the operation to Snowmass where he offers sled rides and exotic, wild game meals at Krabloonik, which is named for one of Stuart's original dogs. Krabloonik is an Eskimo word for "bushy, white eyebrows," an apt description of Mace himself.

That same year, the U.S. Forest Service and the Aspen Historical Society, in conjunction with the Mace family, began restoring the old ghost town of Ashcroft in an effort to preserve the mining history of the once thriving mining boom town. Greg Mace and his Hungarian-born wife Krisi became managers and part owners of the Pine Creek Cookhouse and the Ashcroft Ski Touring center, both of which were owned by Ted Ryan.

One winter the Maces allowed Ted Ryan's daughter and a couple of her friends to spend the night at Toklat Chalet. According to Isabel, the girls didn't know how to start the fire in the wood-burning stove and used kerosene to prime it. "That was the demise of the A-frame," she said. Several of Greg's friends from

Switzerland helped him build the present hut, which is mostly made of stone and steel and remains standing after being slammed by a massive avalanche in the late 1980s.

Greg Mace died in 1986 in a climbing accident on the Maroon Bells. The peak adjacent to Star Peak in the Elk Mountains south of Ashcroft was named Greg Mace Peak in his honor. Stuart survived his eldest son by seven years.

Former Castle Creek Valley naturalist Trevor Washko, once a resident guide of Ashcroft and dedicated disciple of Stuart's, described Mace's burial: "Stuart Mace died at his home, Toklat, on August 4th 1993 at the age of seventy-four. At sunset on August 6th he was placed in a spruce/pine coffin made by his son, Kent, and buried in a grave dug by his family and friends near the base of Castle Peak, the mountain that first brought him to this valley as a young mountaineer in 1936. His grave-site, hidden amongst wildflowers, is modestly marked with a small cement slab poured by Stuart forty years before. It simply reads, 'Toklat' and holds the paw print of his first lead dog."

I insist that man can't, doesn't and shouldn't own land. He can use it, but he should only use it if he cares about it.

—STUART MACE

IN JANUARY 2004, hoping to preserve Toklat as an enduring nature amenity, the Aspen Center for Environmental Studies launched a capital campaign to acquire the Toklat property, including three acres and the 5,000-square-foot lodge. The Catto Charitable Foundation stepped up with a significant lead gift challenging ACES to complete the $3,250,000 campaign.

Many contributions were given and the campaign was successful. By the fall of 2005, the transfer was made, and in the spring of 2006, the "Catto Center at Toklat" opened its doors to the public. Classes and events will be run from now on by ACES, which will utilize Toklat and further the vision that Stuart and Isabel described for a nature sanctuary given to experiential education.

"We anticipate that Toklat's compellingly dramatic setting could become ACES most persuasive site," announced ACES. "At Toklat we will focus on the challenge of being committed to an ethic that embodies responsible stewardship of our resilient but finite and exploited biosphere. Our central focus at Toklat will be the elevation of environmentalism to a broadly held worldview."

Given the many achievements of the remarkable Mace family, and the new vision under ACES, Toklat clearly defines what may be called "Stuartship." ❖

THE DEANE FAMILY

OF THE T-LAZY-7 RANCH

ANYONE FAMILIAR with the Maroon Creek Valley knows the T-Lazy-7 Ranch. Llamas perch on the roof of a shed blinking sleepily at passersby, horses graze in grassland meadows, a huge log lodge stands among a grove of old spruce trees, and hoe-downs, barbecues, and snowmobile tours are offered by "down home" folks. The T-Lazy-7 also holds a rich history of Aspen and its early beginnings as a frontier town.

Josiah W. Deane was among the earliest pioneers to cross over into Aspen from the high passes. Born in Massachusetts in 1853, Deane came to Leadville in 1878. He made the trip to Aspen over Independence Pass on snowshoes in May 1880 as a member of B. Clark Wheeler's town survey party. Wheeler brought Deane, an attorney, to look after the legalities of the mining properties Wheeler had bought for his client, David Hyman, a Cincinnati capitalist who would later figure prominently in Aspen's development as a silver mining district. Deane, the first lawyer to set foot in Aspen, provided legal clout to Wheeler's Aspen Town and Land Company, which "jumped" Henry Gillespie's previous townsite claim.

Upon their arrival at the tent camp, then called Ute City, Deane and Wheeler immediately faced a contest to Wheeler's townsite claim by squatters and a group of pioneers who predated his visit. There was talk of forcefully taking properties, but according to historian Malcolm Rohrbough in his book, *Aspen: The History of a Silver Mining Town*, Judge Deane stopped the insurrection by arguing the validity of property rights. Deane convinced the squatters that if Wheeler's townsite lots could be seized this week, then town lots with improvements might be taken next week. The conflict simmered down, but claims and counterclaims on the townsite controversy "became Aspen's first political issue," wrote Rohrbough.

Deane and Wheeler said they represented a well-financed corporation that would benefit the camp in the long run. They attempted to ameliorate the conflict with the "jumpers association" by pledging to invest in roads and a smelter. Desperate for such improvements, some of the opposition favored the compromise, especially when it meant getting on with the business of mining and town building. Eager miners were none too patient when the next big strike might be just a few days, or a few shovelfuls, away.

Once the compromise was reached, Deane helped Wheeler survey the townsite and change the name of the fledgling mining camp from Ute City to Aspen. The first name had been given in deference to the native Indian nation that held rights to the valley until 1881. The name Aspen celebrated the quaking aspen trees in the upper Roaring Fork Valley.

Josiah Deane set up a law practice in Aspen. He and a partner built one of the city's first log houses, which they used as a law office. Deane also established a charcoal pit and produced charcoal for blacksmithing. Supported by Wheeler, Deane acquired a large parcel of land along the southern boundary of the townsite and developed the first subdivision in Aspen, known as the Deane Addition, a tract of land between the original townsite and the foot of Aspen Mountain. Deane Street, just below old Lift 1, still bears the name of the man who filed the subdivision.

In May the pasture below T-Lazy-7 Ranch becomes a sea of dandelions.

THE JUDGE

Great grandfather came here in 1881
He'd always been a miner and he had a miner's son
He snowshoed o'er the mountains from the town
*   of Leadville*
And he wintered up in Ashcroft while snow was cold
*   and still*
Early the next springtime, snow melting in the sun
He staked out a townsite where Aspen was begun

And he wouldn't leave the mountains
*   or the valley that he loved*
He stayed here all his lifetime;
*   was the first County Judge...*

—BUCK DEANE

WHEN PITKIN COUNTY was incorporated on February 23, 1881, Deane was appointed its first judge by Governor Frederick W. Pitkin, for whom Pitkin County was named; Deane would later serve as Pitkin County Attorney. Judge Deane married Lottie B. Cruikshank, an opera performer who had entertained in Chicago. They had a child, Harry Deane.

Harry Deane grew up in Aspen and married a woman named Selma. The couple lived in Aspen for several years, then moved around the state and eventually settled in Nevada, where Harry engaged in mining. They had one son, Harold Alexander Deane, shortened to the acronym HAD, who was born in Steamboat Springs, Colorado, on August 9, 1910. Years later, in the early 1950s, Selma came to live at the T-Lazy-7 Ranch until she passed away in 1963.

As a boy "Had" Deane spent summers in Aspen with his grandfather, the Judge, who owned a cabin at Weller Lake Campground on the Independence Pass Road. Judge Deane had worked on the Independence Pass road in the early days and he shared his stories with his grandson. Judge Deane died on March 14, 1930 and the *Aspen Times* reported the passing of one of the town's foremost pioneers:

"Judge Deane was about seventy-six years of age and was a remarkable man physically and mentally. In the organization days, he stood foremost in all things for Aspen's betterment, giving the full force of his excellent legal training for the good of his community. In recognition of this, an addition to the city of Aspen and a street in this addition bear his name. During the famous Apex suit, which made legal history for mining, Judge Deane took an important part in that great battle. For several years, Judge Deane followed mining in Utah, Arizona, New Mexico, and Nevada, returning to Aspen in about 1911 and residing here since that date."

"Together with the [*Aspen*] *Times*, he carried on the primary movement for the establishment of the Independence Pass Highway and was chief spokesman at all the early meetings to establish our present splendid highway system. Dr. Bartlett, J. D. Brunton, and Judge Deane were the authors of the first highway bill to be passed by the Colorado Assembly in 1913. Indeed at all times did Judge Deane stand at the top of all endeavors to promote and prosper his home town, county, state, and nation. A staunch Republican and coming from old Pilgrim stock, he was ALL-American at all times and in all places. He was a man among men and his passing is regretted by every man, woman, and child in Aspen. He is buried in Red Butte Cemetery."

After working a few years as a mountain guide in Colorado, Had Deane settled in Chicago where he worked for Tamms Industries. Had graduated from Northwestern University in nearby Evanston and decided to pursue a career in the Midwest. But Colorado was in his blood, and in 1938, he left Chicago for the mountains he loved and had known as a boy.

"Had Deane was twenty-eight years old when he decided he was going to retire out West and look for someone to marry who also wanted to get away. That was me," recalled Lou Deane in a 1990 interview featured in *The Story of Aspen* by Mary Eshbaugh Hayes.

Louise Glover Deane (Lou) was born September 13, 1911, to John and Marie Glover and raised in Memphis, Tennessee. For much of the 1930s, she was a stage actress on Broadway, playing leading roles on the *Great White Way*. She also appeared in several motion pictures. "My mother's side of the family was always a little more straight-laced," said Buck Deane, "but when she was fourteen my mother kind of took off and went to New York and did live radio and theater. And she

Buck Deane, troubadour.

"My mother's side of the family was always a little more straight-laced," said Buck Deane, "but when she was fourteen my mother kind of took off and went to New York and did live radio and theater. And she had a baby while she was there," he said, referring to his late half brother, Tony.

—BUCK DEANE

had a baby while she was there," he said, referring to his late half brother, Tony.

"She lived with Shirley Temple; that was her best friend. She was in a film with W. C. Fields. She went to California to go into films and she and one other actress were picked to do a part that would have made one of them a major star. The director and a buddy of his made a bet that she would take a shower in the nude in front of them. My mother wouldn't do that to have the job and she lost the part. The other lady got the role and became a major star. She made her choice and she was a strong woman," said Buck with a note of pride. "She moved to Aspen, but when she heard that John Ford was shooting a Western somewhere she would say, 'You know, I'd like to go down there,' just so she could be there. But she never kept any of those ties. She was the solid force, the one that was always there for us."

The Rick Deane family (L TO R) Jesse, Landon, Rick and Besha.

IN THE FALL OF 1938, Lou and Had Deane moved to Aspen. They stayed at Waterman's Cabins where the old Agate Lodge later occupied part of a city block on Aspen's West End, which is now the site of multimillion dollar homes. Later, when the land was redeveloped, Buck Deane moved the original Waterman 1A Cabins to Carbondale.

After living in Aspen for a year, Had and Lou bought the T-Lazy-7 ranch from the John Sievers family, for whom a rugged mountain peak is named in the Maroon Creek Valley, just west of the ranch. The old homestead included 300 acres and a distinctive brand: "T-Lazy-7."

"Mrs. Sievers had a problem with asthma and they would take a sabbatical from the ranch and stay at the Hotel Jerome, where her health would improve," explained Buck. "When my folks moved into the Sievers' place, it was a one-room cabin with a dirt floor, no running water, no electricity and the ceiling had pole rafters draped with burlap. They pulled that burlap down and found six inches of fine dust, which probably explained why Mrs. Sievers was having trouble breathing."

Had and Lou contracted with Leroy Waterman to build a little home behind the ranch where the Willow Creek ditch flows. Simple and rustic, the home had a little shower room with a peaked roof and a stove to heat water. Running water came from gravity flow from the ditch. The cabin burned down that Christmas Eve, but the foundation, fireplace, and shower house remain. The Deanes gradually built up the ranch to a point where it could house all the guests the gregarious Had Deane invited to share his and Lou's hospitality.

"Had invited all his friends to see our ranch," Lou explained. "He had so many friends, I finally said we had to have some paying guests. Had was too generous. He would let anyone ride our horses. So one day I went to the Aspen Times office and had some cards printed up that advertised horseback riding by the hour. I thought Had would never speak to me again, but we were in business."

An early promotional brochure for the T-Lazy-7 Guest Ranch states the Deane's philosophy: "Our ranch welcomes you 'IF'... you enjoy superb scenery, horses for riding our beautiful trails, fishing our tumbling mountain streams, or just relaxing by our large pool. We plan breakfast, lunch, and dinner rides with great camp cooking. Our chuck wagon dinners include singing, dancing, and just plain fun."

A CCORDING TO BUCK DEANE, "Had worked for Tamms in Chicago three months a year, during the winters, and he had a lot of friends. He was a great storyteller. He was a big man—6' 1" and 220 pounds. He played football for Northwestern University and for the Chicago Bears. He always rolled Bull Durham tobacco and he could do it in a wind. He smoked cigarettes until they would get down to his lips and sometimes there was no tobacco in them and he would be telling a story and he would light that thing up again and smoke it and it hung there on his lip. People loved him. He had a story for everything. He was something…"

On an upper section of the ranch just below Maroon Lake, the Deanes expanded the guest ranch and opened the Maroon Bells Lodge. A brochure from the 1950s described the lodge: "Our meals are excellent…we raise our own beef, chickens, and vegetables, as well as maintain our own milk herd. There's lots of cream and homemade butter at T-Lazy-7. Our guides and wranglers are lifelong mountain men…. Breaking horses at the ranch is a daily task and each week we hold an impromptu rodeo…. You will find every moment packed with something interesting to do—or you can just loaf in that grand Colorado sun…. We enjoy teaching the children to ride, handle horses and cook over a campfire. They will learn a lot about outdoor life and the young ones thrive on good food, fresh air and daily rides or hikes into the upper regions…. The country made famous by Teddy Roosevelt!"

The Deanes later sold the Maroon Bells Lodge to Henry Stein, one of Had's old Chicago friends and a college buddy from Northwestern University. Then the Deanes bought the Strong Ranch meadow, just below T-Lazy-7, from Clyde Mecham.

"My dad loved horses and they started with about ten," explained Buck. "When he died in 1962, we had 186 head of horses up there. That's a lot of horses. They had some cattle, too. One summer in the early '50s my father contracted to graze some Texan longhorn steers on the place. The steers arrived on the train and were unloaded below the Hotel Jerome at a stockyard. They were all slicked up and there was about a foot of fresh snow on the ground and they thought they would all die. Those steers started jumping out of the corrals and some ran up toward Independence Pass, some downvalley. They were wild and it was like trying to herd deer. I remember going up to the Bells later with my dad and he sat down with binoculars and started looking up in the spires and saying 'Yep, I can see six of 'em. Oh, there's a couple more.' We hired cowboys from Meeker and everywhere and they rounded up cattle, and when they shipped them out they were fat and slick and there was none of them missing."

Throughout the years, the ranch appeared in movies like *Devil's Doorway*, starring Robert Taylor, and in TV commercials for 7-Up and General Motors. The T-Lazy-7 became a Western icon that put Aspen in the limelight.

After Had Deane died in 1962 at the age of fifty-two from a cerebral hemorrhage, Lou and her sons, Buck and Rick, ran the ranch as an Aspen landmark with miles of fishing streams and horseback trails, chuckwagon dinners, sleigh rides, snowmobile tours in the winter, and a rustic guest lodge. Buck's country-western band performed at dances. Rick has been a mainstay volunteer of Mountain Rescue Aspen for decades. The Deane's eldest son, Tony (Lou's child from a previous marriage), was a rescue team member who died in an avalanche in Utah in 1958.

"Those steers started jumping out of the corrals and some ran up toward Independence Pass, some downvalley. They were wild and it was like trying to herd deer. I remember going up to the Bells later with my dad and he sat down with binoculars and started looking up in the spires and saying 'Yep, I can see six of 'em. Oh, there's a couple more.'"

—BUCK DEANE

FOR THE DEANE BOYS, growing up on the ranch was a dream. "We fished a lot," said Buck. "There were some great beaver ponds where you could really see them. We grew up hunting. I got my name Buck because we were raised on deer meat and I really liked deer meat. I have early recollections of playing on the ranch in a family that was right there, the best mom and dad, totally supportive. Kids walked up to the ranch from Aspen sometimes to play, but I was used to doing for myself."

When skiing became the dominant tourist activity in Aspen, the Deanes were right in step as Buck recalled. "My older brother came home one day and said 'I gotta show you this new thing.' I said 'What is it?' He said, 'It's called skiing.' I said 'Yeah!' He took me outside and put these boots and skis on and he pushed himself through the snow and said, 'You want to try it?' I said 'Yeah', and that was my first time skiing."

As the T-Lazy-7 grew into a popular resort, the Deane boys worked with wranglers and cowboys who were holdouts from a bygone era. "We spent a lot of summers in the mountains," said Buck. "I loved being out in the mountains. The ranch attracted workers, many of whom were old broken down cowboys, people you just don't see anymore around here, guys who were brought up on ranches, rode rodeos and got kicked in the head, and had broken bones. They were some real characters and they all had stories. And I spent all my time with these guys. What a way to grow up. We were maybe a little red-neck up there, but mostly pretty understanding about the hippies. I met a lot of people on the ranch from different walks of life, so I had a broader scope of life than most people might think. A lot of the opportunities and growth I had were due to the ranch and its guests."

BUCK PICKED UP THE GUITAR as a senior in high school and said it took him a year to learn three chords. He began his professional career as a musician and performer after his first nerve-wracking solo performance in the old Bier Stube at Aspen Highlands in the 1960s. His band became known as "Buck Deane and the Buckin' Strings."

The forty-year-old lodge at the T-Lazy-7 burned down one night in 1991 and was rebuilt in 1992. When the old lodge burned, Lou escaped wearing her nightgown but lost all the historic photographs and memorabilia collected over a lifetime. The new lodge, designed by the Deanes and built by contractor Jack Kaufman, is a spruce log building with a big dining hall, bar and a stage. There are two huge rock fireplaces on the first level and three guest rooms upstairs. The standing dead spruce logs came from the Grand Lake area. Wagon wheels from as far away as Kansas are employed as chandeliers, and an antique doctor's buggy is suspended from the ceiling. Other antiques provide a rural, historic ambiance. Horseshoes are fashioned into door handles.

Lou Deane died Thursday, April 1, 1993. She was eighty-one. Her death ended an era on the ranch and allowed a deep-seated animosity to erupt between the two surviving brothers that eventually landed them in a court battle for control of the ranch.

Today the T-Lazy-7 is under the management of Rick Deane and his wife Landon, offering traditional trail rides, fishing, hiking, hay rides, and a large, heated pool occasionally visited by black bears. Winter is also a big season for the ranch, with snowmobile tours to the Maroon Bells and Independence Ghost Town, horse drawn sleigh rides along Maroon Creek, cross-country skiing, ice skating, and live country-western music and dancing.

Buck Deane lives on an 80-acre ranch near Carbondale. He teaches skiing for the Aspen Skiing Company and plays music with his popular country-western band, performing a repertoire filled with original songs that provide a sense of his own pleasure in his mountain home, a pleasure shared by residents and visitors alike. ❖

COLORADO

There's a high mountain valley way up in Colorado

Where crystal clear water runs down from cold winter snow

Beautiful meadows where wildflowers grow

And a deep pine forest where my melodies go…

Mountain melodies on high where the peaks meet the sky

And a man can be free and he almost can fly…

—BUCK DEANE

T-Lazy-7 country. Maroon Creek, looking northeast toward Aspen from the crags of Pyramid Peak, shows the proximity of wilderness to the urban context of the Roaring Fork Valley below.

9 Ski Dreams for Castle Creek

S KI DEVELOPERS THINK BIG. They look over vast, mountainous terrain and see ski runs, lifts, and resort facilities. Castle Creek has drawn ski developers whose grandiose visions never got off the drawing boards, but inspired hundreds of ski enthusiasts and raised millions of dollars in capital investments.

Two major ski dreams, if realized, would have dramatically changed the look and feel of the Castle Creek Valley. One was focused on the Mt. Hayden massif, the other on Richmond Ridge. In both cases, world events and the changing development climate in Aspen conspired in their downfall.

MAGNIFICENT MT. HAYDEN

W HILE ASHCROFT languished in the aftermath of silver mining in the 1930s, another industry–skiing–was poised to make Ashcroft a destination resort with international prestige. The mountain West was a prime location for winter resorts that could capitalize on deep winter snows and glaciated mountains. Chance meetings and fast friendships came together with plans for a European-style ski resort that could have become the biggest in the U.S.

Theodore S. "Ted" Ryan was introduced to skiing in the 1920s and fell in love with cross-country skiing on the "Maple Leaf Trail" in the Laurentian Mountains of Canada. In 1935, Ryan skied in Europe for the first time, and his view of skiing was forever changed. He met a young man there named William M. L. "Billy" Fiske, III, a student at Cambridge University and the former captain of the U.S. Bobsled Team, which had competed in the Winter Olympics of 1932. Fiske and Ryan shared a close bond from their mutual love of skiing and together attended the Winter Olympics in Garmisch, Germany, in 1936. They marveled at the expansive ski slopes and alpine terrain, and they vowed to establish a ski area in America that could be the equal of those in Europe.

That summer, during a visit to Pasadena, California, Fiske met T. J. Flynn, a die-hard Ashcroft promoter who tried to interest the young man in silver claims in Colorado. Fiske wasn't interested in silver, but rather in the photographs Flynn showed him of the area where the mines were located. The mountains resembled those in Europe, replete with high snowy basins. Fiske decided to explore the area.

Fiske and three friends flew a single-engine airplane to Glenwood Springs (Fiske was the pilot), where they set down unannounced on a golf course. They spent the next three days exploring Aspen and Ashcroft, relishing in the sights of Aspen Mountain, Little Annie Basin, and Mt. Hayden. Their guide was Billy Tagert, a true character of the upper Roaring Fork Valley who had run away to Aspen as a boy in the late 1800s (see pg. 156).

Fiske and friends knew they had found a gem in the Elk Mountains and were eager to return to Pasadena and report their find. Lifting off from Glenwood Springs required that the golf course temporarily drop some power lines so the

Fiske and three friends flew a single-engine airplane to Glenwood Springs (Fiske was the pilot), where they set down unannounced on a golf course. They spent the next three days exploring Aspen and Ashcroft relishing in the sights of Aspen Mountain, Little Annie Basin, and Mt. Hayden.

The first ski descent of Mt. Hayden by André Roch and the Los Alamos Ranch School Ski Team in March, 1937.

97

plane could clear the makeshift field. As soon as he returned home, Fiske called Ted Ryan in New York and told him of his discovery, extolling the virtues of the Elk Mountains as the motherlode for American skiing. The men joined in a partnership and soon formed the Highland Bavarian Corporation, the first ski company in Colorado. They acquired options on the Tagert Lake Ranch along the Independence Pass road near Difficult Creek and on the Highland Ranch at the junction of Castle and Conundrum Creeks.

I N OCTOBER 1936, twenty men were employed to construct the Highland Bavarian Lodge, a 40- by 70-foot building that cost $10,000 and stands today as Aspen's first ski lodge. The lodge would hold sixteen people in eight double-decker beds in two rooms. There was a large kitchen to provide for the appetites of the first skiers in Aspen, who paid $3 for private ski lessons or $.50 for group lessons. Room and board was $7 per night. The architect was George Kauffman, and the artist who furnished the Bavarian figures under the eaves of the main building was Walt Disney artist Jimmie Brodrero. A barn behind the lodge housed four horses and a sleigh, plus accommodations for resident manager T. J. Flynn and mountain experts from Europe who would serve as teachers and guides.

André Roch, a famous Swiss mountaineer, ski enthusiast, and engineer was hired that winter by Fiske and Ryan to study the area for potential ski sites. Roch (pronounced *roke*) studied the climate and snow conditions, aspects and elevations, avalanche potential, and lift alignments with his assistant and fellow Swiss, Gunther Langes. The men spent six months in the area and were paid $125 per month for their expertise. In particular, they scouted the Aspen-Ashcroft area, plus Hunter Creek and Aspen Mountain. Roch's conclusion was that ski runs on Aspen Mountain would be superior to anything then available in the U.S. Mt. Hayden, he said, could furnish skiing exceptional to anything in the world!

For Mt. Hayden, Roch described a ski resort complex stretching south along Castle Creek from the Highland Bavarian Lodge across the eastern side of Mt. Hayden, through Cathedral Basin, beneath Castle Peak, across Montezuma Basin to Pearl Basin, and beyond Cooper Basin to Taylor Peak and Green Mountain. A vertical drop of 5,100 feet was possible, speculated Roch, on a ski area that would dwarf any other ski area in the world at that time. The plan included a huge hotel on the ridge of Mt. Hayden and a tram from Ashcroft to Electric Peak, at over 13,000 feet, that would climb 4,000 feet in 3 1/2 miles.

Roch thought Ashcroft was a more attractive location for a base resort than Aspen, in part because of the depressed and dilapidated condition of Aspen, which was falling into ruin. Ashcroft was uncluttered and ripe for the development of a complete alpine village. Land was available for cheap and there were only a few residents to disturb during construction. Roch's enthusiasm was shared by Ryan and Fiske, whose dream it was to build a world-class ski area.

The Highland Bavarian Corporation began acquiring land in the Ashcroft area and at the base of Little Annie Basin, across the Castle Creek Road from the Highland Bavarian Lodge. Billy Tagert ran the first crude lift: a horse-drawn sleigh. He drove loads of skiers up the Little Annie Road to the Little Annie Mine. They were charged $.50 for the ride. From Little Annie Basin, skiers could either make a run down Little Annie back to the Highland Bavarian Lodge or attach climbing skins to their skis and hike to the present location of the Sundeck restaurant. From there, they could ski down the front of Aspen Mountain into Aspen on a looping

COURTESY OF SAVILLE

ABOVE **Before WWII, Ted Ryan leads a group of skiers up Little Annie.**

RIGHT **Early Aspen ski enthusiast Billy Fiske flew a Hawker Hurricane in the Battle of Britain. Fiske was mortally wounded in the air but managed to land his plane before dying.**

system of old wagon roads.

The Highland Bavarian Lodge officially opened in December 1936, and on February 27, 1937, the lodge sponsored the first annual Winter Sports Carnival, attracting 200 men, women, and children for a day of skiing on five to eight inches of fresh snow. Awards were handed out at a dinner banquet that night by Roch, and Langes entertained with his accordion.

Ryan and Fiske began talking with railroad representatives, encouraging them to improve the rails into Aspen and build hotels for the skiers. They invited the Dartmouth Ski Team to test the skiing and spread the word. The long abandoned townsite of Ashcroft was deeded to the Highland Bavarian Corporation, with all delinquent taxes canceled. Just as the momentum was growing to realize Roch's Mt. Hayden plans, World War II exploded in Europe.

THE HISTORY CHANNEL

A vertical drop of 5,100 feet was possible, speculated Roch, on a ski area that would dwarf any other ski area in the world at that time. The plan included a huge hotel on the ridge of Mt. Hayden and a tram from Ashcroft to Electric Peak, at over 13,000 feet...

BILLY FISKE, a pilot, immediately joined the Royal Air Force of Great Britain to fly fighter planes. He was mortally wounded during the Battle of Britain over the English Channel in 1940, but managed to land his Hawker Hurricane at an airfield south of London before he died. Fiske was the first American killed in action with the RAF and was honored by a plaque at St. Paul's Cathedral in London.

"With Billy dead in 1940, I guess many lost heart for putting money into recreational purposes, especially when the country was gearing for the war effort," Ted Ryan was quoted in *Memories Worth Saving: The Story of Ashcroft*, by Charlene Knoll.

Fiske's death dampened plans for the ski area, but T. J. Flynn, the old promoter, tried to fill Fiske's shoes and by partnering with Ryan. With ski development abated, Ryan encouraged families to settle in the Ashcroft area, but only if they pledged full-time residency. The Highland Bavarian Corporation wanted people who would contribute to the area, not draw wealth away from it. Families would be helped to build homes on lots that included a plot of land to grow vegetables, raise a few chickens, and keep a cow. Visitors would be consigned to hotels and lodges.

The proposed tram project from Ashcroft to Electric Peak had been approved before the war, and the American Steel and Wire Company had estimated construction costs at $1.5 million. The Colorado State Legislature had created the Mount Hayden Tramway Commission to oversee the project. A tourist railroad had also been planned, but was scrapped when the demands of the war began to demand natural resources. The architectural flavor of the resort, as conceived by Ryan and architect Elder Husted, was Bavarian. However, that was before rising anti-German sentiment made that style less attractive. They agreed to use log construction in keeping with the historic charm of Ashcroft.

When Pearl Harbor was attacked in 1941, all plans were laid aside. Ryan immediately attempted to join the service, but a crushed leg from a ski accident classified him 4-F. Instead, he joined the Office of Strategic Services (OSS), a forerunner to the Central Intelligence Agency (CIA), and served on the Gold Coast of Africa and Italy. Following the war, plans for Roch's visionary ski resort were delayed and later abandoned altogether. Another Ashcroft dream had died.

EDITOR'S NOTE: *The following was a typewritten manuscript composed in the winter of 1936-37 by André Roch, describing the potential for skiing on Mt. Hayden.*

André Roch
ASPEN HISTORICAL SOCIETY

A FIRST DOUBLE CHAIRLIFT is proposed from Ashcroft to Monument Station [midway on Mt. Hayden]. It gives a drop of 2,200 feet (680 m.). From Monument Station, five different main runs and many more variations are available. This first part of the lift will be run under any weather conditions. This lift alone gives more runs and more possibilities than at Aspen.

The second chairlift should reach the summit of Electric Peak. It is very important to reach this peak because it is the key point of the area for two reasons: first, it gives access to a run down Cathedral Lake area and to Pine Creek, which is magnificent; second, it enables one to ski downhill, without having to climb, to a pass in front of Ski Hayden Peak and gives access to the runs on Sandy Creek, Sawyer Creek, and Hayden Ridge.

This second part of the lift goes so high (13,600 ft.) that it could not be run in bad weather or in too strong a wind. However, this splendid ski area would not be developed into its proper capacity without it. Furthermore, it would be a wonderful summer excursion to descend to Cathedral Lake or to American Lake for hiking or fishing. Skiing should be possible at the upper part through June.

There is yet a possibility of skiing down into Conundrum Valley, but this run should be most of the time in bad conditions on account of the wind. Beside the two main chairlifts, there are many possibilities of T-bar lifts, which could be built later on in the area of Cathedral Lake, American Lake, and Sandy Creek. A bus service should be organized in the Castle Creek Valley to bring skiers back to the start of the chair lift.

The area of Ashcroft should be carefully planned in order that the runs would remain free from houses and hotels. The valley is long and broad, large enough to combine hotels, bungalows, and parking places with the ski runs.

—ANDRÉ ROCH

"ASHCROFT OBER ASPEN"

TED RYAN saw his grand plans for a ski resort in Ashcroft die, but he could not let go of his vision of Ashcroft as a ski destination. If not alpine skiing, then Ryan would return to his roots and promote cross-country skiing.

The Ashcroft Ski Touring center was opened in December 1971 by Ted Ryan, still president and major stockholder of the Highland Bavarian Corporation, which owned most of the land around Ashcroft. Ryan, by now a retired publisher and former Connecticut Congressman, had offered the corporation's land in Ashcroft to the 10th Mountain Division for ski and mountain training during World War II. He had hoped that Tenth troopers would return after the war and help develop Ashcroft.

The elite mountain troops did train in Ashcroft, but after the war, instead of helping Ryan realize his dreams in Ashcroft, the veterans flocked to Aspen and developed Aspen Mountain. Again Ashcroft had been abandoned and forgotten in the rush to realize the potential of Aspen. Ryan, however, persisted in advancing the skiing potential of the upper Castle Creek Valley, focusing on a cross-country ski area that he called "Ashcroft Ober Aspen." According to an early brochure, there were "No lift lines...no lifts! Guided tours into God's high country...quiet tracks along the valley floor...."

Ryan envisioned an experience similar to alpine skiing where skiers had all the comforts and conveniences of groomed, maintained trails, equipment rentals, lessons, food service, and lodging. He contracted with Sven Wiik, the country's foremost cross-country ski coach with Olympic qualifications who was then coaching at Western State College in Gunnison. Wiik developed the first twelve miles of trails for Ryan and compared it to his Scandinavian Lodge in Steamboat Springs for excellent terrain and snow conditions.

The trails led skiers through open meadows and among stands of aspen trees with incredible views of the Elk Mountains. Skiers could tour along Castle Creek and through the ghost town of Ashcroft. Wildlife could be seen and a nature ethic was enhanced by a strict code of preservation instilled by Ryan. The trails were also designed to skirt potential avalanche slopes. The Kellogg Cabin and Mace Hut (Toklat Chalet) were made available for overnights on guided tours. One of the early ski runs was named "Fiske" for Ryan's old friend.

The Ashcroft Ski Touring center needed a warming house and a restaurant, so the Pine Creek Cookhouse was fashioned from an old trap-shooting clubhouse that once occupied a hog pasture at today's Airport Business Center (ABC). The three A-frames on the site were built by Earl Kelly and were later sold to Dave Farny, who ran a boys' camp at Pine Creek called "The Ashcrofters" in the 1960s (see pg. 129). The Cookhouse first opened under the direction of Hungarian émigré Krisi Mace. The restaurant seated twenty-four and had ski-only access.

Today, the Pine Creek Cookhouse and Ashcroft Touring Center are owned by John Wilcox, an Emmy Award-winning independent television and movie producer who expanded the center's ski terrain, rebuilt the cookhouse after a fire claimed the original structure, and added a sleigh ride behind a team of Belgian draft horses. Wilcox built a home in the upper Castle Creek Valley in the late 1990s, at the foot of Cooper Basin. During the winter, he and his family use snowmobiles or a family-sized snowcat to access the large log home.

Ashcroft Ski Touring now has about thirteen miles of cross-country and snow-

Ski touring along along Castle Creek at the Ashcroft Ski Touring Center.

shoe trails. The trails vary from intermediate trails on the valley floor to advanced trails on either side of the valley. Where possible, the trails are groomed for both diagonal gliding and ski skating. Night ski tours are available after a gourmet meal at the Pine Creek Cookhouse, and headlamps are issued to skiers willing to brave the cold. The experience of gliding down a trail under the stars on a dark winter night is a foremost attraction of today's Ashcroft Touring Center.

LITTLE ANNIE SKI AREA

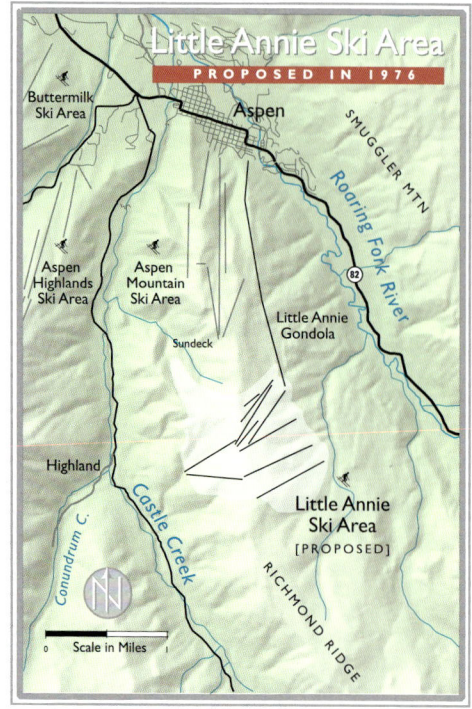

VAST MOUNTAIN BASINS with open glades amid stands of aspen and forests of spruce and fir provide Little Annie Basin a dramatic setting. Situated below Richmond Ridge and popularly known as "the backside" of Aspen Mountain, Little Annie hosts an enclave of second homes and secluded cabins, many of them located on old mining claims. Views from the ridge reveal the Mt. Hayden massif to the west and Difficult Creek and the Sawatch Range to the east.

First a mecca for silver miners, later a grandiose ski area development plan, and now a rural community, Annie Basin describes a rich history dating to the early 1880s when silver miners followed promising veins deep underground.

According to legend, a huge forest fire swept along Richmond Ridge in the early 1880s. Fanned by strong, prevailing southwest winds, the fire scoured much of the ridge and burned an enormous quantity of timber. It was rumored that the fire had been set by Ute Indians in protest of settlement in the valley; others blamed careless or conniving miners who may have set the blaze themselves and blamed it on the Utes. Lightning may have been the actual cause. Regardless, the forests burned and cleared vast sections of land that now bloom in summer wildflowers and provide powder skiing in the winter.

Throughout the mining days, Little Annie Basin remained mostly undeveloped and served as a ski area for early Aspen skiers, particularly those who stayed at Aspen's first ski lodge, the Highland Bavarian. In 1959, Waddy Catchings devised a scheme to introduce lift-served skiing to Little Annie Basin. He convinced a group of investors to purchase 750 acres of patented mining claims along both sides of Richmond Ridge in Hurricane Gulch and Little Annie Basin. Catchings named the project "Little Annie" and formed the Little Annie Ski Corporation.

Catchings' dream was thwarted by high costs and bureaucratic red tape, so in 1976, he sold the properties to Dave Farny. Farny revitalized the Little Annie project by bringing in a group of local investors, including a number of prominent Aspenites. The Little Annie Ski Area engendered the most intensive study of a proposed ski area in the history of Colorado. It was subjected to the Colorado Review Process (CRP), a new and comprehensive land use study designed to allow affected local, state and federal governments, and concerned agencies, to participate in the development review process.

Through the lengthy and detailed CRP, the City of Aspen, Pitkin County, various agencies of the State of Colorado, and the U.S. Forest Service had an opportunity to address the social, economic, environmental, and political implications of the Little Annie development. Over thirty consulting firms were called in to analyze and evaluate all aspects of the proposal.

The Little Annie Ski Area called for a 19,000-foot-long, six-passenger gondola originating on Ute Avenue, near today's Aspen Club & Spa, to a point beyond the Sundeck restaurant at the top of Richmond Ridge at 11,300 feet. The gondola would take twenty-eight minutes to reach the topmost lift station with a capacity of 2,250 passengers per hour. From there, skiers could choose from a variety of runs on 700 groomed acres. The ski area would have incorporated a total 3,400 acres within its boundaries, with 1,200 skiable acres. Runs radiating from the transfer station were to be served by triple chairlifts. A 1,200-seat restaurant, 500-seat cafeteria, meeting facilities, performance venues, and other summit facilities would make the ski area unique for its 360-degree views and multi-use opportunities.

Little Annie had a budget of $8 million and was promoted as a ski area designed to function independent of the automobile. Alpine and cross-country skiers and sightseers would catch a town shuttle and ride the gondola, without driving a car in Aspen. All ski runs would be at high elevation to maximize snow quality, and primary egress after skiing would be by the gondola.

The Little Annie Ski Area would have created the most European-like ski area design in Aspen, said promoters, reflecting the original vision of André Roch. A plum that was dangled by developer Farny to entice hard-core local skiers was a proposal to limit some slopes on the new ski area to skis 200 cm or longer. This was during the "Short Skis Suck" campaign, and it won Farny some support. Season pass prices were also adjusted to attract local support by undercutting the Aspen Ski Corporation's prices.

Aspen was then recoiling from a ski area and lodging boom of twenty years that had soured residents on more and bigger ski areas. While the Little Annie proposal called for reduced automobile traffic and air pollution, it came at the wrong time. Environmental goals aside, the project was too big for the community to swallow. The review process became time-consuming and enormously expensive, with the onus of mitigation on the proponent.

While the ski area plans were innovative, local governments and residents who opposed it eventually carried the day. The Pitkin County Planning Commission voted unanimously against the ski area in 1976 in deference to a growth management study from 1974 that warned against large developments and their spin-off impacts. The U.S. Forest Service had required approval from local governments in order to issue an approval, so the project was effectively turned down.

The *Aspen Times* lamented: "We think the benefits of an additional, independent ski area on Aspen Mountain are greater than the evils, and we are sorry the planning commission didn't grant preliminary approval to enable the applicant to make the additional studies needed to resolve some of the objections raised by the commission in its resolution of denial."

Farny eventually settled with investors by dividing the land holdings among them. These were mostly old mining claims that were later developed as homes or vacation cabins. The Little Annie project was scuttled, and Farny moved to Telluride.

Today, the open bowls of Little Annie Basin are served by a guided snowcat powder skiing franchise from the Sundeck. Cross-country skiers hike the bowls, as in the old days, and alpine skiers use snowmobiles as lifts. Several avalanche fatalities have occurred in uncontrolled portions of the former ski area. ❖

A plum that was dangled by developer Farny to entice hard-core local skiers was a proposal to limit some slopes on the new ski area to skis 200 cm or longer. This was during the "Short Skis Suck" campaign and won Farny some support. Season pass prices were also adjusted to attract local support by undercutting the Aspen Ski Corporation's prices.

10 Aspen Highlands

THE 'LOCAL'S SKI AREA' GOES BIG TIME

BY JAY COWAN

THE LONG, RHINO-BACKED ridge that bunches up between the Castle and Maroon Creek Valleys was created in the titanic upheavals of mountain building. For the last two million years, the ridge has just hunkered there being slowly sculpted by the elements into a beautifully corrugated work of earth, stone, water and woods extending for miles off the main spine of the Elk Range. Crowned by several 12,000- and 13,000-foot peaks, the ridge rises so vertically above Castle and Maroon Creeks that it seems to levitate.

Because it points almost due north, the ridge's long, steep flanks catch the brunt of the sunrise on one side and the sunset on the other. This makes for dramatic lighting, whether it's cast upon the gaudy gold and green brocades of autumn or the brilliant snows of winter. Only in the last 10,000 years, with the coming of Early Man, the Ute Indians, and early surveyors and the prospectors, were there any humans around to enjoy the light on this ridge, which was pretty much devoid of people until the 1950s. That was when it became known as "Aspen Highlands."

WHIP JONES OPENS AN ERA

WHIPPLE VAN NESS JONES first came to Aspen from St. Louis in 1947 on a ski trip and he returned for the Goethe Bicentennial in 1949. With a Harvard business degree and a love of the outdoors, Jones liked what he sensed was happening: "When I saw all that Walter Paepcke, who organized the Goethe Bicentennial, was doing in Aspen, I bought a house here," said Jones in an interview six months before his death on June 29, 2001. In 1954, Jones built the Smuggler, one of the first ski-lodges in town.

At about the same time, Had and Lou Deane bought the T-Lazy-7 Ranch. The Deanes and Henry Stein also owned 280 acres called the Lower Ranch, including what is now Highlands Village. Then the Deanes and Stein had a falling out. "Had Deane approached me and said 'Whip, I want you to buy the Lower Ranch.' I said I couldn't afford all that land, but he said 'Yes, you can', and gave me some figures and an easy payment plan," laughed Jones. "So I bought it."

In 1957, Jones was approached by Deane, Dick Wright, and the Pat Henrys about starting a ski area on Sievers Mountain, directly west of Deane's T-Lazy-7 Ranch. That plan was vetoed by the U.S. Forest Service. Later, local Forest Service supervisor Paul Hauk talked to Jones. "I suggested to Whip that he check out the potential in his 'backyard', since it was obvious from across the valley on Sievers Mountain that the lower Highland Peak country had definite possibilities for the next major area near Aspen," wrote Hauk in a 1978 Aspen Highlands Ski Area Chronology.

Highlands had already been the site for some of the first organized skiing in the valley. Early Aspen Ski Club races were held on the Castle Creek side, above the old Highland Bavarian Lodge near Conundrum Creek. And native Aspenite Glenn Beck,

The Aspen Highlands base area at après ski.

in *Aspen: The Quiet Years*, recalled the 1930s when there was a nice little slope at the present base of Thunder Bowl that he said "was just right for beginners."

JONES INSISTED for his whole life that he only bought the ranch to build a house and raise horses, but he soon found himself walking the ridge above it with Paul Hauk, wondering if it would work as a ski area. "The most influential person in the early history of Highlands was Paul Hauk," said Jones, without hesitation. "He suggested it and we walked the whole mountain together and decided where to put the runs."

Next, Jones filed a special use application with the Forest Service for 4,200 acres of Forest Service land immediately adjoining his ranch to the south, running for approximately two miles along Highlands Ridge between Castle and Maroon Creeks. Then he went to Willie Hodges and Edgar Stanton, who were the president and vice-president of what was then called the Aspen Ski Corporation, which owned and operated Aspen Mountain. Jones told them that the Forest Service thought the next ski area should be at Highlands and that he wanted the ASC to develop the mountain. "Willie Hodges and Edgar had roomed together at Yale," said Jones, a Harvard man. "They both said, 'No, we can't do it because we've got our hands full with Aspen Mountain.' And I said, 'Well, okay, if you don't want to do it, I will.'"

That exchange foreshadowed a pattern of prickly relationships that would persist between the Highlands and the ASC for another thirty-five years. "So I hired Dick Durrance and Friedl Pfeifer [legendary skiers living in Aspen] to give me an opinion on whether the skiing would be feasible or not, and they both walked it in the winter and came back and told me 'Yes'."

When Jones received final Forest Service approval on April 16, 1958, he undertook the project himself. That summer he built the longest double chairlift in the world and started clearing trails with bulldozers and a crew of chainsaw-wielding Cherokee Indians from Bunch, Oklahoma. The latter were employed primarily on terrain the machinery couldn't tackle—pitches that were described by one of the Cherokee crew leaders as being "steep as a cow's face, and her a-grazin."

Highlands opened informally in late November of 1958, and officially on January 17, 1959. "The competition, terrain variety, and spectacular views provided by Whip's excellent area helped put Aspen on American skiers' 'must' list. Whip deserves 'kudos' and 'thank-yous' from skiers and all the businesses that benefited from his effort and persistence," wrote Paul Hauk.

A SPECIAL AMBIANCE

THE SKI SCHOOL at Highlands started off flamboyantly. It began with Norwegian ski idol and 1952 Olympic sensation Stein Eriksen as the director, performing his famous layout back flips for onlookers once a week. "Stein established our image first," noted Jones. "He did a good job and brought over some very fine Norwegian instructors who are still in town and well-liked today."

Almost immediately, Highlands established a reputation for being Aspen's "maverick" area. That wasn't really intentional, allowed Jones with a smile. "But it developed that way

ASPEN HISTORICAL SOCIETY

ABOVE **Viviane and Whip Jones, the original developer of Aspen Highlands.**

BELOW LEFT **Fred Iselin jumps and Freddie Fisher sings. Two characters that made Aspen Highlands the "maverick ski area".**

RIGHT **Aspen Highlands towers above Maroon Creek.**

because we brought in a number of people who fit in that category." Legendary Aspen musician Freddie Fisher headed the list. The brilliant jazz clarinetist and iconoclast performed with his son King and local piano virtuoso Walt Smith at Smith's Hindquarter Restaurant with its Freddie Fisher room, upstairs at the Highlands base-lodge. Fisher was often urged by local police to walk, rather than drive, home to Aspen following his well-lubricated gigs. He also had a ready answer for anyone who asked if he skied: "I'm too poor to go up and too smart to come down."

The original Highlands après ski bar was the notorious Bier Stube. Later it was called the Christian Endeavor, sharing the name with a Methodist society for young people. "We had this beautiful piece of stained glass from the society that said Christian Endeavor," recalled Jones, "and when we were building Highlands we put it up over the bar. I don't think that's what the original society would have had in mind, but people in Aspen loved it."

IT WASN'T JUST THE BAR PATRONS and musicians who danced to a different drummer at Highlands. The original head of the ski patrol was also unique. "There's no question that Charlie Bolte was the biggest character I ever knew at Highlands," said Jones. "On the job he had a fondness for explosives. And after work, he was quite a prominent member of the customers at the bar. He also came up with the idea, maybe at the bar, for our famous race, "The Bash for Cash."

This was a deranged, mass-start event where everyone took the most direct line to a pot of money at the bottom of one of Highland's steepest runs. "We started it each week by blowing up a case of dynamite," recalled Jones, "and that was a hell of a charge." At the behest of lawyers and insurance companies, both the dynamiting and the races were stopped long ago, but their spirit (and a faint whiff of mayhem and cordite) still lingers.

The fabled Swiss ski-racer and impresario Fred Iselin took over the Highlands Ski School with dazzling élan in 1964. Iselin's energy, whimsy, and joy permeated everything he did on skis. One of his early stunts was to put a battered dummy in the snow alongside the trail to illustrate the plight of those who didn't take lessons. And he was regularly photographed making swooping arcs down the slopes with one ski kicked high in the air and a mischievous grin spread across his face while a clutch of mod-looking women (whom he called "dolls") beamed at him.

When the Loge Peak chairlift opened in January of 1964, it was one of the wildest rides in America, delivering skiers to 11,675 feet, atop the longest vertical drop (3,635 feet) in the country at the time. The original Loge chairlift contained a section of dangle time where you hung suspended over a chute near the top that emptied away below your feet in what seemed like an unimpeded plunge all the way to Maroon Creek, 3,500 feet straight down. Turn away from that clammy-handed view and you were confronted with one almost as dramatic, because straight ahead were the high, icy temples of Pyramid Peak and the Maroon Bells.

FUNKY AND FAMILIAR

THE ORIGINAL HIGHLANDS base-lodge, which held the restaurant and bar, was an over-lapping A-frame building, echoing the shape of the surrounding peaks and designed by noted Aspen architect Fritz Benedict. The Highlands base area always had the look and feel of modest national park buildings with Bauhaus overtones, and it grew by fits and starts. It originally had a creek running through and a small lake, both of which were soon drained or diverted. The small Heatherbed Lodge and stables were built across the road in 1959, and then came the Chateau Kirk (later renamed the Highlands Inn) in 1961. A Savoyard-styled behemoth, it sat halfway between the bottom of Thunderbowl and the bottom of the Exhibition chairlift. Next came the Maroon Creek Lodge and the Chamonix riverside condominiums, then nothing more. For years, this was a strong element in the Highlands appeal. It felt more like a ski-club operation than a major franchise, and was always loved and guarded by locals.

The Cloud 9 Restaurant, built at the top of the Cloud 9 lift in 1962, was one of the most dramatic mountain aeries in the country, with a wraparound sun deck hovering high above Maroon Creek and bathed in full frontal views of Pyramid Peak and the Maroon Bells. One night in the winter of 1967, the building burned spectacularly to the ground, with the flames visible from Aspen.

Cloud 9 was replaced with a smaller building that became the site for the ski patrol's infamous deck jumps: big gelandes made while pulling toboggans and clearing forty feet of sun deck. Viewers tried to ignore the fact that these were the same crazy bastards who would be hauling them down the mountain if they had an accident. The deck jumps have recently been revived, and the restaurant is one of the best and most intimate on any of the local mountains. The view still rules, and you can pop next door to the ski patrol room to find out where the untracked powder is.

In the meantime Highlands also constructed the larger and less scenic Merry-Go-Round restaurant on a flat, protected site at mid-mountain. It has ringside seats for watching bump and aerial competitions, or just everyday skiers scrambling down runs like Scarlett's and Gun Barrel that empty directly onto the restaurant's sprawling front deck.

While, happily, not too many new buildings cropped up each season at Highlands, every year the skiing expanded a little, with more trails cut and lifts added or moved. Much of this stemmed from the incentive of individual ski patrol and trail crew members who have always loved the mountain and devoted lots of their waking time to tweaking and improving the skiing. Chief among these happy zealots has been Mac Smith, who signed on as a patrolman at Highlands in 1973, and by 1978, at the tender age of 26, was the patrol director. "Every day on the mountain creates a feeling of arrival, a place in the soul that says you're home," observes Smith, who has skied the area since he was little.

Smith already knew Highlands well as a kid and started ducking into the woods and out-of-bounds when he was still in high school. It was a popular, albeit illegal, pastime, but Smith took his adventures one step further. Once he was on the patrol, he immediately started lobbying to expand the ski area boundaries to include terrain that he knew could be great. Of the 4,200-acre permit, Highlands was using only 540. Much of the rest was afflicted with serious avalanche danger and cordoned off from the main lift-served slopes. Smith thought they could change

Cloud 9 was replaced with a smaller building that became the site for the ski patrol's infamous deck jumps: big gelandes made while pulling toboggans and clearing forty feet of sun deck. Viewers tried to ignore the fact that these were the same crazy bastards who would be hauling them down the mountain if they had an accident.

—JAY COWAN

Hiking to Highland Bowl requires a measure of stamina, but the powder skiing and fine views are big paybacks.

some of that, and Whip Jones agreed.

Not everyone else did. Many felt it was too risky, while others wanted to keep it all for themselves. "Sharing experiences is where it's at," says Smith. "When we first opened Steeplechase, a lot of people opposed it. But seeing friends on it is great. I've made a billion turns in my life. Now it's nice seeing other people get a chance."

BEFORE LONG, under Smith's prodding, Highlands had dropped the ropes into the so-called "5 Towers" chutes into the Castle Creek Valley from near the top of the Loge Lift. Christened as Steeplechase, these 700 to 800-vertical-foot plunges dangle down toward the valley like icicles, and if all the snow on them were to melt at once, they would be waterfalls. Still regarded as some of the best skiing on the mountain, when they joined the area's official menu they were a big step into a new dimension of adventure skiing for Highlands. Just getting back to mid-mountain on the notoriously abrupt and whippy Grand Traverse at the bottom carries its risks.

In 1987, Highlands opened the poacher's paradise known as Olympic ("Oly") Bowl that drops off the opposite side of Steeplechase toward Maroon Creek. When this west-facing bank of tenderly gladed lines is topped with two feet of whipped-cream powder and the air is full of crystals, Oly Bowl is nirvana with the props to prove it. The early-morning back-lighting conveys a hint of the divine, the pitch compels you forward without thought, and behind it all lurks the movie-set backdrop of Pyramid Peak and the Bells, so excessive as to risk cliché.

THE END OF THE BEGINNING

A T THE HEIGHT of its business in 1975-76, Highlands generated 321,000 skier days, well ahead of Aspen Mountain and Buttermilk. The base buildings had expanded to include a ski shop and offices.

Life was good. But then lengthy and expensive antitrust litigation against the ASC, which owned the valley's other three ski areas, led to a Pyrrhic victory for the Highlands. While the court case dragged on, legal costs deprived Highlands of money to spend on new lifts and stay competitive. By the time they received their damage award, lawyers took a lot of it and Highlands ran up against revised land-use regulations that stymied their effort to build a 300-room hotel at the base. Without the hotel, plans to fund infrastructure upgrades on the mountain stopped.

Not only did expansion at the area grind to a halt, but the resort actually began to devolve. In a time when skiing was booming in a valley where real estate was worth more than in Manhattan, Highlands was literally tearing down buildings. In the early '80s, the crumbling edifice of the Chateau Kirk/Highlands Inn was razed to make room for the hotel development that was never approved. Ironically, the Kirk's demolition created more parking at a time when the area was losing customers. By 1993-94, skier days had dwindled to an anemic 106,000. While most other areas were loading up on high-speed lifts and more resort amenities, Highlands was a resort frozen in amber. Its once "colorful" platter-pulls and Vietnam-era chairlifts tended to dawdle and stop a lot. There wasn't enough snowmaking to ensure egress from the mountain in early and late seasons, and there wasn't a fern bar or snooty sit-down restaurant to be found on the entire mountain.

Obviously, some of this had an up side. For many locals it was an amazing throwback, an echo of skiing's roots in the valley. No more silly frills, just good hard-core skiing with fewer people on the slopes than at the supermarket. The mountain still had major vertical, some of the steepest terrain around, and no one got too carried away with grooming, so the snow was soft and the powder lasted. Plus you knew every lift op and patrolman by name and drinking habits. It was the closest many people ever got to having their own private mountain, and at bargain rates.

This wasn't the business model Highlands had in mind. It was the only major area in America that was almost vanishing in front of everyone's eyes. So in 1993, Whip Jones donated the ski area he founded to Harvard University, which then sold it to Houston-based developer Gerald Hines. Hines soon struck the deal Whip Jones had attempted thirty-five years before when he convinced the Aspen Skiing Company to assume operation of the Highlands Ski Area.

ALAN BECKER

ABOVE **Highland Bowl skiing**

RIGHT **Trail crew art; wild, quirky, and a little bit brazen**

THE HIGHLANDS MAKEOVER

WHILE HINES wrestled with Pitkin County over the extent of permissible development at the base, the ASC started work on the mountain. They began by consolidating and upgrading lifts, eventually paring eleven antique conveyances back to four new, fast and shrewdly placed ones. Said patrol director Mac Smith at the time: "It's a chance to go from the Flintstones to the Jetsons." And he was right. Two high-speed quads now deliver skiers from bottom-to-top in seventeen minutes, about one-third of the old travel time.

By 1998, a kind of stark minimalism obtained at the resort. Most of the old lifts were gone, as were all of the original buildings. The last to pass under the blade were the Maroon Creek Lodge and the base-lodge A-frames, but not before heavily initialed and carved sections of the Christian Endeavor's ceiling were salvaged.

Then, after years of haggling, Hines Resorts finally received the okay to build Aspen Highlands Village. "I am proud that the village is literally a gateway to the Maroon Bells-Snowmass Wilderness, one of the most beautiful and revered wildlands in America," said Gerald Hines. "We knew we had a very great responsibility to the community and to the generations that would follow, because this wilderness is one of the great scenic beauties of the world. Nothing could compete with such a creation of Mother Nature. That is why we designed the Village to be its own enduring attraction."

In the summer of 1998, Hines Resorts broke ground and began work on the Highlands Center base-lodge, which was purchased by the ASC and opened in 1999, with escalator service to deliver skiers slopeside from an underground parking garage. By the fall of 2002, most of the village rising up around the cobbled central plaza was complete, housing a whole new era of lodges, restaurants, and shops.

THE STEEP AND DEEP

EVEN THE SKIING at Highlands, which defines a big-mountain experience, has been upgraded. The lifts are now thoroughly modern and there is good snowmaking and a consistent carpet of grooming on the Daytona-styled cruisers where skiers most appreciate it. And the area is still essentially deserted, the very model of wide-open Western skiing.

The skiers at Highlands are usually pretty familiar with the mountain and not long on fashion shows or posing. Mostly they come for the goods, and they go straight to them. Says patrol director Mac Smith: "We get a lot of good local athletes here and that's the best kind of clientele. They're easy to deal with, there aren't many accidents, and you know they really appreciate all this stash kind of terrain we work hard to open up."

The area is continually clearing out testy new lines all over the mountain. Recent additions near the bottom include Bob's Glade, Golden Horn Woods, and the P-Chutes, all on steep, tricky northwestern exposures. Up higher on the moun-

ALAN BECKER

For many locals it was an amazing throwback, an echo of skiing's roots in the valley. No more silly frills, just good hard-core skiing with fewer people on the slopes than at the supermarket. The mountain still had major vertical, some of the steepest terrain around, and no one got too carried away with grooming, so the snow was soft and the powder lasted. Plus you knew every lift op and patrolman by name and drinking habits.

tain are brilliant riffs in thick timber like Moment Chutes, Twilight Zone, and Boomerang Woods.

Management has also moved boldly into the once forbidden zone of Highland Bowl for some of the best hike-to skiing in America. The crown of the Highlands permit is 12,386-foot Highland Peak, rearing up on the far southern perimeter of the Highlands boundary. From the top of the Loge Lift, all the way to Highland Peak (thirty minutes of steady hiking), epic skiing drops off either side of the ridge. It can also be extremely dangerous, especially on the Maroon Creek exposures, where in the winter of 2000 an avalanche on that side claimed the lives of two local skiers. Many experts have concluded that the Maroon Creek side is too unstable to ever be opened by the ski area and is no longer included in Highlands' permit boundaries.

HIGHLAND BOWL, a huge, caldera-shaped basin with the eastern side sliced off, empties into the Castle Creek drainage. The exposures in the bowl range from south to east to north and funnel into a great white hole at the bottom. It is stunning skiing—high, wide, and handsome, and also stop-and-think steep, ranging from 30 to 48 degrees in pitch. Many people poached it over the years, but no one was more familiar with it than the Highlands patrol. They've seen it slide big a number of times, including in 1984, when it killed three of their members who were doing control work for a planned National Ski Patrol figure-eight contest. Chris Kessler, Tom Snyder, and Craig Soddy are now remembered by runs named after them on the Steeplechase section and by a memorial at the top of the ridge.

Highland Bowl represents one of the biggest avalanche control challenges in American skiing. Yet in 1998, cautiously and carefully, using early-season compaction and finely placed explosives, the Highlands patrol began pushing back the ropes. By the 2002-03 season they had successfully opened the whole bowl to droves of delighted patrons, eager to storm the 600 to 800 very vertical feet, catch the radical road out to the Grand Traverse below Steeplechase, and come back and do it again.

In the end, a run down almost any line in Highland Bowl is really a microcosm of the whole Highlands experience: intoxicating air, a dramatic sweep of porcelain snow and ethereal peaks, and a sky so blue it could burst. Then pick a pleat, any long seam of snow and space, where a Whip Jones or Fred Iselin or Mac Smith might go. Something wild and quirky and a little bit brazen, because that's all there is: a sense of adventure, a vision, a will, a line. Work the line, the bumps, the ridges and tight cruxes, and emerge swooping across the broad alluvial flanks at the bottom, loose and free and screaming for more.

Because that's the Highlands way. ❖

EDITOR'S NOTE: *Jay Cowan grew up in Aspen and has skied Highlands more times than he can remember. A free-lance writer, he specializes in skiing and outdoor travel, and is the author of* The Best of The Alps. *Jay is currently editor-in-chief at* Sojourner Magazine *in Aspen.*

Highland Bowl with its famous backdrop of Pyramid Peak (L) and the Maroon Bells (R).

11 Mountaineering in the Elk Range

BY LOUIS DAWSON III

FERDINAND HAYDEN and his "Rover Boys" were perhaps the first white men to discover recreation in the Maroon and Castle Creek Valleys. In 1873 and '74, they scampered up mountains, walked ridges, and explored the valley floors in pursuit of their survey. The Ute Indians, who called the two valleys their domain until 1881, may not have had a word that easily translates into a contemporary definition of recreation, but they found spiritual connections and physical challenges in these dramatic drainages of the Elk Range.

Recreation today is widely defined as play, a form of fun. The idea is expressed by in-line skaters on the Maroon Creek Road, picnickers at Ashcroft, climbers on the ridges of Pyramid Peak, skiers linking turns on Mt. Hayden. Recreation equates to a great variety of sports and activities that allows us to distance ourselves from our normal lives and feel a sense of rejuvenation.

The following section of *Aspen's Rugged Splendor* traces two primary recreational activities—mountaineering and skiing. The section closes with a trails and roads description that acts as a guide and an invitation. Knowing where to go may be the first step in discovering how recreation and rejuvenation are two of the greatest renewable resources of these valleys.

EDITOR'S NOTE: *Louis Dawson is a recognized guidebook writer,* Dawson's Guides to Colorado's Fourteeners, *and ski mountaineer. He moved to Aspen with his parents in 1964, at 13-years-old, and caught the climbing bug at an early age. Dawson spent his next twenty-five years in devoted relationship with the Elks. He went on to become the first person to ski all of Colorado's 14,000-foot peaks.*

Chris Davenport, who in 2006-07 made ski descents of all the Colorado Fourteeners within a 12-month period, ascending 14,018-foot Pyramid Peak. In April, 2006, he and Neil Beidleman and Ted Mahon repeated the renowned Landry Route (see pg. 127). Dropping over 4,000 feet, it is one of the longest extreme ski descents in North America.

NEAL BEIDLEMAN

TRANSITS AND SILVER: THE PRAGMATIC ERA

THE CLIMBING HERITAGE of the Elk Mountains is rich and compelling. Beginning with government surveys in the late 1800s, and on through modern rock climbing, peak ascents, and ski mountaineering, valley residents and visitors have amassed an impressive list of accomplishments. What is more, the Elks have served as a training ground for dozens of world-class mountaineers.

Beginning in the late 1800s, mountaineering as exploration and sport gained popularity on Eastern Colorado monoliths such as Longs Peak and Pikes Peak. Blocked off by the Continental Divide, Western Slope ranges drained by the Roaring Fork River, such as the Elk and Swatch Mountains, lagged a decade or so behind the rest of Colorado as climbing destinations.

In 1873, two government survey parties penetrated the rugged Elk Mountains. One group, led by Lt. George M. Wheeler, made only minor forays into the backcountry. Another team, led by Dr. Ferdinand Hayden, performed detailed documentation of geology and topography and spent two summers in rugged splendor, motivated by a wealth of wondrous backcountry terrain—theirs to tread and map. It was obvious to the Hayden team that the stupendous rifts of the Castle and Maroon drainages defined the topography of the Elk Mountains and provided the deepest access.

"Castle and Maroon Creeks, and their branches, are probably without parallel for ruggedness, depth, and picturesque beauty...the remarkable and unique forms of the peaks, and the extreme ruggedness, all conspire to impress the beholder with wonder," effused Hayden in his report.

Mountain surveyors of the 1800s had no aerial photos or GPS satellites; they collected data the hard way: on horseback and foot. In large unsurveyed areas such as the Elks, it was necessary to climb a number of high-points with a bulky barometer and 40-lb transit, then measure the summit altitude and location using air pressure and triangulation. (Triangle Peak and Triangle Pass are both named for a "triangulation station" Hayden used in upper Conundrum Creek.) In the pursuit of mapping, the Hayden team became the first Anglo climbers in the Castle and Maroon Creek area, and in the entire Elk Range.

Fifty-four mountains in Colorado equal or surpass elevations of 14,000 feet. These peaks are known as "Fourteeners," and the quest to explore them has driven much of Colorado mountaineering. The obvious royalty of the Elk Range are its six Fourteeners: Pyramid Peak (14,018 ft.) and the two Maroon Bells at the head of Maroon Creek, North (14,014 ft.) and South (14,156 ft.); Castle Peak (14,265 ft., the highest in the Elks) at the head of Castle Creek; and Capitol Peak (14,130 ft.) and Snowmass Mountain (14,092 ft.), both promontories on the same massif, about 12 miles northwest of Aspen.

The significance of the Fourteeners was not lost on the early surveyors. Pyramid and the "Bells" dominate the land from many viewpoints, including a startling view of Pyramid from the Roaring Fork Valley just before entering Aspen from the west on Highway 82. These lofty Fourteeners were soon roughly verified by triangulation from surrounding locations, and climbs were attempted.

In 1873, a member of the Wheeler Survey made a bold attempt at climbing

"Hardly where you would think of skiing, but in fact, the North Face of North Maroon Peak has become a modern classic ski descent route. From mid-winter through late spring, the face will periodically come into condition and can see several descents a year. The steepest pitch hovers around 45 degrees, which is quite reasonable by modern standards."

—NEIL BEIDLEMAN

The pioneering of new routes in the Elk Mountains has increasingly involved challenging ski descents of the major peaks. Shown here is the Neal Beidleman and Bob Perlmutter June, 2005 route on the North Face of North Maroon Peak.

North Maroon Peak. He got close to the summit (the report claims within 200 feet), and was turned back by terrain beyond the ken of an 1800s climber. That same year the Hayden Survey summited 14,092-foot Snowmass Mountain. Their description of that climb clarified the foremost geologic obstacle that would come to define Elk Range mountaineering, namely, loose rock: "The slopes consist of immense fragments...When we reach the crest, we find it also broken in masses and pillars...an industrious man, with a crow-bar, could...reduce the height of the mountain one or two hundred feet....," wrote one of the climbers.

In terms of mountaineering, the top achievement of the Hayden Survey was a climb of Castle Peak, which attracted the explorers because they knew it to be the high-point of the Elks (14,265 feet). Most modern climbers scale Castle from the north via "walk-up" ridges, or from the southwest on a route that is mostly a hike. For some reason, probably their inexperience with judging climbing routes, the Hayden party chose an amazingly difficult route on Castle's southerly reaches—a route that even today is rarely climbed because of its complexity and loose rock.

"Our only way of surmounting the lower cliff was in finding a crevice...we climbed...putting the back against one wall and feet against the other and alternately raising the points of support and thus slowly and painfully making progress upward," is how Henry Gannett of the survey party described part the route. Such "chimneying," to describe the technique in modern climbing argot, takes incredible strength and coordination, not to mention the desirability of having a rope around your waist in case you slip. For North American climbers to tackle near-vertical terrain in 1873, unroped, with leather-soled boots, was a time warp.

The survey era closed in 1875 when the final reports were published. A few years later Elk Mountain mountaineering reached a new height of pragmatism, when in 1879 prospectors discovered mineral "blossoms" on the slopes of the Elks. A huge mining boom ensued. The town of Aspen grew to be the third largest city in Colorado, with Ashcroft on Castle Creek not far behind. Then, after fourteen years of frenzied digging, the demonitization of silver in 1893 brought about a rapid decline in population.

While mining would seem a far cry from climbing, prospectors of the short-lived silver boom era made fundamental contributions to Castle and Maroon Creek mountaineering by inaugurating a tradition of bold exploration. Equipped with little more than a wool coat and squashed felt hat, with perhaps a lick of jerky in a pocket, they crawled every square inch of the Roaring Fork Mining District.

This treasure-hunting mountaineering was not all a sullen tromping in search of riches. At the start of the mining era, Aspen was a town of men, with a small number of idolized women. One legend describes how in the early days of the camp, the males decided to throw a winter holiday party for the few ladies in residence. They needed oysters for a special entree, but the only oysters were in Leadville—fifty miles over the mountains. No problem. The scrappers donned their 12-foot-long skis, trekked to Leadville, and returned with the goods.

To this day, when you stomp through the high country, you will find prospect holes, cabin foundations, and the remains of industrial operations in the most unlikely places. Carried on by second and third generation locals who became mountaineers, or adopted by newcomers who tapped into the area's adventure ethos, the miner's spirit lives on in today's exploratory mountaineering.

Additionally, the miners built roads and trails. Such routes are now the transportation grid of the high country, and mountaineering as we know it would be impossible without them. A good example of such hand-hewn access to the alpine is Montezuma Mine Road (built in the early 1880s) on upper Castle Creek, which provides the traditional approach to Castle Peak.

ABOVE **Mountaineer and author Louis Dawson III**

RIGHT **Ski touring toward Pearl Pass above the Tagert and Green-Wilson huts.**

MODERN TIMES: MOUNTAINEERING FOR FUN

I N THE LATE 1800S and early 1900s, mountaineering in North America gradually changed from enterprise to recreation. This modern era entered the Castle and Maroon Creek drainages in 1908 with the enthusiastic explorations of two men: Percy Hagerman and Harold Clark.

Percy Hagerman was the son of J. J. Hagerman, who was a shareholder in the famous Molly Gibson silver mine in Aspen and became famous for his Colorado Midland Railroad. While Percy lived in Colorado Springs, he had business interests in Aspen and was somewhat familiar with the surrounding Elk Mountains. Moreover, he inherited exploratory fever from his father, which he applied to mountaineering.

Hagerman's friend Harold Clark was an Aspen lawyer and fanatic fisherman who knew the backcountry above Aspen as well as anyone. In the early 1900s, the key to Elk Range climbing was the approach. Rather than driving a car, you rode a horse or hiked up valleys such as Castle Creek, then entered a confusing array of side drainages. Signs were rare and maps inaccurate. Thus, it was Clark's navigation that clinched the pair's successful pioneering.

Even with Clark's expertise, one of the pair's first exploits was the result of a mistake. In 1907, they set out to climb Snowmass Mountain. Standing at Snowmass Lake, they mistakenly identified the stupendous arête to their left as the route to the Fourteener, rather than correctly identifying the true peak (an uninspiring bump on a ridge high above the lake). They climbed their error: a first ascent of an extremely aesthetic ridge to a classic summit, now named Hagerman Peak.

No doubt learning from their Snowmass mischance, in the summers of 1908, 1909, and 1910, Clark and Hagerman returned for many successful climbs in the Elks. They became organized and proficient horsepackers, and established a series of base camps throughout the range. They referred to these camps by number, much as modern Himalayan climbers refer to their aeries.

From a climber's view, the most important peaks of a range are the highest. Thus, while Clark and Hagerman scrambled many other peaks in the Elks, they kept the Fourteeners on their short-list. In 1908, from "Camp 2," the pair made the first ascent of North Maroon Peak. Just as the Hayden team chose a less obvious and more difficult route on Castle, Hagerman and Clark ended up on North Maroon's difficult north face instead of the easier east face.

As most, if not all, early 1900s climbers sought the easiest routes, the fact they often ended up on harder terrain in the Elks is not without significance – it drives home the point that the Castle and Maroon Creek peaks are unusually broken and convoluted. Route finding is difficult. Vertical rock is too broken and loose for safe climbing. Lower angled ledges and ramps, where most mountains would provide safe travel, are covered with unstable rubble. Accidents are common.

MORE THAN A DOZEN PEOPLE have fallen off the Maroon Bells to their death, with a somewhat lesser number reaching their demise on Pyramid. Sadly, most of these accidents take several common forms.

Unlike most other mountains, it is virtually impossible to use a rope as a safeguard against falling off Pyramid and the Maroon Bells. Good anchors are rare (modern climbing usually requires some means of attaching the rope to the mountain). Ironically, the rope itself becomes a hazard as it knocks rocks on the climber below. Thus, climbers are forced to work ropeless on pitches where a slip can send them hundreds of feet to certain death. Other common and often fatal mishaps result from bombardment of rubble from above (usually dislodged by human feet) and from sliding falls down steep snow and ice fields. Still more misfortune comes from lightning, altitude sickness, snow avalanche, and plain stupidity such as climbing until night, then descending in the dark without a flashlight (this is not conjecture; it's happened!).

Hagerman and Clark climbed before accidents became commonplace. Nonetheless, the harsh environment tempered their attitude. "This climb is not without danger," Hagerman wrote of North Maroon Peak. Considering these were the days before you could call a rescue helicopter on your cell phone, Hagerman's words were serious indeed. His successful career implies a healthy dose of caution. Modern rescue services aside, this is a good thing for today's peak baggers to emulate.

The next phase of Elk Range alpinism could be termed the Colorado Mountain Club (CMC) years. Organized in 1912 to "render readily accessible the alpine attractions of this region," CMC has been a powerful force in Colorado mountaineering, and more recently, environmental politics. In CMC's inaugural year, club president James Rogers asked Percy Hagerman to write a memoir of his climbs in the Elks. He did so, and the subsequent manuscript, *Notes on Mountaineering in the Elk Mountains of Colorado*, became the bible of Elk Range climbing until more comprehensive guidebooks appeared in the 1930s.

The club inaugurated a tradition of organized trips that brought a variety of Front Range climbers to the Elks. The area thus became established as a mountain recreation mecca (albeit of a primitive nature, as the first mechanized skiing began later, in the 1930s).

Albert R. Ellingwood and his protégé Carl Blaurock were the two main activists of the CMC era. While at college in England, Ellingwood learned to climb with advanced European technique. He brought those skills to Colorado. One of the most important climbing routes in the Elks is the half-mile ridge connecting North and South Maroon Peaks. This traverse was pioneered in 1936 by Ellingwood, and if you've been there, you know the man was ahead of his time.

Starting from North Maroon Peak, you must downclimb about twenty feet of broken terrain. Then the first route decision is in front of you. A series of large blocks and rubble piles form the crest of the ridge. For hour after tedious hour, you "micro navigate" as you decide if you're going over the top, right, or left of each obstacle. If you make a wrong decision, you tiptoe to a dead-end where you stand on dangerous rubble where a slip will send you flying. So you backtrack and try again – and again. The route has become easier in recent years. The path may be marked; the rubble tamed by hundreds of boot soles. Yet the essence remains the same: it's complicated—a bad decision can kill you.

ABOVE **Out of the mist, Graeme Means scales the west ridge route on Pyramid Peak.**

RIGHT **1920s climber Carl Blaurock celebrates on the summit of yet another Colorado Fourteener.**

COLORADO HISTORICAL SOCIETY

ARL BLAUROCK was one of North America's most devoted alpinists. When he started climbing in his late teens (circa 1912), the sport had changed from pragmatic to pure fun, and Blaurock embraced the new ethos with fanatic vigor. Indeed, he might have been Colorado's first "climbing bum," as his vocation, crafting gold teeth, appeared to have the sole purpose of supporting his fifty-year career as an alpinist.

Most of Blaurock's alpine life consisted of simply getting out and climbing, first ascent or not. Thus, while he made a number of "premiers" on North American peaks, he is remembered more for his attitude and the sheer volume of his climbing. In terms of the Castle and Maroon Creek Valleys, his enthusiasm certainly contributed to the popularity of CMC outings to the area. Perhaps the greatest insight into Blaurock's personality comes from an endearing personal habit: he would attempt a headstand atop every peak he summited, most often with hilarious success.

The golden age of "scramble" mountaineering in the Elks came to a close in the 1940s. Ellingwood, Blaurock, and others had visited most non-vertical routes. Now exploratory climbing around North America was turning to high-angle technical climbing, using ropes and special techniques. Elk Range peaks such as Capitol yielded a bit of such "vertical challenge," but after encountering the loose rock of the Elks, most climbers returned from such sport with a few more white hairs—and solid resolve to never return. However, steep technical climbing is only part of the mountaineering panoply. There are other ways to enjoy the appealing summits of Pyramid and the Bells.

In 1920, Blaurock and his longtime climbing partner William Ervin were sitting atop one of Colorado's southern Fourteeners. They counted up the ones they had climbed out of the total (there were considered to be 49 Fourteeners then as opposed to today's 54), and resolved on the spot to climb every 14,000-foot peak in the state. Three years later they completed the project and started a revolution in the process.

EFORE THE CONCEPT of a list, climbers enjoyed the Fourteeners as relaxed, congenial outings, each for its own sake. Blaurock's and Ervin's idea raced like an avalanche through the climbing world. Soon the CMC newsletter was publishing an annual accounting of those who made all the summits, and "list tickers" swarmed to the Fourteeners like silver boom prospectors. Today, during any summer weekend, hundreds of climbers enjoy popular and easy trails such as that on Colorado's highest peak, Mount Elbert. Harder climbs such as the Castle and Maroon Creek Fourteeners get less traffic, but are still climbed hundreds of times every summer.

While being a healthy muscle-powered sport, Fourteener-bagging has its downside. The shear number of feet on the trails has resulted in a surprising amount of damage to fragile alpine tundra. While this is being remedied through education and trail building, it is still a problem. To do their part, climbers should stick to established trails or less popular routes, or climb during winter and spring, when snow protects delicate alpine slopes.

Beyond environmental concerns, snow is the most important ingredient in the modern mountaineering history of the Elk Mountains. In late winter, thick snow covers and cements much of the terrifying rubble. Taking advantage of this, a small number of hardened climbers have established winter wall routes that would be suicide in summer. Furthermore, the sport of climbing mountains, then descending on ski or snowboard (known as "ski alpinism" or "ski mountaineering") fits well with the snow covered Elks. Thus, winter sports form a large portion of the modern history of these mountains.

WINTER MOUNTAINEERING AND SKI ALPINISM

WHILE MODERN CLIMBING is about aesthetics and plain fun, it is still about challenge and exploration. The great ranges such as the Himalayas or Alaska have the toughest weather and most virgin terrain. Still, when you climb to 14,000 feet in Colorado during a February storm, you could be anywhere in the world. "If you want training for the great ranges, just climb Fourteeners in winter," said Michael Kennedy, who pioneered many winter routes in the Elk Mountains during the 1970s and 80s, and went on to become a respected Himalayan veteran.

Nevertheless, mountaineering on snow is not just about winter. The Colorado mountains define a snow environment from as early as October through June, or sometime into early July. Winter can be cold and biting, with dry, light snow and unstable avalanche conditions, but as the months of April and May segue into spring, the snowpack warms and compacts into "spring" snow conditions. Avalanche danger is much easier to predict and avoid at this time, and it is easier to climb and ski on the firm snow. The spring snow season is when most snow climbing and ski mountaineering are done in the Elk Mountains.

In the late 1920s, the popularity of skiing was increasing everywhere in North America, and dozens of ski "maestros" visited or immigrated from Europe to teach skiing and assist in developing the industry. Among these was Otto Eugene Schniebs, who came from Germany in 1927.

Schniebs traveled the country promoting skiing, which he claimed in his stylish accent was "not choost a shport, but a vay off life." He networked with virtually all other ski promoters and surely knew of and was attracted to the commercial skiing gestating in the Aspen area. Indeed, Schniebs may have been an originator of the area's reputation, in that he had visited as early as 1936, and "climbed many of the mountains and ridges, among them the beautiful Mt. Hayden…and Castle Peak," he wrote in *American Skiing*, his classic how-to ski book.

In the spring of 1939, Schniebs organized a crew of three, who staged a virtual military expedition to the Castle Peak area of the Elks. First, the locals assisted by dynamiting avalanche debris off the Castle Creek Road so the skiers could drive to snow closure near the end of the valley. Then the expedition spent thirteen days moving 1,600 pounds of supplies (including fresh eggs and movie cameras) twelve miles to an old cabin at timberline below Castle Peak, where Schniebs set up his

…Schniebs may have been an originator of the area's reputation, in that he had visited as early as 1936, and "climbed many of the mountains and ridges, among them the beautiful Mt. Hayden…and Castle Peak," he wrote in American Skiing, *his classic how-to ski book.*

NEAL BEIDLEMAN

Ted Mahon makes first turns off the summit of Pyramid Peak on the Landry Route.

base of operations. (This cabin would later burn down, to be replaced by the Tagert Hut, a popular modern destination for ski mountaineers in the Braun Hut System.)

Schniebs and his friends hammered the Castle Creek Elks for a month. They skied from high on Castle Peak several times, then enjoyed snow-climbs and descents on dozens of orbit peaks. Their boldest climb was a pioneer ascent of 13,521-foot Star Peak via a technical snow route. The crew cut turns on every ski-able slope they could reach and enjoyed the classic high traverse over Pearl Pass toward Crested Butte. Schniebs was certainly the most aggressive snow season mountaineer of this era in the Elks, but another man would end up having a bigger part in the ski industry, and no small amount of influence on mountaineering.

Andre Roch was a Swiss mountaineer and ski resort consultant hired by investors trying to start a ski industry in the Aspen area. He first visited during the winter of 1936-37 (possibly preceding Schniebs' first visit). Roch was on the prowl for ski terrain and the locals led him to Aspen Mountain, then brush-covered, riddled with open mine shafts, and splotched with tailings piles.

Imagine the day: breaking out of the timber at the top of Aspen Mountain, Roch looks down the weed-covered hill with a bemused expression on his face. This was not a European alpine ski mountain. Then he looks up. He is immediately slapped in the face by Hayden Peak, a huge hunk of snow-covered geology looming from across the Castle Creek Valley. To a skier from the Alps, Mt. Hayden must have looked like heaven. Roch made the first ski ascent and descent of Hayden that winter and promoted the mountain as the best in the area—a true world-class venue for a ski resort. He even created an elaborate schematic for ski runs and a summit tramway, which was blueprinted and distributed.

WHILE MT. HAYDEN was never developed as a mechanized resort, Roch was correct in his assessment of the mountain's potential. It is big and steep, yet with slopes less riven than neighboring peaks. By being slightly lower, it is protected from wind by nearby higher ridges, thus having better snow cover throughout the winter. Result: the Aspen area's most popular ski mountaineering destination.

After Roch and Schniebs, and as World War II passed, Hayden and Castle peaks reigned over a dormant land. During the War, the U.S. Army formed a mountain warfare division known as the 10th Mountain. Troopers chosen for their mountaineering abilities and experience trained near Leadville for two winters. Many 10th Mountain soldiers visited Aspen, some even skiing over the Continental Divide from Leadville in February of 1944, via an incredibly alpine route that was years ahead of its time. While the bulk of 10th Mountain Division soldiers trained at Camp Hale, a small group lived and trained in Ashcroft and practiced their skills in the surrounding mountains.

A number of these rugged soldiers returned to Aspen after the war, often with ski-related lifestyles in mind. In terms of ski mountaineering, newspaperman Bil Dunaway (former owner/publisher of the *Aspen Times*) and architect Fritz Benedict were the most influential of the bunch. Dunaway was a gifted skier. He raced in Europe for the French National Team, where he learned the craft of ski mountaineering and became well known for making the first ski descent of Mount Blanc, Europe's highest peak.

Dunaway spent many a spring day skiing on Mt. Hayden and other slopes in the Castle Creek drainage. He befriended most of the area's younger mountaineers, including Fritz Stammberger, Michael Kennedy, and Lou Dawson, and was a big influence in what these men later accomplished in mountaineering.

Fritz Benedict was not as committed a ski mountaineer as Dunaway. Nonetheless, he realized how terrific the European style of ski mountaineering could be, with hut lodging, camaraderie among the lodgers, and plentiful terrain for play. He envisioned such skiing for the Aspen area and became a founder of the expansive system of backcountry ski huts in the Aspen area.

The huts north of Aspen are part of the 10th Mountain Hut Association. The six huts to the south form the Alfred Braun Memorial Hut System in the Castle Creek headwaters. Use of the Braun huts is an important part of Castle Creek mountaineering, and the story of the Braun Huts is an important piece of Elk Mountain history.

Dunaway was a gifted skier. He raced in Europe for the French National Team, where he learned the craft of ski mountaineering and became well known for making the first ski descent of Mount Blanc, Europe's highest peak.

CHRIS CASSATT

ABOVE LEFT **10th Mountain Division ski troopers practice turns with a ninety-lb. backpack on Cooper Hill near Camp Hale.**

ABOVE RIGHT **Esteemed Aspen climber and German immigrant Fritz Stammberger was the inspiration behind the annual "America's Uphill" race on Aspen Mountain. Stammberger made several mountaineering firsts in the Elk Range and disappeared on a solo climb in Pakistan in 1975.**

WHILE THERE WAS a fair amount of ski mountaineering done on the Castle Creek Elks through the 1950s, winter mountaineering on Pyramid Peak and the Bells proceeded at a slow pace. In January of 1958, the first winter ascent of North Maroon was made by Peter Hofer, an Aspen ski bum with roots in European mountaineering. Hofer got to know a trio of hardy Aspenites while frequenting the Red Onion Bar, and talk turned to visiting North Maroon's summit. The names of Hofer's companions have faded from his memory, but other details of the trip stick in his mind.

"In those days, you were an Aspen old-timer if you hung around for just one off-season," he said. "I knew these guys by first name and we just decided to go up there and try it. It was supposed to take a weekend, but we ran into horrible weather and stayed out four days. Two guys quit and went home. The other guy and myself waited out the weather, then climbed the Northwest Ridge. It was tough."

Hofer and his friends didn't realized they had done an important winter ascent and their "first" went unknown for years. In a way, Hofer's climb was the beginning of a new era in Elk Range winter mountaineering. Gear was improving and a liberal recreation ethic was taking hold. It was okay to be a ski bum or climbing bum in Aspen, and you could be revered more for your devotion to mountain sport than for your college degree or vocation. Here were the ingredients for a strong mountaineering culture.

While Castle Peak had received its first winter ascent by Roch many years before, and it had been skied from near the summit by Schniebs and possibly by Roch and others, skiing from the exact summit required modern attitude and technique. In the early 1960s, an Aspen lodge owner named Rick Richards bought land in Montezuma Basin and installed a small ski tow for a summer ski training camp on the permanent snowfield known as the "Montezuma Glacier." Richards would plow the Montezuma jeep trail every June, then ski with his groups into July. Legend holds that a young racer attending one of the ski camps did the first summit descent of Castle, via the upper East Ridge and a couloir on the North Face—a now classic route that is done many times each year.

FROM THE 1960S to 1975, snow season mountaineering in the Elk Mountains was defined by one man: Fritz Stammberger. Stammberger was an imposing man with a weightlifter's physique, thick German accent, and the poise of a rugged individualist. After emigrating from Germany in the early 1960s, he settled in Aspen as a job printer, ski instructor, and all-around activist. He once chained himself to a tree to prevent a building from going up, and marched in a parade with a sign reading "Public Castration for all Bycicle Thiefs [sic]."

In terms of alpine activism, Fritz was a committed alpinist and a bold skier. In 1964, he became the man with the highest ski descent of the time when he skied from 24,000 feet on Cho Oyu in Tibet (after making the first oxygenless ascent of that 8,000-meter peak, the seventh highest mountain in the world).

While living in Aspen, Stammberger spent countless days climbing the Elk's Fourteeners and skiing mountains such as Hayden Peak. His training was legendary. To prepare his hands for winter climbing, he would ski without gloves and walk around town with dripping snowballs clenched in his huge fists. Almost any winter morning you could see Stammberger's tall figure striding impossibly fast up the ski area on his touring skis—his favorite training, now memorialized in the popular "America's Uphill" ski race held every winter up Aspen Mountain Ski Area.

Like a Nietzschean Übermensch, Stammberger would wait until the cold and snowy season, then make first winter ascents of mountain walls as visionary and difficult as any climbs of similar size done elsewhere in the world. In 1969, he made the first winter climb of Pyramid Peak, one of the last Colorado Fourteeners that awaited a winter ascent. In March of 1972, he skied with Aspen restaurateur Gordon Whitmer to the north wall of 14,130-foot Capitol Peak, where the pair made a bold direct ascent of the face, again a winter first.

Mixed in with Stammberger's aesthetic and playful spirit was a good measure of self-promotion and one-upmanship. He was obsessed with trekking and climbing in the Himalayas, and the only way to raise money for such trips was to make a name for himself. He had heard of the European extreme skiers who were creating their own legends. Why not make his own? Fritz could ski and climb as well as anyone, so he did.

On June 24 Stammberger cramponed up the North Face of North Maroon Peak, donned his planks, and skied back down. Even by today's standards, the descent wasn't easy: Stammberger fell over a fifteen-foot cliff and skied narrow slots exceeding 50 degrees. While Stammberger's Maroon Bells descent was too far from North American ski reality to receive much press, it was an inaugural event of modern "extreme" ski alpinism in the United States.

After his Maroon Bells descent, Stammberger endured a frustrating series of failures in the Himalayas. He eventually met his end while solo climbing in 1975 on Tirich Mir in Pakistan. Dunaway and other Aspenites launched a search, but Stammberger was never found and is presumed dead.

By the late 1960s Aspen's mountaineering culture was going full tilt. Individuals like Dunaway were the old guard; Stammberger was a one-man show; and a loosely knit group of young climbers in their twenties lived a carefree life on the streets and in the bars of Aspen. Style in those days told it all. A pair of scuffed mountain boots was as common as polished cowboy boots are today. It seemed like everyone wore a faded backpack that looked like it had grown from their shoulders. Instead of real estate and breast implants, talk in the bars was often about climbing.

With the inspiration of Fritz Stammberger, Aspen climbing bums turned their attention to ski alpinism. They spent scores of days at the Braun huts, and the traverse over Pearl Pass from Ashcroft to Crested Butte was an ever-popular endeavor. Those with steeper terrain in mind spent days on Hayden Peak. With this foundation, many in the loosely knit Aspen crew went on to become nationally recognized mountaineers. Michael Kennedy made notable ascents in the Himalayas and took a local mountaineering magazine to worldwide prominence as he shepherded *Climbing Magazine* for more than two decades. Steve Shea went on to star in a ski

MICHAEL KENNEDY

Chris Landry arrives at the summit of Pyramid Peak in May, 1978.

film called *Fall Line*, the first of hundreds of subsequent "extreme sports" films that have become somewhat of a genre.

The 1970s closed with another gateway event in the Maroon Creek Elks—a happening that would profoundly influence North American ski mountaineering up through the present.

CHRIS LANDRY grew up in the Aspen area, and while somewhat of a loner, he became an accomplished mountaineer while climbing with the Aspen group. Landry was also a terrific skier who raced during high school. After practicing in the Elks by skiing ever-steeper lines, he set his sights on Pyramid Peak. The line Landry chose on the east face of Pyramid was easily a generation beyond the descents of Fritz Stammberger. Super steep, with a number of 60 degree sections, the face is long and discontinuous. Just getting up the wall is a dangerous, technical crampon ascent, and is seldom done.

After climbing the route with Michael Kennedy in the wee hours of May 15, 1978 (Kennedy was along for support and photography; he did not ski), Landry started down at 8:30 in the morning. "I didn't decide to ski until I got to the top," Landry recalls. "I knew all along what I wanted to do, but it wasn't until that moment I knew I would." On the 60-degree, 15-foot-wide patch of thawing crud near the summit, Landry sometimes had to stop and back up in order to gain enough room to make his next turn. Several times slabs big enough to knock him down would break loose, resulting in at least one narrow escape. Much of Landry's skiing on Pyramid was performed within several feet of 300-foot cliffs. The crux of the route was stopping above a near-vertical ice face, changing mode to crampons, downclimbing a short distance, then changing to skis again.

"I'm still shocked by it," Landry stated a few months after making the descent. "It was the first time I'd ever skied something where, if I fell, I died. I wonder sometimes—like anyone—exactly what I was doing there." Landry went on to make notable descents in California and Washington, and then retired from extreme skiing after a near-death fall on Denali in Alaska.

With a past rich in exploration, adventure and risk, the 1980s and '90s have been a time of transition in mountaineering in the Elks. With the area's high cost of living and change to a second-home population, the cohesive and self-reliant climbing community of the '60s and '70s has largely dissipated. Aspen's climbing community is now largely a "culture of guiding" wherein a few strong mountaineers attend to well-moneyed neophytes.

What's more, mountaineers have come to realize that many other ranges in North America are equal in stature to the Elks, but have better rock for climbing and snow climates with less avalanche danger. Yet extreme skiing is still defined by challenge and risk, and the Elk Mountains offer plenty of both. Again, consider Pyramid Peak.

On Pyramid's east side, next to and south of Landry's route, is a gigantic ramp of snow known as the Gendarme Face, which drops from a small saddle just a few feet south of the actual summit. The first section of the route averages 55 degrees and includes 60-degree pitches as it drops 2,000 vertical feet. These angles are the steepest it is possible to ski, and even then such "skiing" is more of a controlled fall. Below that, the "easy" skiing takes you down another 2,000 vertical feet of terrain steeper than the black diamond runs at a ski resort.

After practicing in the Elks by skiing ever-steeper lines, he set his sights on Pyramid Peak. The line Landry chose on the east face of Pyramid was easily a generation beyond the descents of Fritz Stammberger. Super steep, with a number of 60 degree sections, the face is long and discontinuous.

S KI ALPINISTS have known for three decades that the Gendarme Face is the best line in the Elks, and perhaps the best in Colorado. Perfunctory attempts were made at first descents, but the sun-blasted east-facing snow on such routes is only in skiable condition several weeks a year, and the climb is always a major endeavor. More than anything, such a route requires every facet of your day to be perfectly orchestrated. You miss one note and your whole song falls down the mountain.

Crested Butte residents Frank Konsella and Jay Prentiss knew the program. After researching the Gendarme Face route on Pyramid and making a 1999 attempt, they returned in 2000 and nailed every note. They camped at the base of the face, started their climb at midnight, and made a consummate first descent. The two are experienced and well-traveled extreme skiers, and they called the route the "best descent we had ever made." In amusing understatement, the pair named their route "Frank's Angst."

Prentiss and Konsella's assessment is correct. Throughout the world, drops this long and continuously steep are a sought after prize. For example, the Orient Express couloir on Denali in Alaska, one of the classic extreme descents of the world, is only about a thousand feet longer than the Gendarme. Thus, the Elk Mountains still provide a sensational arena that asks the best of its players.

Beyond route and summit, beyond challenge and risk, mountaineering is about relationship. While challenging the steeps, climbers and ski mountaineers reach a unique bonding with their partners, the land, and the spirit. Other ranges than the Elks are safer or easier for alpinists. Other ranges are better known. Yet the stupendous Castle and Maroon Creek mountains continue to yield that most important part of alpinism: connections that are mystical in their power.

ABOVE **One of the best extreme skiing lines in Colorado is the East Face of Pyramid Peak. The Landry route from the summit is in red on the right, while the K/P Gendarme Face route is in green on the left.**

RIGHT **A young camper and packhorse at "The Ashcrofters", a 1960's mountaineering school and boys camp at the site of the present day Pine Creek Cookhouse.**

"THANKS DAVE" • A REMEMBRANCE OF THE ASHCROFTERS

EDITOR'S NOTE: *As one of the leading mountaineers of the Elk Range, Lou Dawson got his start at a unique mountain camp in Ashcroft. What follows is a personal account of that experience.*

As part of our camp experience, we would bake ourselves in a wood-burning sauna, then climb a hill by the pond next to the cookhouse, hang from a pulley and take a wild slide down a zipline to a big splash in the frigid water. We would run around in our sagging wet underwear, smeared with mud from the pond, and repeat the routine over and over again …

AROUND 1966, at fourteen years old, I became obsessed with mountaineering. As I devoured climbing literature like a starving wolf on a deer kill, it was obvious to my parents that if their "mountain boy" didn't get proper training, he'd kill himself by tying into a length of clothesline and dangling off one of the numerous and tempting cliffs around Aspen.

Nine miles up the Castle Creek Valley from our home, Aspen outdoorsman Dave Farny was operating "The Ashcrofters," a mountaineering school and boys' camp now legendary among the climbing cognoscenti. Several alumni went on to become famous climbers, including Henry Barber, who had a big influence on American rock climbing in the 1970s. My parents sent me there during the summer of 1967, with hope of instilling sanity into my quest for mountain adventure. My experience accomplished their goal, but it was so much more.

The location of the camp was exquisite. It occupied the site of today's Ashcroft Ski Touring Center and Pine Creek Cookhouse (most of the existing buildings were extant in 1967 and used for the camp). Dave's wife Sherry fed everyone in a classic dining hall that is now the Pine Creek Cookhouse.

As part of our camp experience, we would bake ourselves in a wood-burning sauna, then climb a hill by the pond next to the cookhouse, hang from a pulley and take a wild slide down a zipline to a big splash in the frigid water. We would run around in our sagging wet underwear, smeared with mud from the pond, and repeat the routine over and over again like a tribe of nascent savages. Other camp activities included a challenging ropes course and soccer games in a rock-studded field scattered with dried cow pies.

ASPEN HISTORICAL SOCIETY

Farny was a somewhat severe individual, but even he smiled at the exuberance demonstrated by a bunch of thirteen- to sixteen-year-old boys getting their first taste of testosterone-induced wildness. Dave did finally get enough of our behavior. I had long "hippie" hair when I arrived at the camp. After a particularly rowdy zipline session, he sat me down on a log and gave me a marine haircut, thus eliminating about six months of shag.

Dave and Sherry Farny and their young family in the early 1960s at "The Ashcrofters" mountaineering school and camp for 13–15 year-old boys.

My hip mother was furious, but I took Dave's barbering in stride. I liked having someone take an opinionated stance on my appearance, as the permissive 1960s were often too unstructured for this wandering teen.

Indeed, while Farny was often derided by liberal Aspenites, his organizational skills and rigidity were exactly what made a camp like The Ashcrofters a fantastic haven for teenagers. What cinched Dave's success was his wife Sherry. His opposite in demeanor, she would spend hours with groups of boys when they returned from the field, letting them vent their teenage angst and share what they had learned.

The 1960s were a halcyon time for outdoor education, with virtually no standards for guide skills and risk management. This made the camp special, as our adventures were 100 per cent real, rather than contrived by rigid rules as they are in much of present-day outdoor education. Besides enhancing the experience, this cavalier attitude resulted in many amusing stories and one sad accident. On a tragic Ashcrofters outing in 1965, a participant, Robert B. Rossetter, drowned during a stream crossing. The Mountain Rescue cabin on Main Street, Aspen, which was donated to Mountain Rescue by the Rossetter family, is named in memory of their son.

"Loose" is how former Ashcrofter guide Jim Ward described the outfit. "There was the raft trip on the Yampa during the first session of each Ashcrofter summer," recalled Ward. "Farny would have everybody drink straight out of the river and they'd all get the runs a few days after the trip. After every float we'd stop in Dinosaur, Colorado, and get a 'brontosaurus burger' at the drive-in, on which Farny would later blame our intestinal distress. As for myself," confessed Ward, "I had quite a bit of experience in the outdoors, but my climbing experience was rather limited. Prior to working for Farny, I'd gotten my experience with ropes working for a sign company in Minnesota."

THE VALUE OF THE CAMP far exceeded any recklessness, but there were some wild times during my stay. We spent a solo night in the woods called a "survival," during which we were allowed a small survival kit, but no sleeping bag. It was suggested that in order to stay warm we could build a fire in a hole, cover up the hot coals with dirt, and sleep on top. Most of us did exactly that. The next day, back at the camp, we noticed faint wafts of smoke rising from nearby conifer forests. The wafts soon plumed into forest fires—at the exact locations of our "fire beds." It turned out we'd built a number of fires in flammable conifer duff .The next thing we knew, the guides and older kids were pressed into work by the Forest Service as impromptu firemen.

In another instance, a group of kids during my session went for a hike on their own. They ran across an abandoned mine, entered the shaft, and found a box of old dynamite sticks. Not knowing that aged dynamite can explode at the slightest touch, they carried a handful of sticks out of the mine and posed for goofy camera shots, including one memorable image of a young man pretending to smoke a stick of dynamite like a cigar.

But beyond all the funny stories, there were formative experiences in the mountains. From our cabins at Pine Creek, we could quickly hike up the hill to the Cathedral Lake trail and into the Maroon Bells-Snowmass Wilderness. Our outings required scrambling around on dangerous and majestic 14,000-foot peaks like Pyramid and Capitol, skinny dipping in high mountain lakes, and tromping classic alpine trails like Buckskin Pass. One such trip included a climb of Pyramid Peak that sticks in my memory like it was yesterday.

Pyramid is a tough, dangerous mountain, covered with loose rock and draped by precipitous cliffs. Our guide/instructor deviated from the standard route and kept us on a direct line. Soon he had a rope out and was taking turns belaying us up a vertical cliff that was like a boulder studded gravel pile. As each kid took his turn on the rope, he would knock at least half a dozen large rocks down the face.

These bombs would soon achieve artillery velocity, then hit ledges below with terrifying booms. A flinty smell wafted up from the depths as we cowered to the side, awaiting our turns. It was scary and exhilarating and made our arrival on the summit a special event.

Ever since then, I have been extra careful with the loose rock of the Elk Range. Indeed, the fact that I am still alive and have accomplished what I have as a mountaineer is a testament to lessons learned from Dave Farny and his Ashcrofters. ❖

The beauty of the Maroon Bells is a deceptive allure to loose rock, narrow ledges and icy snowfields. Even the most experienced mountaineers have perished on these peaks.

12 The Deadly Bells

THERE IS A SIGN on the trail from Maroon Lake to Crater Lake that gives casual hikers a final warning. THE DEADLY BELLS, it reads, briefly describing the risks inherent in the mountains beyond. Few of the hikers who read the sign will imperil themselves on a high mountain ledge; most visitors don't get that far. But every year there are injuries and sometimes fatalities for those who pass that dire warning.

No words can safeguard hikers or climbers from the dangers they unknowingly face—hypothermia, dehydration, frostbite, lightning, exhaustion, drowning, falling. Even experienced mountaineers fall victim to poor judgment, unforeseen circumstances, lapses in attention, or just plain bad luck. The annals of Aspen's Mountain Rescue team are filled with such tragedies.

Consider the following anecdotes as a warning and a prod for heightened awareness. The rest is up to the individual through attention to proper caution, training, fitness, preparation, orienteering skills, equipment, and clothing. Here are some examples of what happens when things go wrong for people who stroll past that warning sign on the Crater Lake Trail and find themselves in a life-and-death struggle for survival.

"A CLOSE CALL"

EDITOR'S NOTE: *The following is excerpted from a* Denver Post *feature from the mid-1950s. It details a near-death climbing accident, a true "cliff-hanger" written by long-time Aspen resident and lodge owner Ralph Melville. The article was titled "I Slid to the Brink of Death."*

I LIVE AND RUN A BUSINESS in Aspen and I suppose I've climbed my share of mountains. This day—it was Aug. 5, 1956—we started out at dawn and climbed Maroon Bells Peak, 14,000 feet up in the snow and a real mountain climber's mountain. It was about 1 p.m. when the three of us—Mary Lou Hayden, 25, a waitress; Loren Jenkins, 19, a University of Colorado student (now Senior Foreign News Editor at NPR); and myself—started back down. I suggested the glissade when I noticed my two companions were tiring. I should never have done it.

But I did, unstrapping my crampons from my boots so I could slide and holding my ice ax out behind me to control the run. Then away I went and everything was fine for a second or two.

Suddenly, though, I whirled out of the snow and onto a patch of bare, shining ice. This is the most dangerous surface for a glissade, and I leaned back heavy on my ax to slow down and stop. But the point of the ax only flicked the top of the ice, and I shot down that slope faster and faster like a bullet looking for a target.

Then one foot whipped out from under me and I lost all control and I knew I was gone and something snapped and then...

...I came to in a haze of pain and blinked up at the glaring, blinding sunlight dancing off the white walls of Maroon Bells. I looked around, slowly, and discovered I had fallen into a steep ice run, pitched like a chalet rooftop, which ended 200 feet below me in a sudden-death drop of nearly 2,000 feet. That 200 feet between me and the drop-off was gleaming ice—slick, silent, deadly.

Above me was the rim of ice and snow over which I had skidded. The only thing that stopped me from sliding down from that rim to the ice precipice below was a wedge of rock that jutted out from the ice. My legs had jammed in the wedge and pain shot up from them. Something must be broken.

Pain and fear and the great awful silence flooded over me in pulsating waves of weakness and panic. I realized with a shock that I'd have to fight this out alone—that my companions were gone and that it would be hours, probably the next morning, before anyone summoned by them from Aspen could reach me to help. My ice ax, crampons, and rope were gone. I had nothing to work with. What could I do?

An icy wind ripped down on me and I knew then that I had another bitter enemy, the cold. I still had my rucksack and I opened it, looking for an extra jacket. But the sack slipped away from me and I watched—hypnotized—as it slithered down across the ice beneath me to the precipice, soared out into nothingness, and disappeared.

SAW THAT AND KNEW I HAD TO DO SOMETHING. Across to one side of the slope where I was pinned in the rocks was a protected point. If I could reach it, I might keep out of the wind and live through the night.

Carefully, I twisted my legs free. My right leg seemed to be okay, but the sharp pain from the left told me something in it had snapped. Biting my teeth and holding the leg with my hands to keep it stiff, I stood up to test it. But my knee collapsed, and I spun off the rocks onto the ice and down toward that terrible void...

When I regained consciousness this time, I felt out with my hands, trying to find something to hold on to. My right hand closed around a small rock. But my left was hanging in mid-air! I turned my head slightly and looked directly down into that great white hole. I was right on the brink of that horrible drop to death!

I was afraid to move, afraid that even the slightest shift would send me hurtling down that hole to the valley floor far beneath me. Icy water ran down across me and sprayed out into space in a filmy mist...and still I did not, could not, move.

There was more pain, this time from my side. Needles of it stabbed into my body every time I breathed. I tried to figure the time, but I had no idea how long I had been unconscious. I saw deep shadows develop on the rocky peaks above me, and then it was twilight...and still I did not move. And everything was so quiet.

Then came the dreams; strange, wild fantasies of delirium: I was riding my horse along a narrow ledge above the clouds when the horse reared, tossing me out into space where I kept falling, falling, falling...

In a flash of reality, I saw a tiny figure far below me. A tiny figure in a red sweater. I tried to yell, but my jaw ached and I could not open my mouth. All I could do was groan. I was on the horse again, this time on a mountain trail. And the horse threw me and I tumbled down, down, down...

The figure in red was closer now, chopping steps in the ice walls of the gaping hole. Now I knew! The figure in red was death, coming for me. When it reached me, I would be dead! My right hand ached from clutching the small rock. The twilight was colder. I saw a star, cold in the deepening blue of the evening sky, high

Nearing the summit from a rocky aerie on the west ridge route to Pyramid Peak, mercurial mountain weather changes the nature of a climb. Climbers usually start in the dark to reach the heights before typical afternoon storms make for lethal exposure.

above me.

"Melville"... my name drifted faintly up from below. "Melville"... The figure in red was waving and I blinked my eyes, trying to focus them on the figure. Then I saw—it wasn't death, it was Mary Lou. Mary Lou!

I watched as she chopped at the ice, coming up step by step. I wondered how long I could last, whether I could wait for her. I could hear her now—chopping at the ice. Then I could hear her breathing, gasping from the exertion. Then her hand was over the brink before me, then her head, her face.

And she said, "You're all right now, Melville," and she smiled.

Ralph Melville was rescued from his fall. He had suffered a shattered kneecap, three broken ribs, jaw and arm fractures, a sprained back, shock, exposure, and bruises and cuts from the ice and rock. Mary Lou Hayden made a daring solo rescue while Loren Jenkins ran to Maroon Lake and notified rescuers. Mary Lou received the Carnegie Hero Fund Award for the year's most heroic rescue.

Pitkin County Mountain
Rescue volunteers practice
rescue procedures on the
lower slopes of North Maroon
Peak.

"THE BELLS" CLAIM GREG MACE

I N JULY 1986, forty-three-year-old Greg Mace decided to climb the Maroon
Bells with two fellow Mountain Rescue team members, Tom McCabe and David
Floria. Mountain guides Flint Smith and Jerry Begley joined them. The group
planned to summit North Maroon Peak and explore for a helicopter landing site on
the Maroon Bells for use in future airlift rescues. Mace, son of the legendary Stuart
Mace, was then head of Mountain Rescue Aspen.

Greg Mace was a seasoned mountaineer who had learned many of his skills
from his father during childhood. Growing up in Ashcroft, he had been surrounded
by mountains and he loved the challenges they presented. On his first rescue on Mt.
Hayden in 1973, before he had been admitted as a member of the rescue team,
Mace, then thirty, staged a solo rescue where he was the first to respond. Alone, he
exhumed the body of a sixteen-year-old boy from a fatal avalanche and from then
on was dedicated to helping others in the mountains. Mace succeeded Fred Braun
as Mountain Rescue leader and bore that mantle with serious dedication.

According to Hal Clifford, in his book *The Falling Season*, Mace and his
friends met on a July day at the Maroon Lake parking lot and hiked to the base of
North Maroon Peak. "Because Greg was permanent rescue leader," wrote Clifford,
"he always carried a radio. Yet he'd left his at home this day; it wasn't working
properly. Tom [McCabe], expecting Greg to have a radio, didn't bring his.
It wasn't a big deal; they could climb without one."

The group followed the standard route to the summit of North Maroon Peak
at 14,014 feet and discussed helicopter landing sites and rescue routes. Then they
traversed the ridge to the south and summited South Maroon Peak at 14,156 feet.
On both summits, states Clifford, Flint Smith pulled a golf club out of his pack
and, in a hacker's dream, drove a golf ball so far it disappeared from sight.

"DEATH ON THE MOUNTAIN"

EDITOR'S NOTE: *The following published account from September 1952 illustrates the high stakes of climbing the Maroon Bells.*

Two college men, ending their vacation, were climbing the treacherous Maroon Bells near Aspen, Colorado. They could have turned back with two friends at 5 p.m. Wednesday. But exhilarated by their adventure, experienced Alpinists Larry Hackstaff of Denver and Gordon Schindel of Kansas City continued climbing. At 7 p.m., they started down, sliding in tandem over icy snow.

Then the adventure became a fight with death. They fell and rolled dizzily downward, only saving themselves by falling against rocks. Hackstaff blacked out and awoke alone Thursday morning. Delirious, he walked a few steps and fell off a 100-foot precipice into a crevasse.

After a twenty-eight-hour hunt, rescuers found both men, 100 yards apart, at 1 p.m. Friday. Hackstaff, with battered face and broken leg, took three days to regain consciousness. Schindel was dead. ❖

The group hiked down the south ridge of Maroon Peak and, a short distance from the summit, decided to descend into the West Maroon Creek Valley, 4,000 feet below, via the Grand Couloir, a snow gully that drops off steeply from the ridge in a narrow declivity. Smith volunteered to establish a belay for the first steep pitch, but the others declined and began preparations for the descent.

According to Clifford's account, Tom McCabe and Greg Mace stopped to strap on crampons, the spiked attachments to boots that assist in gripping snow and ice. David Floria and Jerry Begley headed down together, plunge-stepping by thrusting their heels into the soft snow with every forward step. Floria and Begley practiced self-arrests by enacting a fall, rolling over on their stomachs, and braking their slides with their ice axes. By the time McCabe and Mace started down, the others were 500 feet below.

Mace apparently stumbled on the descent and attempted a self-arrest with his ice ax. McCabe watched as Mace plunged his ax deep into snow. However, when his inertia tugged against the anchored ice ax, Mace lost his grip on the handle. The safety leash on the ice ax—a band of stout webbing—slipped over his hand. With the ax still embedded in the snow Mace slid, then tumbled. Apparently, his crampons caught in the snow and turned a slide into a tumble from which there was no recovery.

Clifford writes that Mace tumbled rapidly toward Begley and Floria, who at first moved into his path to stop his fall, then moved quickly back as they realized how fast Mace was moving. At thirty miles per hour, the impact could have been deadly and one or both men could have been knocked down like bowling pins. Mace tumbled past them into a deep groove worn into the snow gully by warm weather. He disappeared around a corner.

Begley and Floria worked their way down Mace's track until they could see him. They shouted to McCabe and Smith, who were still above them, that Mace was alive. Then all four men hurried to his aid.

Clifford reports that Mace had tumbled headlong into a pile of rocks at the end of the snow gully and, by the time McCabe reached the scene, only Begley was at Mace's side. Recognizing the severity of Mace's injuries, Floria had hurried immediately into the West Maroon Creek Valley where he would run ninety minutes to the Maroon Lake parking lot, then drive seven miles to make a distress phone call. The others gathered in the snow gully, picked up Mace, and laid him carefully on a rock ledge. He was spitting blood and his left side had been severely impacted by the collision with the rocks.

Smith had a medical kit, but nothing to drain the fluid welling up in Mace's chest. The three men had to roll Mace onto his left side to drain the fluid before his lungs filled. The cramped ledge was too small for all four of them, so the three men took turns to be with Mace who was fully conscious and expressed shock and dismay that this could be happening to him.

It was on McCabe's watch, after the sun had set, that Mace stopped breathing. The men took turns with Cardio-Pulmonary Resuscitation (CPR), but to no avail.

"A few minutes later," after Mace had died, wrote Clifford, "they heard the whap-whap-whap of Bert Metcalf's helicopter coming up the valley."

Mace's body was loaded into a litter and flown out by helicopter. The others hiked down in the deepening dusk, minus a friend, a leader, and an experienced mountaineer.

HEINZ PAGELS FALLS FROM PYRAMID PEAK

EDITOR'S NOTE: *Pyramid Peak is notorious as one of the most difficult and dangerous of the Colorado Fourteeners. Loose rock and vertical exposure require acute awareness while climbing. The following describes a fatality on Pyramid that claimed the life of a prominent physicist.*

HEINZ PAGELS was a regular visitor to Aspen in his role as a theoretical physicist connected with the Aspen Center for Physics. He was a professor at Rockefeller University in Manhattan and executive director of the New York Academy of Sciences.

On a summer day in the late 1980s, Pagels and a young physics student to whom Pagels had served as dissertation advisor climbed Pyramid Peak from the standard approach up the north cirque. After a lunch break at the top of the 14,018-foot summit, Pagels and his companion began the tricky descent down a series of small ledges comprised mostly of loose rock.

Ted Conover, in his book *Whiteout: Lost in Aspen*, interviewed Pagels' companion, "Seth Lloyd", and described the fatal descent:

… He and Heinz had been descending along a narrow ridge. There was a path in the middle of the ridge, with steep drops on either side. Heinz was in the lead, Seth a few paces behind. Heinz, forty-seven, had previously climbed Pyramid seven times. He was a tall, slender man who had some weakness in his ankles from a childhood bout with polio. As he made a small hop over a gap, he landed on a rock that proved unsteady and lost his balance. Almost before Seth could notice, he was gone, sliding down a steep, gravely chute and then dropping out of sight.

BERNICE DURAND

Heinz Pagels

Seth called to him repeatedly, but got no reply. There was no question of following his path down the couloir, because there were no hand- or footholds. Seth, hearing only silence, ran down the trail to see if he might intercept Pagels' route. But the trail angled away from where Heinz would be, and sheer cliffs blocked the way. Despairing, Seth ran the rest of the three miles down to the trailhead, near the Maroon Bells parking lot, and waved down a shuttle bus. The driver used his radio to call the police, who called Aspen

---

"A DOUBLE FALL"

A FREAK double fall apparently killed R. Peter Isto, 51, of Lakewood, as the Maroon Bells claimed their fourth victim in ten days," reported the *Aspen Times* in August 1965. Isto was climbing South Maroon Peak with a partner when he slipped on wet rocks and fell to a ledge 100 feet below, suffering a serious head injury. His partner checked his condition, then went for help. A rescue team under the leadership of Fred Braun returned that night.

Darkness postponed the rescue on this the third consecutive weekend that rescuers had answered calls to the Maroon Bells. When Isto's body was recovered the next day, it was on a ledge 50 feet below the one where his partner had seen him last, indicating that he had rolled off only to fall again, fatally the second time.

Two weeks prior to Isto's death, three members of a four-man team died during an attempted climb on the west side of the same peak. Braun was quoted saying that restrictions on climbing the Bells should be considered in the wake of five deaths that summer. ❖

The imposing North Face of Pyramid Peak is always on the climber's left as they ascend the west ridge, seen in the sunlight on the right side of the massif.

Mountain Rescue; the first ones on the scene ascertained that a team on foot would take hours to arrive where Heinz had probably fallen, and that, with sunset impending, they might not even find him, so vast was the terrain. They ordered in a helicopter and advised Seth to go home, shower, and change, and return within two hours…

…The rescue personnel scattered from the parking lot when the 'copter arrived, and it set down in the middle. Seth climbed into its Plexiglas bubble, along with the pilot and one of the rescue team's top climbers. The climber was famed for having recently hung off a helicopter skid to rescue someone from a ledge; he carried rope and other equipment, which seemed a hopeful sign. The helicopter lifted off toward the high valleys…

…Their return was desperately awaited for the answer it might bring to the question no one had dared to discuss openly: was he alive, or was he dead? In the best of all worlds, I could imagine the 'copter carrying Pagels himself. He had managed to save himself by grabbing on to a branch or getting his shirt snagged on a rock, just as they do in cartoons…

…Twenty minutes later, as the rotor slowed, the wind died down, and dust settled, Seth climbed slowly out of the helicopter's bubble. He walked toward me, and everyone else walked away. He appeared scared and stony-faced and looked at me for a long time before saying, 'He's dead.'

THERE WAS A LOT MORE TO BE DONE, and unfortunately, only Seth could do it. With a sheriff's deputy and a psychologist, we drove to the house of Heinz's wife, Elaine Pagels, a well-known professor of religion at Princeton, and their children, ages three months and two years, where Seth broke the news. The next day the local papers called, and the day after that, *The New York Times*… Seth had to retell the story of the fall to each of the reporters, again to the police, and then, numerous times to Heinz's associates at the physics institute and at Rockefeller University.

There was a funeral service. There were more visits to Elaine. There was a trip with Elaine to the coroner's office, where she had asked to view the body. But the coroner persuaded her not to: 'It would give you the wrong idea of how he died,' he said, which was instantaneously. Heinz Pagels had fallen between fourteen hundred and two thousand feet, the height of one to one and a half Empire State Buildings." ❖

12 Mountaineering Firsts

DAWSON SKIS PYRAMID

By Louis Dawson III

EDITOR'S NOTE: *Pyramid Peak is Lou Dawson's favorite Elk Range Fourteener. By the 1990s he had climbed Pyramid more the thirty times, many of those in winter, and made two ski descents from the summit.*

F ANY ONE PLACE DEFINES my life as an alpinist, it would be the Castle and Maroon Creek Valleys. When my family first moved to Aspen in the 1960s, we built a house on Castle Creek. I worked as a teenage apprentice carpenter on the project, but my mind was elsewhere. As flies bit my neck in that muggy creek bottom, I would sometimes smell the alpine air blowing down from Castle Peak, Pyramid, and the Maroons. It was like opening your freezer on a hot day and feeling the cold air chill you down. I would lift my gaze and imagine myself on a mountainside, ice ax in hand, questing for the heights.

As life would have it, my father hired a lanky teenager named Chris Landry, who would later make his name as an extreme skier. He and I worked together much of that summer. While a quiet man, Chris spoke enough of climbing for me to know that he was a master of the sport. Over the years, Chris became known for his astringent personality. I got my first taste of that when I asked him if he would teach me to climb, and he gave me a simple answer: No.

As setbacks often do for the zealot, Chris's answer strengthened my resolve. I became a climber, and for a few decades devoted my life to the sport. Yet living in Aspen was also about skiing, both at the resorts and in the backcountry. I learned there is nothing like climbing to the top of a high summit, then pushing off with ski poles to make a glorious descent. When conditions are good, it has to be the closest thing to flying you can do with your feet on the ground. Thus, as happens with many alpinists, my climbing and skiing came together. I became a ski mountaineer.

From Alaska to South America, but mostly in North America, I climbed up and skied down hundreds of peaks. Occasionally I would find myself atop a Colorado Fourteener, my ski tips literally hanging off the summit. I soon found that Colorado's Fourteeners and high Thirteeners were extraordinary places for skiing. The high altitude snow lasts longer in the spring, the summits feel "real," and the descents can be epic drops. Sometimes you make turns for more than 3,000 vertical feet on these peaks. If you hit it right, you carve perfect God-smoothed snow that makes the best machine-groomed resort slopes feel like rock fields. Other times, the climbing and skiing are more challenging than fun—but still rewarding.

In the spring of 1987, my friend John Quinn suggested we drive around the state and ski as many Fourteeners as we could. After a few days, we slipped into a routine. The guidebooks of the time had no snow-season route information, so we spent evenings poring over maps and photos. The next day would find us driving back roads in search of obscure trailheads. Once we found a parking spot, we would plant the bumper of John's truck in the snowplow swale, sleep on the seats for a few hours before a 3 a.m. start, then "bag another 'teener." Usually back down by late morning, we would drive into a nearby town, catch a late breakfast,

I learned there is nothing like climbing to the top of a high summit, then pushing off with ski poles to make a glorious descent. When conditions are good, it has to be the closest thing to flying you can do with your feet on the ground. Thus, as happens with many alpinists, my climbing and skiing came together. I became a ski mountaineer.

Lou Dawson negotiates an unpredictable snow crust, caused by wind, in Pearl Basin.

then do it all over again. We skied from the summits of nine Fourteeners that way. It was one of the best of our many ski trips together.

Back in the Roaring Fork Valley, John and I sat on the porch of my mobile home. While basking in the glow of our journey, we did what all mountaineers do in such situations: we imagined future trips and lofty goals. "You know, Lou," John said, "you ought to go and ski all the Fourteeners. That would be a cool project—you'd probably be the first guy to do it." Bingo! My destiny was nailed to the trailer-house wall.

WITH VARIOUS PARTNERS, and sometimes solo, I climbed and skied another nine Fourteeners that spring, then did a few the next winter. This was a good start for the project, yet my pace would slow to a crawl. I had made a fundamental mistake in strategy —I'd left most of the harder peaks until last. Capitol Peak; the cliffy Crestones in southern Colorado; windy Longs Peak near Estes Park; all incredibly difficult, some with unreliable snow cover, some requiring overnight backpacking. One of the Crestones took me seven tries. Other peaks yielded partial descents and I returned when their summits were skiable. Looming above all those "adult" mountains, Pyramid Peak jutted into my dreams like a gigantic spike tearing up from the core of the planet.

In 1988, I skied a route on the west side of Pyramid. This incredible journey took a fabulous system of narrow couloirs, starting from about 150 feet below the summit. While this was a bonafide descent, it did not count as a "list tick" for my Fourteeners project. I have always adhered to the classic view of ski mountaineering where the climb of the mountain and launching off the top made the perfect day. My personal rule was, if it was possible to ski from a summit, I would not claim a descent of the peak until I'd launched from the apex. Chris Landry had skied from the top of Pyramid during his 1978 pioneer descent. Thus, I had to return.

In May of 1989, Aspen carpenter Jeff Maus and I planned another trip to Pyramid. Our strategy was complex—in some ways not as elegant as Landry's—in other ways more logical. We figured we could start from the top using Landry's route, then escape to a 13,000-foot saddle where we could ski easier terrain down the north bowl of the peak. Neither of us was a skier of Landry's caliber, so our plan allowed a summit ski descent while using as small a section of his fearful route as possible.

Our plan fell short in its complexity; it would require complicated route-finding. In addition, because of the cliffy terrain and possible avalanche danger, we would do some of our skiing while roped. Doing so makes the descent much less fluid, slower, and harder because of technical issues and the distraction of skiing on a leash. While many of my other Fourteener descents had been runs of freedom— fluid descents on perfect snow—this would be an exercise in problem-solving.

MICHAEL KENNEDY

THE POINT OF NO RETURN

OUR DAY on Pyramid begins much as any other successful Fourteener climb and descent—with suffering. At 12 a.m., my alarm stings me awake. Still half asleep, I drive with fanatic care to the locked gate on the Maroon Creek road. Time is critical. Jeff has slept in his car at the gate. He is awake and ready—a committed partner. I open the gate with a combination I had finagled from somebody (the road is driveable but officially "closed"). We shift to 4-wheel-drive, then bounce over huge piles of frozen avalanche debris still covering the road.

We drive to the end of the road and, by the pools of our headlamp beams, hike dry ground up the valley from Maroon Lake. Normally I'm somewhat cheerful during these "alpine start" approach marches, but not this time. The setting is peaceful —even the birds are sleeping—but as the hulk of Pyramid Peak rises to our left through the darkness like a prehistoric beast, my buoyant thoughts are crushed. I know the mountain too well. We are here for reasons beyond fun.

We reach snow and ski up to the steep west flanks of the peak. It feels as if we've walked across a parking lot smack into a vertical brick wall. Skis back on our packs, we crampon up frozen snow into the huge basin at the base of Pyramid's wicked North Face: a wall that's seen more climbers falling than climbing.

For this trip we had deliberately picked a day just after a big storm, so we'd know the rocks would have maximum cover. The new spring snow is compacted and frozen on the lower part of the climb; just the conditions we want. As we climb higher, we find ourselves punching ankle deep holes in loose, unconsolidated snow. Rather than tight-frozen avalanche-safe crust, we will be on snow that could fall down the mountain; snow that is difficult, perhaps impossible, to climb. We will suffer.

We are on a comfortable saddle, perched at 13,000 feet. A 1,000-foot wall of nearly vertical snow is between the summit and us. Rock outcrops and cliff bands stud the face. These features define the ski route and we must find a line that goes around them. The cliffs leave no room for error. Even a small avalanche will launch you into oblivion. We uncoil our rope, cinch in, and as the eastern sky lights up, Jeff takes the first lead.

Jeff climbs above me until his stretched rope tugs at my waist. He has found no anchors. If he falls, he'll tumble down past me, taking a "screamer" at double the rope length. He jams his skis, tail-first, into the soft snow and attaches the rope to this dubious mooring. Jeff brings in the rope as I climb. In theory, he can catch a slip before it becomes a fall.

Swapping leads, we make our tedious way up the face. The angle varies between 40 and 65 degrees—as sheer as a church steeple roof. My toughest lead traverses under an outcrop. A 300-foot cliff gapes like the maw of a dragon twenty feet down the slope from my feet. I find a crack that looks solid enough to hold an anchor device. I test it with a sharp tug. A rock the size of my head breaks away, rolls between my feet, then launches for a three-thousand-foot flight down the face. After the traverse, I climb steep loose snow. I try to step up, only to have my foot punch back down to the level of my other foot. I scoop the snow above me with my hands, pushing cubic yards down between my legs, toilsome "trenching" that exposes firmer snow for better footing.

The sun has risen—a bad thing. Small balls of snow begin to roll down the wall as the heat loosens what meager cohesion darkness had given the snowpack. Some falling chunks pick up snow as they spin; they become head-sized wads that occasionally slam our helmets and shoulders. We can hear the tinkling of pebbles as they break away from thawing tendrils of ice that cemented them during the night. We hear the blocky thud of larger rocks falling down the north face, which is just around the corner from our route. The thawing snow becomes more avalanche-prone.

THE SUMMIT OF PYRAMID is exactly as you would expect: a tiny ridge about 150 feet long surrounded by cliffs broken with a few climbing routes. Perched there, you feel like a wing-walker doing stunts at an air show. We spend a few moments preparing. I jam a pair of skis in the snow as an anchor and Jeff starts skiing, tied into the rope. I pay out slack from above as he descends. I'm supposed to catch him with the rope if his descent becomes a fall. At what point one thing becomes the other is something we have not discussed. We should have. During the descent, more times than I like to admit, Jeff or I would make a clumsy turn, only to be brought up short on the rope like a trout being hook-set by an angler. "Sorry," would come the shout from above, "I thought you were falling."

During the climb, I had measured the slope at 60 degrees. That's a tough angle to ski. Without special technique, you can't bring your ski tails around fast enough to complete a turn before you accelerate out of control. Today, the mashed potato snow makes skiing even harder. Jeff stands, ready to turn. The lip of a 300-foot cliff is fifty feet below him. With an upward lurch, he initiates. His buried skis follow too slowly. He brings his planks around with a savage motion, then jams his upper arm into the slope to keep from falling backwards. A few of those and he gets smoother, but he never links more than a few turns. He skis out of site to the left, within a few ski pole lengths of the cliffs.

Jeff prepares an anchor station, then shouts up for me to start. The skiing is easier for the second person, as the loose snow is somewhat compacted and removed. Who cares? The rope curves from my waist, 150 feet down to Jeff. If I fall, I'll go 300-feet down the cliffs before the rope catches what's left of me. I find myself doing much the same routine as Jeff. Stand and shuffle in the loose snow, then launch a desperate jump turn—or perhaps two. I'd still call it skiing, but it's not the Big Burn at Snowmass.

The altitude saps our strength. The sun is a gigantic heat lamp, the snow a perfect reflector. Sunscreen mixed with sweat drips into my eyes and stings like battery acid. My skis push a pile of snow down the face. The pile gathers speed and widens into a loose snow avalanche. It pours over a cliff with a booming sound, gathering momentum and more volume. A gigantic rushing roar comes from below.

Avalanches occur more frequently as the sun heats the snow; we start at least twenty huge slides and twice as many small ones. My nerves burn until they sputter and smoke. Skiing with my fearful, tight body is a futile exercise. I pause and close my eyes. Only a calm mind will get me out of this. I force myself to think of family back home. I vow that once this is done I won't need to return.

There is only one way out. We continue our tiptoe descent, anchoring the rope whenever possible, stomping platforms with our skis, making gingerly turns, and sidestepping down when nothing else works. Dangerously late in the morning, with legs too tired and minds too gone, we are back at the 13,000-foot saddle. We can

So close, yet so far. 14,018' Pyramid Peak, as seen from the the Aspen Golf Course on Hwy. 82, reminds us of how much true wilderness surrounds Aspen.

see down most of Landry's route from here. Our avalanches have scoured it and now jagged rocks jut from ragged ice and snow. Standing above this Stygein pit doubles my pulse rate.

We coil our rope, turn from Landry's route, and descend the north bowl. Pyramid does not relent. While safer from avalanches and falls, the snow in the bowl is pure guano—ten inches of muck topped by fist-size warts of ice. With quads burned beyond recognition, we suffer through hundreds of flailing jump turns. You could only call us "skiers" with the loosest of definitions. The snow improves as we descend and for the last thousand vertical, we link normal turns. They feel strange; too easy. The angle is wrong. Instead of a mountainside, there is air behind our ski tails. The suffering is over. Perhaps now, even as Pyramid frowns down upon us, we'll even have a bit of fun.

HIGHLANDS RIDGE

NEAL BEIDLEMAN'S MOUNTAINEERING "PLUM"

EDITOR'S NOTE: *Neal Beidleman gained widespread respect in the climbing world from the heroic depiction he received in John Krakauer's book* Into Thin Air. *Beidleman was a Mt. Everest guide for Scott Fisher's Mountain Madness expedition in 1996. He was credited by Krakauer with saving several survivors during an ill-fated climb of the world's highest mountain, which resulted in nine deaths from four separate expeditions.*

HIGHLANDS RIDGE IS A DRAMATIC symbol of wildness for the Aspen area, a lofty, rugged and forbidding example of the rugged Elk Mountains. This stark escarpment of rock, snow, and ice defines high risks/high rewards mountaineering in the Maroon Bells-Snowmass Wilderness. Neal Beidleman refers to Highlands Ridge as one of the most difficult and challenging winter traverses in Colorado. His two attempts on the ridge in 1995 and 1996 are indicative of the rigors of a high-altitude endurance feat that turned him back both times.

For Beidleman, the Highlands Ridge traverse begins in the parking lot at Aspen Highlands Ski Area and climbs to Loge Peak, where the now popular hike to Highlands Bowl sets off on the precipitous ridgeline. From there the ridge runs almost due south over a jagged line of peaks, couloirs, and basins, ending at the head of Conundrum Creek, over ten miles away.

Beidleman describes the ridge as uniquely difficult due to sustained elevation, length, route finding, and level of difficulty. It should be noted that Beidleman's attempts were made during the very depth of winter when the days were short, temperatures low, and snow conditions tenuous.

EARLY ONE MORNING on a December day in 1995, Neal Beidleman, Jeff Maus and Jeff Hollenbaugh started out in the dark from the parking lot of Aspen Highlands with packs and skis. Hiking up the mountain with climbing skins was their only choice because the lifts wouldn't open until long after the team had made its way to the top. Once they reached Loge Peak, accessing Highlands Ridge meant violating the ski area boundary, which is not something they wanted to do during operating hours. By getting an "alpine start," the team would avoid boundary hassles and get a jump on a very long day.

"We figured that was the only fair way to do it, climbing 4,000 vertical feet as a warm-up," said Beidleman. "Our intention was to make it all the way back to Coffeepot Pass and then ski back down Conundrum Creek. It was really, really cold that night in late December, probably 15 below. We tried to time our traverse to as close to the Solstice as possible to make it a real winter traverse. It was cold and it was winter. This route hadn't been done before in the winter, so we thought it was a good goal, a real plum."

Beidleman, Maus and Hollenbaugh reached Loge Peak as the sun was coming up, then spent the day skiing, hiking, and climbing the ridge traverse to a point just past Hunter Peak, a distinctive triangular peak that straddles the ridge at about the halfway point. "It's a real, true knife edge and the rock up there is just abysmal and the snow in the depths of winter was all sugary and tenuous," described Beidleman.

The team worked its way past Hunter Peak and bivouacked for the night. Beidleman and Maus had brought sleeping bags, but not Hollenbaugh. He had

Highlands Ridge as it leaves Aspen Highlands Ski Area. To the right of the skier are Pyramid Peak (14,018 ft.) and the South Maroon Peak (14,156 ft.) and North Maroon Peak (14,014 ft.).

packed a warm down jacket and a 750-ml. bottle of Jim Beam. They fabricated a makeshift shelter and huddled together for warmth. "We found enough snow in a little hollow to dig a shallow cave," explained Beidleman, "then used our skis as the roof. We got inside and we sat there. Jeff shivered and I snored."

As Beidleman and Maus wrapped themselves in their sleeping bags, Hollenbaugh snuggled with his bottle of whisky. "He wouldn't bring a sleeping bag but he brought the whiskey, and a lot of it," Beidleman recalled with a smile, "and we gave him a lot of grief. The two Jeffs broke out Power Bars and I broke out a whole, oven-roasted chicken from City Market and polished it off for dinner."

In the morning, at first light, the team faced a difficult decision. "The weather was really sour—very windy—and we weren't sure how much it was going to snow," said Beidleman. "We were very aware and concerned about avalanche conditions if we tried to get off the ridge. Not knowing exactly what was going to happen, we went a little further along the ridge, then bailed down into a high basin in East Maroon. We broke trail all the way back down to Maroon Creek and ended at T-Lazy-7. It turns out we were pretty close and there were just two more peaks [Hilliard and Keefe]. We probably could have made it."

In 1996, they tried it again. "We were going to bivouac as far as we could and we were determined to do it, no matter how long it took," said Beidleman. "If we were out three or four days, that was acceptable."

A S BEFORE, the team started with a hike up Aspen Highlands, but this time even earlier than before. They crested Highlands Peak in the dark and began working their way carefully across the ridge. It was still dark when they stopped to negotiate a technical section. "There was one ridge we had to cross on a steep spot, so we stopped to drink something and we put our packs down. Then we started off, but Jeff [Maus] said 'Hold on a sec. I dropped my pack.' So I said, 'Okay, so pick it up.' Then we waited, but he didn't come. We asked, 'Well, how far did you drop it?' He said: 'I don't see it.'"

Maus explored below the ridge in the dark, but he could not find his pack. The ridge dropped off steeply, so he could not see below without considerable risk. His pack was nowhere in sight. It was pitch dark and the headlight only pierced the night a small distance.

"We weren't going to wander down there in the dark where we couldn't see, so we set up a small, two-man tent and crawled in," explained Beidleman. "When the sun came up, we started down and still didn't see his pack until we were well below the ridge. The pack was about 1,500 feet down the Maroon side in one of the rarely skied bowls."

The team had no choice but to retrieve the pack, and since Beidleman and Hollenbaugh would not let Maus go alone, they made a team descent. "We took all our gear, not knowing whether we would come back or not, and we went down, careful of some dangerous avalanche conditions," recalled Beidleman. "By the time we got to his pack, it was kind of late in the morning and we were tired and we looked back up at the ridge and said, 'No.' So we skied out and that was that. Jeff felt pretty bad about it, although we laugh about it to this day."

The following year, 1997, a third attempt of Highlands Ridge was made as a solo by Jeff Hollenbaugh. According to Beidleman, the full route took Hollenbaugh more than twenty-four hours, and he did it nonstop, through the night. "So, he got the carrot," said Beidleman, satisfied that his friend and companion had scored a major first in local mountaineering. "Jeff had great conditions and he nailed it."

Beidleman regards Highlands Ridge as either a "skier route" or a "very strong snowshoer route". Skis are problematic on the ridge traverse, but are better for the long trudge out of the Conundrum Creek Valley, he explained. "The ridge has been tried a bunch of times, but it's so far, so long—more than ten miles—and after all the bends and curves, it's a lot longer than that. Even in the best of snow conditions, you have to take off your skis and you might need crampons. Skis are almost a detriment on parts of it, but if you get all the way to Coffeepot Pass and don't have skis, you're hosed. But I have another goal," said Beidleman, studying a map. "If the ridge went well, then the ultimate route would be to make a horseshoe out of it and come back over Castle and Cathedral Peaks, over Electric Pass and then finish with a ski down Mt. Hayden."

Beidleman, who grew up in Aspen, has been mountaineering since he was thirteen. He got his start through the Outdoor Education programs offered during his Aspen public school years. Today, married and with two young children, Beidleman works as a freelance mechanical engineer designing "everything from space crafts to avalanche shovels." The "Avalung," a breathing apparatus worn as a life vest and marketed to skiers navigating avalanche terrain, is a design Beidleman worked on for Black Diamond.

Always active in mountaineering, Beidleman has currently set his sights more on local adventures than long distance expeditions. He gives high ratings to the mountaineering experience available on Highlands Ridge.

"The ridge presents difficulty in an overall sense because of altitude and length. It's an extremely difficult ski route. If you're not ready for the exposure and some of the moves, you're going to have problems. You have to know where to go because you don't just stay on one side of the ridge; you cross back and forth, and there are fifty or a hundred of those kinds of places. If you're not moving fast and you make the wrong decisions and have to backtrack, you can be up there forever. The rock is not solid and the snow conditions can be horrendous. Your security is with your partners."

NOW THAT HIGHLAND BOWL is open for skiing from Aspen Highlands, hikers stream uphill to reach some of the most challenging, lift-served ski terrain in North America. Every year, skiers venture farther along the ridge, said Beidleman. The well-known "Five Fingers" area beyond Highland Bowl and the chutes of Maroon Bowl and other alluring drops on the west side of the ridge are drawing increasing numbers of skiers and snowboarders. Two avalanche deaths on the west side of the ridge in 2000 attest to the potentially high risks.

Still, wildlife is more likely to be encountered on the ridge than day-trippers, as Beidleman explained. "We followed several mountain sheep up there. Following their tracks is a good way to go. We saw them standing at the top of the ridge at dawn, butts to the wind. They are really tough and looked right at home."

Beidleman allowed that one of the only mountaineering routes he has done that's comparable in duration and difficulty to Highlands Ridge is a route he contrived with Jeff Hollenbaugh when they linked all the "Fourteeners" in the Elk Range with no vehicular support. They did so by running, walking, and climbing half a dozen high summits during a thirty-five-hour marathon.

"We started with Capitol Peak (14,130 ft.), then crossed into Pierre Basin and climbed Snowmass Mountain (14,092 ft.), up a very steep, seldom-done face right to the summit. Then we went down into Snowmass Creek, up Juanita Basin to the backside of South Maroon, climbed the south ridge of South Maroon (14,156 ft.) and traversed the ridge to North Maroon (14,014 ft.). From there, we hiked down to Maroon Lake and up and down Pyramid Peak (14,018 ft.) by the regular route; this we did at night. Then we went back to Maroon Lake and down to East Maroon Creek, then up over Triangle Pass to Conundrum Hot Springs. Here we got in the wrong basin and ended up climbing two 13,500-foot summits on the ridge to Castle Peak (14,265 ft.), which we also climbed. We did all this during the Perseid meteor shower and it was quite a show. I'll never forget being on the summit of Pyramid at 1:30 in the morning and just lying there on our backs watching the meteors blaze across the sky."

Beidleman still has his sights set on a winter traverse of Highlands Ridge. It is the kind of mountaineering challenge he loves. "Highlands Ridge is maybe unique in Colorado for the kind of terrain, for being that long and that high and that continuous with no easy egress. It is a really wild place, and once you start, you are committed." ❖

13 Ski Huts of the Elk Range

A RUNAWAY BOY from Leadville, ten victims of a head-on plane crash, and mountaineers from many walks of life are memorialized in a system of remote mountain ski huts radiating from Castle Creek. These huts furnish lodging for backcountry skiers seeking high routes through the Elk Range and have become cherished for their backwoods character and remote settings.

The Braun Hut System and the Friends' Hut provide rustic and comfortably furnished cabins available for rent through a reservation system operated by the 10th Mountain Hut System. Ski-only access during the winter assures a wilderness experience that rewards those who are prepared and capable. Using these huts requires route-finding abilities, knowledge of snowpack and avalanche conditions, experience in the high country above 11,000 feet, and good physical endurance.

FROM "IRON MAN" TO FRED BRAUN

THE ALFRED A. BRAUN Memorial Hut System is Colorado's first ski hut system. Its humble beginnings originated with the Tagert Hut, a small A-frame located on the Pearl Pass jeep trail at the head of Castle Creek. Before the present hut existed, a dam tender's cabin was on the same site and was occupied by a man who tended a dam used for hydroelectric power for the mill of the Montezuma Mine during the mining era. The first known use of this cabin for modern ski alpinism was when early mountaineer Otto Schniebs used it for expeditions during the 1930s. Prior to Schniebs it was visited by a group of Aspen residents for "snow play."

When Schniebs first saw the cabin it was in use by John Stubagger, an old, one-eyed miner known as the Iron Man of Montezuma. Stubagger earned his moniker by his tenacious prospecting, and by helping the Schniebs expedition move their mountain of supplies up to the hut. According to Fritz Benedict, Iron Man kept a pair of Attenhofer skis under his bed, which Schniebs taught him how to use.

In 1946, Jay Laughlin came to the Aspen area from Connecticut, where he worked in publishing. He had convinced the National Ski Association to set up a hut committee to build and maintain ski huts in the central Rockies of Colorado. Laughlin repaired Stubagger's old cabin for use as a hut, which by then was owned by well-known Aspenite Billy Tagert, who graciously donated the cabin to the Ski Association. Laughlin was assisted in his renovation by several Aspen residents, including 10th Mountain Hut founder Fritz Benedict, who said in an interview: "It was a beautiful little cabin."

In 1953, an educator named John Holden moved to Carbondale to start the Colorado Rocky Mountain School. Holden was active in the Ski Hut and Mountaineering Committee of the National Ski Association, which eventually became the United States Ski Association, or USSA. For the next decade or so,

The Friends' Hut, located at timberline on the Crested Butte side of Pearl Pass, was built in memory of victims of a head-on plane crash in 1980. The hut commemorates a bond between friends in Crested Butte and Aspen. This night-long time exposure shows star tracks circling Polaris, the North Star.

Holden spearheaded the fund-raising and building of three huts above Ashcroft: the Lindley Hut in 1958, a new Tagert Hut in 1960, and the Markley Hut in 1964.

Holden worked with many others on these projects, including students from his school, Ashcroft dog musher Stuart Mace, and an Aspenite named Fred Braun. Braun emigrated to the U.S. from Germany in 1928 and moved to Aspen in 1951, where he operated a ski lodge, the Holiday House, which he ran with his wife, Renate. At the time, the Braun lodge was one of four operating in Aspen. Braun then founded an Aspen chapter of the Colorado Mountain Club. He was a civic-minded go-getter who started Aspen's first ambulance service and in the mid-1950s founded one of the west's first organized mountain rescue teams. In 1965, the same year he incorporated Mountain Rescue-Aspen, Braun built the current Mountain Rescue cabin on Main Street on a lot leased from the City of Aspen for $2 per year. Braun was also a mountaineer who understood, based on his European past, the potential for mountain huts.

N 1967, Holden turned over the operation of the hut system to Braun, who spearheaded completion of the last huts built for the system: the Barnard, Goodwin Green, and Green-Wilson. Over the years, Braun was known to hut users as a friend—and a phlegmatic pain in the rear. He held most other mountaineers in humorous contempt, especially if they did something he deemed stupid, such as falling and hurting themselves—or simply leaving for a trip during what Fred proclaimed as the wrong day or hour.

Braun's reputation was characterized in 1978 by *Aspen Magazine*, when he was declared "best crusty old altruist." According to Hal Clifford, in his book *The Falling Season*, Braun "complained about skiers burning too much wood at the huts and leaving too much of a mess behind, but he loved getting people into the backcountry. When he grinned it was a sort of elfin smile—he didn't always show his teeth—in a round face under a close mustache and a Karl Malden nose. He had just a few wisps of hair left on the top of his head by the time the city celebrated Fred Braun Day on June 20, 1975, but a good patch of white ran around the back from ear to ear. Furrows trickled like mountain rivulets down his high forehead to black eyebrows above deep-set, dark eyes."

Fred Braun, in 1966, at the Mountain Rescue cabin on Main Street in Aspen.

Instead of a computerized booking system, prospective hut users were often treated to a few swallows of Fred's schnapps between sardonic stories about other people's misfortunes, then handed a roll of toilet paper and a candle, warned about the avalanche danger (extant or not), and sent on their way. A nonprofit group, the Alfred A. Braun Hut System Inc., purchased the huts in 1998 from the United States Ski Association. Booking today involves computers rather than cocktails. Fred Braun died in 1988 of old age.

The six high mountain cabins comprising the Braun Huts provide endless skiing and mountaineering opportunities in the Elk Mountain Range. The huts can be skied hut-to-hut or out and back from trailheads in the Aspen area. The Tagert and Green-Wilson huts are often used in conjunction with the Friends' Hut, located on the Crested Butte side of Pearl Pass, as a popular ski between Aspen and Crested Butte. The huts are open each year from Thanksgiving through the end of May. All huts have wood burning heat stoves, firewood, propane stoves, photovoltaic lighting, mattresses, eating and cooking utensils, toilet paper, matches, and cleaning supplies.

EDITOR'S NOTE: *Lou Dawson researched and wrote portions of this section.*

FRIENDS' HUT HONORS PLANE CRASH VICTIMS

WHEN BRENDA BOYD of Aspen turned forty, her friends wanted to throw a special party. Brenda was a ski instructor at Snowmass, a volunteer at the Windstar Foundation, and the mother of two children. She had many friends, so a special birthday celebration was planned at her favorite restaurant in Crested Butte, thirty-five miles across the Elk Mountains from Aspen. On June 17, 1980, Brenda and five friends boarded a six-passenger Cessna 310 and made the half-hour flight to Crested Butte.

The pilot was Robert Pimmentel, thirty-three, a former Aspen resident who had moved to Crested Butte in 1973, where he opened a ski shop. With Pimmentel and Boyd were David Freedman, thirty-two, an Aspen ski instructor; Betsy Hube, thirty-one, a merchandise designer at Sport Obermeyer; Michael Pokress, thirty-three, a real estate agent; and his wife, Ellen Pokress, thirty-one, a waitress at the Golden Horn. The Pokresses had been married eight months. The Crested Butte airport was closed, so they flew to Gunnison, twenty-eight miles south of Crested Butte. The flight was smooth and the scenery beautiful. That night they toasted Brenda with good cheer and friendship.

The next morning, June 18, the group planned to return to Aspen. They boarded Pimmental's Cessna at the Gunnison airport and lifted off in clear weather around 11 a.m. At about the same time, four men in a Cessna 182 were cleared for take-off at Aspen's Sardy Field. Their destination was Crested Butte. Jeff Kest, twenty-six, the pilot, was a rescue chief for the Snowmass Fire Protection District. With Kest were Pat Palangi, thirty-five, Thomas Spillane, twenty-seven, and Rudy Csadenyi. All were employed by the Snowmass Village Property Management Corporation, which was sponsoring the trip as a vacation for its deserving employees.

KEST'S PLANE lifted off into a clear blue sky, and he maintained periodic radio contact with the Aspen airport as he flew south from Aspen, following the deep, narrow valley of East Maroon Creek past towering Pyramid Peak (14,018 feet), which was still covered with snow. Flying just below the snowy ridgelines, the plane climbed gently toward the end of the valley where East Maroon Pass crosses the Elk Mountains at 11,810 feet.

As the Cessna 310, with Pimmentel at the controls, passed over Crested Butte, the passengers could gaze down at the tiny grid of streets and survey the snowy swaths of ski runs on the flanks of Crested Butte Mountain. Pimmental's plane was dwarfed by the cliff faces of Crested Butte Mountain as it banked around the rocky, pinpoint summit. Flying low enough to pick out familiar terrain features, Pimmental flew north of Crested Butte, then veered east of the old mining town of Gothic and began climbing toward Copper Lake and East Maroon Pass, the lowest saddle on this most direct route to Aspen.

Twenty minutes after Jeff Kest's Cessna 182 had lifted off from Sardy Field, air traffic controllers in Aspen failed to make radio contact with him. They knew the plane had approached East Maroon Pass, but that was the last radio contact received. As a routine safety measure, a search plane was dispatched from Sardy Field, which followed Kest's route up the East Maroon Valley. Circling a snowfield near the top of East Maroon Pass, the search plane pilot gasped. Below him on the snowfield lay the scattered wreckage of Kest's Cessna 182. The plane was in pieces

They boarded Pimmental's Cessna at the Gunnison airport and lifted off in clear weather around 11 a.m. At about the same time, four men in a Cessna 182 were cleared for take-off at Aspen's Sardy Field. Their destination was Crested Butte.

just below the Aspen side of the pass.

The pilot wheeled his plane in a tight circle and went back for another look to see if there were any survivors. What he saw on the second sweep caused an even greater shock. There were two planes down in the basin. Pimmental's Cessna 310, which had not been reported missing or in danger, was nearly intact on the snowfield near the remnants of the other plane. It was initially assumed that the 310 had discovered the Cessna 182, circled to look for survivors, and crashed in the attempt.

JOHN CALLAHAN was on Aspen Mountain Rescue at the time. He and fellow rescue volunteer Don Hose were the first to respond to the emergency call at Mountain Rescue headquarters in Aspen. Callahan and Hose drove to Sardy Field and were flown to the crash site by helicopter. The search plane pilot had reported seeing no survivors. As the chopper headed up the East Maroon Valley, Callahan glanced out the window and noticed a small herd of elk running across the valley, fleeing the chopper as its whirring rotor blades reverberated between the steep ridges. Callahan's gaze was soon directed to the crash site. His immediate suspicion was later confirmed.

"I could see the two planes in the snow and knew how it must have been," explained Callahan, recalling the incident almost twenty years later. "Each pilot thought he'd give his passengers the thrill of a steep climb to the pass and then, topping the pass, the whole world would open up to them. Well…it never did. It was a freak thing, split second timing. A few seconds either way and they probably could have avoided hitting each other."

The chopper hovered low and Callahan and Hose jumped out onto the hardened spring snow. Ducking their heads to avoid the spinning rotors, they waited for the chopper to lift off and return to Aspen to ferry more rescuers to the site. Callahan and Hose stood quietly in the high, snowy, wilderness basin as the chopper disappeared down the steep valley. They listened for a voice, a sound, anything to show that life was left in those planes. There was nothing, only the occasional sound of the wind scouring the high ridges.

"I can remember it like it was yesterday," said Callahan. "I can see it all. Don and I started picking things up from the snow, belongings, equipment, scattered pieces of the wreckage, like the heavy instrumentation that was wrenched out of the planes on impact and strewn all over the snow. There were pieces of bodies lying around, lumps of flesh. I had a shovel and began making a pile so we could protect them from wild animals. There was no question they were all dead.

"I walked to a section of the small, white plane; the other one was pretty much intact. I opened a door and there was a body crumpled against it. The undercarriage of one plane had hit the other. It took the top off one plane. During almost twenty years on Mountain Rescue, I probably brought out over 100 dead bodies

ABOVE A fatal, head-on plane crash occurred in 1980 in the idyllic basin of East Maroon Creek, shown here looking north from over East Maroon Pass. The Friends' Hut was built to honor the victims.

RIGHT Graeme and Liz Means rest from their ski tour over Pearl Pass to the Friends' Hut. Graeme designed the hut and helped supervise its construction.

and the incidents all sort of run together. But I remember this one. There's still a propeller blade stuck up there in the basin somewhere. I saw it during a horseback trip fifteen years after it happened."

Investigators corroborated what Callahan suspected. The planes had collided in mid-air as they crossed the pass from opposite directions. The weather had been clear that day and there was no record of wind turbulence. It was assumed that the planes had climbed toward the pass on deadly trajectories and that the pilots had been unable to see one another. The crash brought them to the ground like stones.

"Bits of the six-passenger Cessna 310 bound from Crested Butte to Aspen were imbedded in the four-passenger Cessna 182," came the official report, as stated in the *Aspen Times* later that week. Six bodies from the Cessna 310 were taken out of East Maroon Basin on the first rescue day by chopper and delivered to Aspen Valley Hospital. Three Mountain Rescue personnel remained that night, camping out at the crash site. They recovered the four bodies from the Cessna 182 the following day. All told, ten were killed, nine from Aspen and one from Crested Butte.

"…But I remember this one. There's still a propeller blade stuck up there in the basin somewhere. I saw it during a horseback trip fifteen years after it happened."

—JOHN CALLAHAN

A COMMUNITY-WIDE MEMORIAL SERVICE was held at the Aspen Music Festival tent and attended by hundreds of mourners. The sorrow shared by Crested Butte and Aspen was later expressed by mutual friends who pooled their resources to create a lasting and meaningful memorial in the Elk Mountains: a beautiful mountain refuge.

Friends from both communities formed the Friends' Hut Committee, which acquired the necessary Forest Service permits and raised money to build the "Friends' Hut," which opened in the winter of 1985-86. Upper East Brush Creek, on the Crested Butte side of Pearl Pass, was chosen for the hut site because it was safer for winter access than East Maroon Pass. Building materials were delivered by helicopter to alleviate road scars, and teams of volunteers labored on the log structure, which was designed by Aspen architect Graeme Means, a close friend of the Pokresses.

The hut is a cozy log cabin with a capacity for nine, perfectly suited to intimate gatherings. A guitar and other personal affects of some of the crash victims are kept there and the walls are decorated with pictures of the friends who lived and died in these mountains. The hut serves as a high-mountain memorial for an extended family of friends on both sides of the Elk Range who have been brought together by common tragedy.

TAGERT HUT MEMORIALIZES A RUNAWAY BOY

BILLY TAGERT, for whom the Tagert Hut is named, was a pioneer who, by the time of his death, was said to have lived in the Roaring Fork Valley longer than any other person. He came to Aspen in the spring of 1883 and lived in the valley for eighty-three years.

Tagert was born June 5, 1873, at Echo Canyon, Utah, and as a child moved with his parents to Leadville. Tagert ran away to Aspen, over Independence Pass, when he was nine years old. It was said that he came over the pass barefoot, hitching rides on freight wagons and landing in Aspen as a self-made orphan and street urchin. He got by in Aspen by selling newspapers on the streets and sleeping wherever he could find shelter.

Fearing he would be discovered and sent back home to Leadville, Tagert decided to escape into the wilderness. He hitched a ride on a freight wagon to the Ten-Mile stage relay station downvalley from Aspen, then walked across Watson Divide into Snowmass Creek. He slept in a haystack that night and ate a small head of cabbage for breakfast that was given to him by a passing rancher. Tagert began walking up Snowmass Creek and was offered a ride by Sam A. Williams, a rancher who offered to let him stay and work with him that fall and winter on his Snowmass Creek ranch. Williams had scant food, so Tagert subsisted that winter on gallons of milk he drank from the cow that it was his chore to milk.

In the spring, Tagert met a neighboring rancher, Walter Boram, who invited him to work and live at the Boram and White Ranch, which was also on Snowmass Creek. Tagert remained there for the next ten years and thrived under a regimen of hard work and pleasant living conditions. He learned the rudiments of stock raising, which would benefit him years later. During these years, he was visited occasionally by his mother and sister who then lived on a ranch near Carbondale. When Tagert visited them, he attended school at Catherine and Satank.

As a young man, Tagert began taking an active role in community affairs and was a charter member of the Farmer's Sub Alliance No. 19, which he organized in 1891. During that time he met and courted Cora Terrance, whose family had moved to the Roaring Fork Valley from the Gunnison Country over Pearl Pass. Billy Tagert and Cora were married in 1895 and settled in Aspen; they had two daughters, Nellie and Wilma. Tagert worked as a partner in a co-operative store in Aspen, then started a livery business, which he operated for fifteen years.

Tagert prospered in Aspen, despite the Silver Crash of 1893, raising a herd of purebred Hereford cattle. He acquired various parcels of outlying land, including what is now known as Tagert Lake at the bottom of Independence Pass, just east of Difficult Campground. He also owned the Holden Lixiviation site, which he leased to the Marolt family.

In 1913, Tagert started a stage line between Aspen and Dorchester, a mining camp in Taylor Park. He had won a contract with the U.S. Postal Service for carry-

LEFT **Billy Tagert** (L) **and John Williams** (R) **were partners in an Aspen livery service, shown here in the late 1800s.**

LEFT BELOW **Billy Tagert in 1965 at the door of his cabin near Original Curve in Aspen.**

BELOW **The Tagert Hut, named for Billy Tagert, who donated the original A-frame as the first commercial ski hut in Aspen.**

ing mail and supplies to 150 miners at the Taylor Park Mining Company. Tagert thought the contract could prove lucrative, but discovered that deliveries of items like twenty-pound sacks of oats were problematic and that shipping costs began to outweigh the returns. He and a friend, George Folsom, a deputy postmaster, worked out a scheme to end the contract.

Tagert and Folsom drove the stage over Taylor Pass to Dorchester, stayed overnight with the miners, played cards, and treated the miners to rounds of whiskey. That night, with the miners sound asleep, Tagert and Folsom quietly collected all the postal equipment and hauled it back over Taylor Pass to Ashcroft, where they delivered it to Dan McArthur, the postmaster there. Then they awaited the regular postal inspection.

When the inspector visited Dorchester he received a complaint from the miners about a lack of mail service and later heard Tagert's explanation and his request for cancellation of the mail contract. To Tagert's relief, it came through a few weeks later and he was freed of the obligation after two years of regular service. Tagert later claimed the honor of being the last man to drive a horse-drawn wagon over Independence Pass, which he did in 1915.

In the 1930s, Tagert drove a team of horses for the Highland Bavarian Lodge, owned by Billy Fiske and Ted Ryan, who he guided up Castle Creek, where they explored the ski potential of Mt. Hayden. Cora Tagert died in 1955 and Billy survived her for eleven years, until his death in 1966; he was ninety-three. Billy and Cora are buried at Red Butte Cemetery in Aspen. The Tagert Hut was named in Billy's honor for his tenure in the Roaring Fork Valley reflecting a life of adventure in the Elk Range. ❖

14 Winter Perils

FATEFUL HUT TRIPS IN THE ELKS

WHEN ALLURING MOUNTAIN terrain becomes lethal, the usual reaction is shock. Despite GPS, cell phones, and avalanche beacons, winter is potentially the deadliest season of the year. Avalanche, hypothermia, and frostbite are the primary risks for backcountry travelers in the Castle and Maroon Creek Valleys. Both valleys and their tributaries are especially prone to avalanche where backcountry travelers run a gauntlet of avalanche chutes that can produce massive slides.

Fatalities occur with disturbing frequency in both valleys, with backcountry skiers as the usual victims. The science of avalanche forecasting is obscure to novices and inexact even to "experts," so skiers crossing steep, snow-laden slopes, or skiing beneath them often take their lives in their hands. During the mining era of the late 1800s, men working winter shifts in remote valleys like Conundrum Creek were sometimes killed as they slept or were swept away during the course of their labors (see pg. 66).

Most winter deaths today occur when recreational skiers, snowshoers, or snowmobilers drop their guard and put themselves in harm's way. When Aspenite Jim Fitzgerald was killed in a small avalanche on the Taylor Pass Road on December 31, 1984, his experience and athleticism did little to protect him. The 55-year-old "experienced backcountry skier," as the *Aspen Times* described him, was uncovered hours after being buried. His lone companion, his girlfriend, went for help. Did she know that she was Fitzgerald's only hope for survival? She was either ill-equipped to dig him out or her sensibilities were overruled by panic.

MIRACLE IN THE MOUNTAINS

ONE OF THE MOST SPECTACULAR episodes revealing a lack of sensibility occurred in February 1993 when seven skiers from the Front Range of Colorado ventured up Express Creek from Ashcroft for a two-night hut trip to the Goodwin Greene ski hut near Gold Hill. The event became known by the national media as "Miracle in the Mountains", the miracle being that any of the party survived, which they all miraculously did. Poor judgment and sheer hubris in the face of a major winter storm led to a multi-day rescue effort that mobilized dozens of volunteers, on the ground and in the air. Getting lost in the mountains has rarely attracted the attention these ill-fated skiers received.

"Why did this group of experienced mountaineers venture into the avalanche-threatened wastes above Ashcroft when all common sense should have told them to cancel their trip?" asked the *Aspen Times* in an article headlined: "A Miracle!" And how was it that the lost skiers, who Pitkin County Sheriff Bob Braudis referred to as "human popsicles" survived such a harrowing ordeal?

It began with a two-night reservation at the Goodwin Greene Hut 7.5 miles from Ashcroft at an elevation of 11,800 feet, where the hut lies is a shallow basin

Skiers break trail beneath the snowy ramparts of the Maroon Bells.

at the head of Difficult Creek. The skiers were all considered experienced, fit, well-prepared, and each one had been to the hut on at least one previous trip. The group leader, Ken Torp, had plenty of experience, having climbed Denali in Alaska. Another of the skiers, Elliot Brown, had also climbed Denali and spent time in the Himalayas.

On the morning of the group's departure, the Colorado Avalanche Information Center issued a severe avalanche warning accompanying a major winter storm in the Aspen area that would deliver three feet of snow in Aspen and more in the high mountains. The group shrugged off the warning and set off at mid-morning under heavily overcast skies.

By afternoon, as the skiers reached Richmond Ridge, just below timberline, the anticipated storm arrived and brought blizzard conditions. The skiers were immediately bogged down, exhausted from breaking trail, and disoriented. They dug in for an emergency bivouac that was grueling because the skiers were provisioned for a hut, not a raging storm at 11,000 feet. They had no tents and no sleeping bag covers or ground pads. After their snow cave collapsed in the night, they were forced to take shelter in shallow snow trenches.

"During the first night we were wondering if we were going to make it," confessed Brown, the Denali and Himalayan mountaineer. "The conditions were worse than I've ever seen on any of my expeditions."

The next morning, conditions had worsened. The heavy snow continued falling, but was intensified by high winds. Breaking one of the fundamental rules of winter mountaineering, the skiers split into three groups and went their own ways through the blizzard. The accounts vary as to the reasons for the split, but the ensuing life and death struggle of the three groups revealed a serious lack of cohesion among them and the confusion inherent in a severe storm. In normal winter conditions, skiing back to the trailhead from the bivouac would have taken an hour at most, but it was five days before all the skiers were accounted for.

Breaking trail through thigh-deep snow, collapsing in exhaustion, taking shelter in snow caves and remote mountain cabins, the skiers floundered in fear and panic. Some had frostbite, all were exhausted. After their rescue, some threatened lawsuits against their friends. Contradictory accounts were handed out to a hungry media as friendships eroded into bitter squabbles. One of the skiers said she had been treated like "a beaten Roman slave" by her fellow skiers. Others claimed they had been abandoned by self-serving friends more interested in their own survival than in the needs of the weakest skiers. Survival brought out the worst, not the best, in the group.

Meanwhile, rescuers from Aspen tested their own endurance by scouring avalanche-prone locations throughout the backcountry of Richmond Ridge, Taylor Pass, and beyond. At one point, when the storm was at its worst, the sheriff prohibited rescuers from venturing out at all. Army Chinook rescue helicopters were grounded. "We have fewer options and we are taking more chances," said Mountain Rescue leader Tom McCabe. With each day, the likelihood of finding the lost skiers' alive diminished. The national media were having a field day.

When the storm finally abated and the skiers were found, two groups had wandered ten miles into Taylor Park and another had made it back to Ashcroft. The Aspen community and nationwide television audiences breathed a sigh of relief. The lost skiers received medical attention for frostbite and exposure and confessed to having learned a lesson—the hard way. "We're a little bit embarrassed," Ken Torp told the Associated Press. "We feel like errant school children, but we're absolutely elated to be alive."

Breaking trail through thigh-deep snow, collapsing in exhaustion, taking shelter in snow caves and remote mountain cabins, the skiers floundered in fear and panic. Some had frostbite, all were exhausted. After their rescue, some threatened lawsuits against their friends.

DEATH IN PEARL BASIN

Rescue mission in gale force winds. Searchers form probe lines in Pearl Basin and dig for Teeny Jueng and her dog.

EDITOR'S NOTE: The Aspen Times *headline on January 14, 1988 read:*

THREE LOST IN AVALANCHE NEAR PEARL

At about 10:30 a.m. Sunday, January 10, one day before Colorado Avalanche Backcountry Safety Awareness Week officially began, an avalanche swept 600 feet from a jagged ridgetop in Pearl Basin and covered three skiers.

The aftermath of the slide was noticed by fellow skiers, but their distance from the slide area was too great for a timely rescue.

About forty minutes after the slab avalanche had worked its mayhem, the bodies of Roy Poteet, 31, of Carbondale and John Logsdon, 32, of Boulder, were dug from shallow, snowy graves by their friends.

Still missing is Teeny (Kristyne) Jueng, 38, a Glenwood Springs Councilwoman and Emergency Room supervisor at Valley View Hospital. She is believed dead and buried in the avalanche debris, along with her dog....

THE DAY AFTER THE AVALANCHE, a rescue party set out on a convoy of snowmobiles that raced up the Castle Creek Valley toward Pearl Pass. Each machine towed several rescuers on skis, who rode the crystal wake of the snowmobiles like water skiers. The snowmobiles were laden with packs, ropes, and long, orange probe poles strapped to the sides. Some of the skiers carried avalanche shovels on their backs. As the rescuers raced toward the avalanche site, wind-blown plumes of whirling snow marked the high ridges, indicative of a coming storm.

At the Tagert Hut, two large, black plastic bags cinched closed with nylon straps lay in the snow. They contained the corpses of two of the avalanche victims, Roy Poteet and John Logsdon, who had been uncovered the day before and were brought down from the avalanche site in body bags.

The Tagert Hut served as base camp and command center for rescuers and was littered with backpacks, scattered piles of clothes, and a sleeping bag. A fire burned in the stove and wind gusts rattled the stovepipe. By mid morning two rescuers on snowmobiles pulling trailers hauled the bodies down the trail to a waiting ambulance at Ashcroft.

Pearl Basin, where the avalanche occurred, is over 1,000 feet above the hut, just south of Castle Peak at about 12,500 feet. Ski tracks, mostly overblown by swirling snow, led into the basin. The trail was marked by small, orange flags that fluttered and popped in the wind. A rescuer handed out bundles of long probe poles.

Around noon, Rick Deane, a veteran of Aspen Mountain Rescue, raced to the rescue site on his snowmobile. Deane's machine had a shark's mouth painted on the front, like the cowling of a Flying Tiger. Somehow, Deane had maneuvered the snowmobile over rocks and tundra, muscling the sled into the wind by sheer will. At the rescue site, three human probe lines wobbled in the intensifying wind. Standing shoulder to shoulder, roughly eighteen inches apart, each rescuer probed down ten or twelve feet into the avalanche debris. More than once the probers sunk their shafts to the hilt, plumbing an unknown depth in debris that was later estimated at twenty feet deep. Rescue leaders directed their teams like choreographers: "Forward...probe! Forward...probe!"

In the deposition zone, massive chunks of compacted snow revealed a slab avalanche, the kind that often kills by trauma rather than suffocation. The blocks of the slab were scattered like chunks of broken concrete, some blocks as large as refrigerators. High on the ridge above the rescuers, a deep fracture line zigzagged across the snowpack. The avalanche had broken from a small point release where the skiers had triggered it, then grew into a slide several hundred yards wide.

As the probe teams moved across the deposition zone, several smaller teams with shovels burrowed holes behind them, searching for Teeny Jueng. If a prober met resistance with their pole, a rescuer dug at that spot, excavating a pit ten or twelve feet deep. Several avalanche dogs trained at sniffing out bodies frolicked eagerly around the pits, their tails waging as their trainers set them to the grim task.

THE VICTIMS OF THE SLIDE belonged to a party of thirteen skiers who had rented the Tagert and Green-Wilson huts for the weekend. On Sunday morning, following a light, overnight snowfall, three groups of skiers set out on separate tours. Logsdon, Poteet, and Jueng, with Jueng's dog "Bear," a frisky eighty-pound pup, skied into Pearl Basin, then began climbing up the steep basin toward the ridge of Castle Peak. One of the other parties had visual contact with the ill-fated skiers. No one saw the slide, just the aftermath. One moment the skiers and the dog were working their way up the basin, the next moment they were buried in the slide.

The witnesses sent a skier down the trail toward Ashcroft for help. The nearest radio was at the Mace Hut, half an hour away. Fortunately, Julie Mace was in residence and she made the emergency call. The other skiers raced to the avalanche site, arriving exhausted, breathless, and frightened. With their avalanche shovels

The blocks of the slab were scattered like chunks of broken concrete, some blocks as large as refrigerators. Above the rescuers, a deep fracture line zigzagged across the snowpack. The avalanche had broken from a small point at the top of the ridge and expanded into a slide several hundred yards wide.

Digging a snow pit, like this one below Pearl Pass, is a ritual for savvy backcountry skiers to evaluate avalanche conditions. Pits are dug to the ground in an effort to reveal possible structural weaknesses in the snowpack.

they dug frantically at a ski tip protruding from the snow. About a foot down, they found Logsdon, who was wearing an avalanche transceiver strapped across his chest. One of his friends removed it, switched from transmit to receive, and quickly scanned the area around him. A strong signal led them to Roy Poteet, who was buried beneath four feet of snow. Both men were dead.

Teeny Jueng had not been wearing a transceiver; she had loaned it to another friend on the trip. There was no sign of her or her dog. The slide was so large that random digging was futile and the friends soon gave up. The most shaken members of the group returned to the Tagert and Wilson huts where they attempted to cope with the grim psychological aftershock. Others stood vigil with the bodies.

Julie Mace radioed the Aspen police, who in turn notified Aspen Mountain Rescue. David Swersky, the team's rescue leader, started a telephone chain that quickly mobilized a rescue party. Rick Deane drove his snowmobile to the site, arriving the same time as Julie Mace, who had skied up from the Mace Hut. They enlisted the traumatized survivors gathered around the bodies to form a probe line, but called off the search by late afternoon. They wrapped the bodies of Logsdon and Poteet in body bags and took them down to the huts.

The next day, rescuers braved wind gusts of seventy mph. Conditions were desperate and the rescue was called off again, with nothing to show but scattered snow pits. Rescuers retreated to the Mace Hut, where Julie Mace served hot soup, corn bread, cider, and tea to twenty rescuers. The storm came in that night and covered the avalanche site with fresh snow. High winds built new and threatening cornices on the ridges and the recovery efforts were suspended indefinitely.

During the spring of that year, small rescue parties visited the site regularly to monitor the work of the sun, and on July 18, with most of the snow gone except where the avalanche had piled it 20 feet deep, two rescuers hiked to the site for a look. The day was sunny and warm, a nice morning to be in the mountains, though not for the reason they were there. In the higher reaches of the slide zone, they discovered a furry paw protruding from the snow. They exhumed the dog named "Bear" and probed the vicinity.

Near the place where "Bear" was found, covered by only a foot of compacted, mid-summer snow, lay the body of Teeny Jueng. Warm when she had died, her body heat had dissipated into the snow and melted it, forming a hollow ice cave in which she was entombed. Teeny Jueng and "Bear" were finally taken down from the mountain, six months after they had died there. ❖

EDITOR'S NOTE: *The original* Aspen Times *report was written by Paul Andersen, who participated in the rescue. The discovery of Teeny Jueng's body was described by Ted Conover in his book* Whiteout: Lost in Aspen.

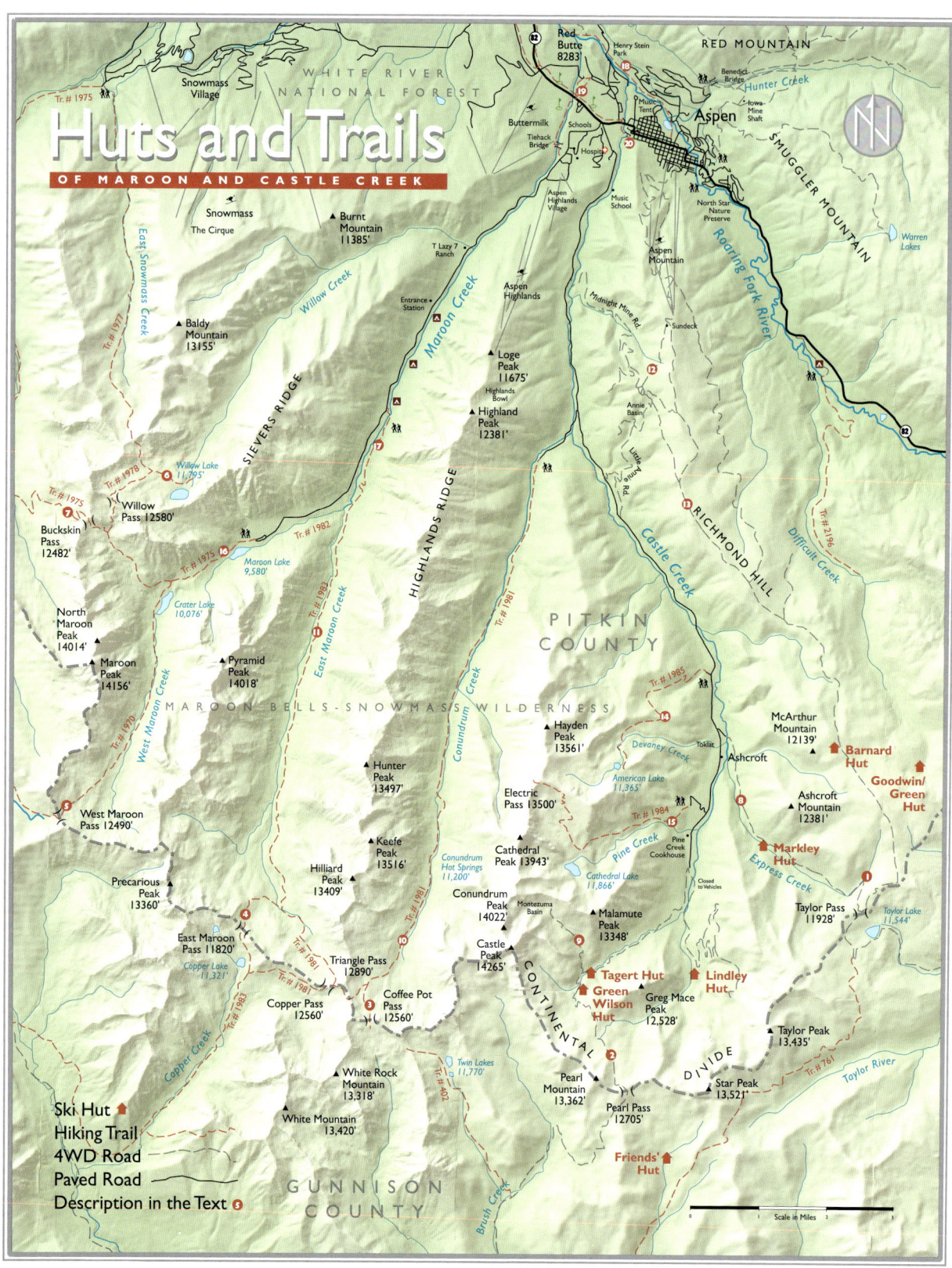

Huts and Trails
OF MAROON AND CASTLE CREEK

WHITE RIVER NATIONAL FOREST

Snowmass Village

Tr. # 1975

Snowmass
The Cirque

Baldy Mountain 13155'

Burnt Mountain 11385'

East Snowmass Creek

Willow Creek

Tr. # 1977

Willow Pass 12580'

Tr. # 1978

Tr. # 1975

Buckskin Pass 12482'

Tr. # 1975

Maroon Lake 9,580'

Tr. # 1982

Crater Lake 10,076'

North Maroon Peak 14014'

Maroon Peak 14156'

Pyramid Peak 14018'

Tr. # 1983

East Maroon Creek

West Maroon Creek

Tr. # 1970

West Maroon Pass 12490'

Precarious Peak 13360'

Hunter Peak 13497'

Keefe Peak 13516'

Hilliard Peak 13409'

Conundrum Creek

Conundrum Hot Springs 11,200'

East Maroon Pass 11820'

Copper Lake 11,321'

Triangle Pass 12890'

Copper Pass 12560'

Coffee Pot Pass 12560'

Copper Creek

White Rock Mountain 13,318'

White Mountain 13,420'

Tr. # 1981

Red Butte 8283'

82

Henry Stein Park

Benedict Bridge

Hunter Creek

RED MOUNTAIN

Iowa Mine Shaft

18

19

Music Tent

Aspen

Schools

SMUGGLER MOUNTAIN

Warren Lakes

Buttermilk

Tiehack Bridge

20

Hospital

Aspen Highlands Village

Music School

North Star Nature Preserve

Roaring Fork River

Aspen Highlands

Aspen Mountain

Midnight Mine Rd

Sundeck

Annie Basin

Little Annie Rd

Entrance Station

Loge Peak 11675'

Highlands Bowl

Highland Peak 12381'

Tr. # 1982

12

13

RICHMOND HILL

Difficult Creek

Tr. # 2196

82

SIEVERS RIDGE

HIGHLANDS RIDGE

Castle Creek

T Lazy 7 Ranch

PITKIN COUNTY

Tr. # 1985

14

McArthur Mountain 12139'

Barnard Hut

Goodwin/ Green Hut

MAROON BELLS-SNOWMASS WILDERNESS

Hayden Peak 13561'

Devaney Creek

American Lake 11,365'

Toklat

Ashcroft

Ashcroft Mountain 12381'

8

Electric Pass 13500'

Tr. # 1984

15

Pine Creek

Pine Creek Cookhouse

Markley Hut

Express Creek

Cathedral Peak 13943'

Cathedral Lake 11,866'

Pine Creek

Closed to Vehicles

Taylor Pass 11928'

1

Taylor Lake 11,544'

Conundrum Peak 14022'

Montezuma Basin

Malamute Peak 13348'

9

Lindley Hut

Castle Peak 14265'

CONTINENTAL

Tagert Hut

Green Wilson Hut

Greg Mace Peak 12,528'

Taylor Peak 13,435'

Twin Lakes 11,770'

2

DIVIDE

Pearl Mountain 13,362'

Star Peak 13,521'

Tr. # 76

Taylor River

Tr. # 202

Pearl Pass 12705'

Brush Creek

Friends' Hut

GUNNISON COUNTY

Legend

Ski Hut

Hiking Trail

4WD Road

Paved Road

Description in the Text **5**

Scale in Miles

15 Exploring the Passes

TRAVELS THROUGH HISTORY

THE BEST WAY to experience the Castle and Maroon Creek Valleys is on foot. Exploring these valleys, their tributary drainages and the high basins and ridges surrounding them is a mountaineer's delight. While trails within designated Wilderness areas are limited to foot and horse travel, other trails and roads are open to limited vehicular access. Signs at trailheads specify prohibited uses.

Following are descriptions of summer trails and roads encompassed by the two valleys, with numbers corresponding to the map on the opposite page:

TAYLOR PASS ❶

TAYLOR PASS was named for Jim Taylor, the namesake of Taylor Peak, Taylor Lake, Taylor Park, Taylor Reservoir, and the Taylor River. The Elk Mountains were first called the "Taylor Range" in honor of this pioneer, who ventured here in the 1860s.

In the summer of 1880, a toll road was built over Taylor Pass, funded by the Roaring Fork Valley Improvement Company, headed by early Aspen entrepreneur Henry Gillespie. The road was built by Stevens & Company. In an effort to protect his investment, Gillespie lobbied against public roads that might compete with his toll road and was accused of trying to bribe Gunnison County officials to protect his interests.

Express Creek Road contours toward Taylor Pass, the first wagon route into the Roaring Fork Valley. Today the road is popular with four-wheelers and dirt bikes.

Public funds finally went to constructing the "Leadville Road" (Independence Pass Road), which was opened to stage traffic in November 1881. Despite the competition, Taylor Pass was used frequently, via Cottonwood Pass from Buena Vista, a route opened by government road builders in the 1870s as a supply route to deliver cattle to the Ute Indians.

A sign posted at the top of Taylor Pass in 1880 read: THIS WAY TO THE ROARING FORK, and for some time the pass was called "Roaring Fork Pass." Just east of the pass, on a round-topped mountain 12,400 feet above sea level, pockets of gold were discovered on

"Gold Hill". A stamp mill and small encampment were established in upper Difficult Creek known as Barr's Mill, the ruins of which may be seen today near the Goodwin Greene Hut. The ore crushing "stamp mill" was disassembled and removed in the summer of 2002, and reconstructed as a display at the Marolt Barn historical site in Aspen.

Before Taylor Pass was connected by road to Ashcroft, wagons were already convening in Taylor Park, driven by pioneers eager to enter the new land of the Roaring Fork. Instead of coming down Express Creek, which the road follows today, these early birds stayed on Richmond Ridge. Once they were directly above Ashcroft, they lowered their wagons down the steep mountainside using winches and ropes wrapped around trees, as Brown and Cowenhoven had done. Express Creek, where the road was built in 1881, was so named for the Express Mining Company.

Once Taylor Pass was completed, Stevens & Co. operated a stage line between Aspen and Buena Vista and charged other users a toll: single animals $1; team and wagon $2.50; 4-horse outfits $5. George F. Elrod drove the first wagon over the new road and Amos Bourquin was one of the first tollgate keepers on Taylor Pass. Later, two stage companies—Rockwell & Bicknell, and Wahl & Witter—ran stage-coaches over the route. Atkinson & Holbrook started a freight wagon-train, haul-ing silver ore and supplies over the pass. It was not unusual to see freight wagon-trains a quarter-mile long and brimming with supplies for the new camps of Ashcroft and Aspen. Four-horse teams usually pulled one wagon; six- and eight-horse teams typically pulled a wagon and trailer.

ASPEN HISTORICAL SOCIETY

Western Stage Lines began operating a stagecoach regularly between Aspen and St. Elmo on Chalk Creek in 1885. This stage service connected with the Rio Grande Railroad below the east portal of the Alpine Tunnel. The Stage Company put on a line of Concord Stages, which the *Aspen Times* described as "the finest in the state," and later extended service north to Glenwood Springs. Stages ran daily in each direction, changing teams at relay stations in Ashcroft, Aspen, Ten-Mile (Watson Divide), and Dinkel's Ranch (Carbondale). During late fall, winter, and early spring, sled runners were attached in place of wheels.

Most emigrants to the Roaring Fork Valley who came over Taylor Pass from the Arkansas Valley stopped at the outpost of Bowman, in Taylor Park, for rest and supplies. At Bowman there were stores, cabins, and stables enough for 150 horses. Travelers were often delayed there by weather or poor road conditions. One stagecoach party was reportedly held up in Bowman for three weeks and enter-tained themselves around a piano. Bowman got its name from Colonel John Bowman, later of Aspen, a colorful frontier character.

ASPEN FOREST RANGER AND HISTORIAN LEN SHOEMAKER recount-ed his father's crossing of Taylor Pass when H. C. Shoemaker made the jour-ney to Aspen in 1885 from Rosita, in the Wet Mountains of south-central Colorado. H. C. Shoemaker traveled through the San Luis Valley, over Poncha Pass into the Arkansas Valley, up Chalk Creek to St. Elmo, over Tincup Pass to Tincup,

across Taylor Park, over Taylor Pass, and finally into the Castle Creek Valley, a journey of over 250 miles. Their "train" used horses, mules, and oxen pulling six covered wagons along with a herd of 150 range cattle and twenty milk cows.

"No serious difficulty was encountered," wrote Len Shoemaker of the expedition. "Their small cavalcade passed one ex-horse thief, dangling from a tree on Texas Creek. They had hard going across Tincup Pass and sometimes met long wagontrains of freighters which were hard to pass. On the six-mile grade between Taylor Pass and Ashcroft, this happened and it took five hours to get by. Some of the wagons had to be unloaded and set off the road until the others went by, then set back and reloaded. Aspen was like a beehive when they arrived; pedestrians, horseback riders and vehicles of all kinds were coming and going on most of the streets. Long jacktrains were packing ore. Hundreds of miners were working around the clock, and when they came off shift at midnight and came down Aspen Mountain with their lamps flaring in the breeze they formed a pleasing and unusual spectacle."

Dorchester, now the name of a Forest Service campground on the south side of Taylor Pass, was an outpost built around 1900 when the gold mines of the Italian Mountain District began producing. By then, Aspen was in economic decline due to the Silver Crash of 1893 and most of the traffic on Taylor Pass was headed out of the Roaring Fork Valley as miners sought work at these new prospects. The last commercial use of Taylor Pass was from 1910 to 1913 when Billy Tagert ran a stage from Aspen to Dorchester, serving the miners there.

The snow cornice at the top of Taylor Pass was a problem to teamsters, who often had to shovel through many feet of snow in July to open the road. Miners on the Taylor Park side occasionally "snowshoed" to Aspen on long skis, the "Norwegian Snowshoes" hewn from single planks of wood. They fabricated toboggans on which they skidded supplies. Progress was especially slow when breaking a fresh trail.

After the last stage crested the pass in 1916, with Billy Tagert at the reins, the road was little used except by fishermen and sightseers who traveled on foot or horseback to fish Taylor Lake and the Taylor River. In the 1950s a pair of miners with a mining claim near Taylor Lake bulldozed the road to their claim and hauled ore in trucks to Aspen.

Today the Taylor Pass Road (Express Creek) is a challenge to even the sturdiest four-wheel-drive vehicles. From the Aspen side, it follows a loose, rocky grade to the top of the pass, then descends into an extremely rugged, rock-filled streambed to Taylor Park. Taylor Pass has become a popular mountain biking route and is often used by off-road motorcycles and ATVs.

A T 12,705 FEET, Pearl Pass is the highest vehicle route in the Elk Range. Pearl Pass is named for the Pearl Mine, one of the first mines in Pearl Basin at the headwaters of Castle Creek. Prospectors first came over Pearl Pass in 1879 from Crested Butte and found gold above Ashcroft before a town was there.

In 1881, Aspen desired telegraph communication with the outside world and Crested Butte was the closest, most direct link to an existing telegraph system. Western Union made a bid to string the lines from Aspen, but the $3,800 price was considered outrageous. Therefore, citizens volunteered their labor to string the line to Ashcroft and then over Pearl Pass. The line was begun in the summer of 1881 and completed that December. The *Aspen Times* described it as the "electric spark connecting us with the busy multitude across the range."

Due to a dispute with the telegraph company, however, the line was never electrified and never used. The company claimed $175 was due for erecting poles between Aspen and Ashcroft and the fee was never paid. The poles above Ashcroft along the Pearl Pass Road were eventually beaten down by severe weather, and now only an occasional metal brace is found.

After Ashcroft was established, a road was built over Pearl Pass, which was first traveled by wagons on September 7, 1882 with a shipment of silver ore from the Tam O'Shanter and Montezuma mines in Montezuma Basin. It would be five years before a railroad would reach Aspen, so the ore was delivered to the Rio Grande railroad depot in Crested Butte, then shipped by rail to smelters in eastern Colorado through the Alpine Tunnel. In 1882, Aspen entrepreneur Jerome B. Wheeler contracted for regular shipments of coke from coal-rich Crested Butte over Pearl Pass until Wheeler's own coke ovens began operating near Carbondale.

Pearl Pass cut the route from Aspen to the nearest railroad by fifty miles compared to the distance between Aspen and Granite in the Arkansas River Valley. Shipping fees over Pearl Pass were reduced by the shorter haul and, for a few years, attracted business. When the railroads reached Aspen in 1887 and 1888, the high wagon passes fell into disuse.

Pearl Pass in mid-summer

During Aspen's "Quite Years", Pearl and other high passes were used for annual picnics and summer outings. Recreational crossings in winter began in the 1950s when Pearl Pass became a backcountry ski route via the Tagert and Green-Wilson ski huts. With the construction of the Friends' Hut in 1985, Pearl Pass was listed as a designated route by the 10th Mountain Hut System.

During the early 1980s, Pearl Pass gained political significance when Crested Butte staged several massive ski tours in protest of a mining proposal by the AMAX Corporation that targeted a molybdenum orebody in a mountain near Crested Butte. Seeking support from Aspen, Crested Butte residents launched the "Save the Lady" ski tours. As many as thirty participants camped in snow caves in Cumberland Basin before crossing Pearl Pass to Aspen where a protest march was held in the mall. AMAX withdrew its mining proposal in 1983.

Another massive crossing of Pearl Pass became an annual event in 1976 when the first annual Pearl Pass Bicycle Tour left Crested Butte with 15 rugged riders who pedaled, pushed and sometimes carried the earliest prototype mountain bikes over Pearl Pass. The bicycle tour grew into epic proportions by the late 70s and early 80s as bicycle frame builders and designers from California joined the tour to test and display new mountain bike technology during a critical growth phase of the sport.

Perhaps the largest number of people ever to cross Pearl Pass under human power occurred in 1981, when over 200 mountain bikers rode the rugged pass to Aspen. A camp-out and keg party in Cumberland Basin, complete with a live band and a barbecue, solidified strong camaraderie, but also made organizers aware that the tour had grown beyond the comfort level of backcountry etiquette. The annual Pearl Pass Tour now averages about twenty riders who cross the pass in mid-September, often in snow.

COFFEEPOT AND TRIANGLE PASSES ❸

COFFEEPOT PASS (12,760 ft.) was named by the Hayden survey party when they found a rusty coffeepot at the top of the pass in 1873. The coffeepot marked the trail for many years at the headwaters of Conundrum Creek and West Brush Creek. The pass is little-used today.

Triangle Pass (12,900 ft.), which is on a connecting ridgeline half a mile from Coffeepot Pass, was named for Ferdinand Hayden's "Highland Triangulation Station," a point from which the surveyor made mapping calculations. Triangle Pass was once planned as a wagon route between Gothic and Aspen, connecting the Conundrum Creek Valley with the Copper Creek Valley. A wagon road was built to Triangle Pass in 1883 by Gunnison County. Pitkin County had agreed to reciprocate with a road from the Aspen side, but reneged, so the pass remained a foot trail on the Aspen side, as it is today.

EAST MAROON PASS ❹

EAST MAROON PASS (11,820 ft.) marks the divide between the East Maroon Valley and the Copper Creek Valley. Traveled by miners in the 1880s from Gothic to the Roaring Fork Valley, East Maroon Pass is the most direct route between Aspen and the Gunnison Country. In 1887, East Maroon Pass became an improved toll road between Gothic and Aspen, with winter sleigh service for a brief time.

When the railroads came into Aspen in 1887 and 1888, the East Maroon toll road fell to disuse and was eventually impassable to all but foot and horse traffic. East Maroon Pass was added to the Forest Service trail system in 1920 when Forest Ranger Len Shoemaker cleared the old road by hand.

In the 1880s, legend has it that a butcher driving a herd of fattened steers over the pass from Gothic to Aspen became stuck in a sudden and intense snowstorm that mired his herd belly-deep. The man butchered the cattle on the spot and buried their carcasses in the snow. The next spring he dug up the frozen beef and packed it into Aspen.

Several mining ventures were started during the 1880s in the East Maroon Valley. Chicago Mountain and Chicago Basin, at the head of the valley, were named for the Chicago Mine. In 1886, an avalanche wiped out one of the mining camps. The Sunset Mine opened in 1887 and cabins were built for miners. A subterranean water pocket, opened inadvertently by mining operations, drowned one miner, whose grave is somewhere in the valley.

The late Matt O'Block, who passed away in the late 1980s, hiked during his college years from Aspen to and from Western State College in Gunnison over East Maroon Pass. His greatest fear was the deep stream crossings when he returned home in the spring. Today, the trail is a popular hiking and equestrian route.❖

On the trail to **Willow Pass**, with **North Maroon Peak** in the near distance

BUCKSKIN PASS AND SNOWMASS LAKE TRAIL 5

FROM CRATER LAKE, the trail to Buckskin Pass trail (12,462 feet) climbs to the west. The pass divides the waters of Snowmass Creek and Minnehaha Creek and is one of the true tests of a hiker's endurance as it climbs steeply through a dramatic landscape of high mountains and lush tundra meadows. The trail goes through the Subalpine, Krummholz and Alpine life zones.

In the early days, no trail existed up Minnehaha Gulch, just a rough track traveled by horseback between Snowmass Lake and Maroon Lake. Percy Hagerman, an early explorer and mountain climber, allegedly named the Pass when his buckskin horse balked on the last switchback. Hagerman recommend that the Forest Service construct a trail over this imposing saddle and Forest Ranger and historian Len Shoemaker surveyed the current trail in 1923 and built it the following year.

Shoemaker claimed to have named the Pass in 1922 when he saw a large buck deer on the Pass. Bighorn sheep, elk and deer may be seen near the summit of the Pass. Beginning in the 1950s, the T-Lazy-7 Ranch used this route for trail rides.

West Maroon Pass

THE HIKER'S HIGHWAY OVER WEST MAROON PASS ⑥

WEST MAROON PASS (12,700 ft.) has become the most popular high pass in the Maroon Bells-Snowmass Wilderness. It follows the Maroon Creek Trail to Crater Lake and bears left (south) past the lake and beneath the steep, striated ridge of South Maroon Peak on the right, and Pyramid Peak on the left. Note the many avalanche chutes coming down from both sides of the valley.

From the top of West Maroon Pass the trail switchbacks down into Schofield Park and traverses through one of the most magnificent concentrations of wildflowers in Colorado. Many hikers going from Aspen hire a van from Crested Butte to meet them at the Schofield Park trailhead. There is a fee, but it beats walking an additional fifteen miles to Crested Butte or hoping for a ride. Pay a little extra and the taxi driver will bring a cooler full of iced beer for appreciative passengers.

WILLOW PASS AND WILLOW BASIN ⑦

Willow Lake

JUST BELOW Buckskin Pass, a trail forks east to Willow Pass, from where the trail drops into Willow Basin and Willow Lake. A ridge walk north from Willow Pass leads to Buckskin Peak (13,370 feet) over the Tundra ecosystem of the Alpine life zone. East Snowmass Pass goes north to Snowmass Creek.

THE PIONEER ROUTE ON EXPRESS CREEK/TAYLOR PASS ⑧

Taylor Lake

EXPRESS CREEK is the most direct route to Taylor Pass. The road turns left off the Castle Creek road eleven miles south of Aspen, just before Ashcroft, and climbs 5.5 miles on a steep, four-wheel-drive road. Taylor Pass (11,928 ft.) offers views of Taylor Lake, Taylor Park and the Collegiate Range. This original pioneer route to the Roaring Fork Valley connects with Gold Hill and Richmond Ridge to the east, Taylor Park to the south, and a route to Crested Butte via Star Pass and Trail 406 to the southwest.

PEARL PASS/MONTEZUMA BASIN/CASTLE PEAK ⑨

PEARL PASS is considered among the three most difficult four-wheel-drive passes in Colorado. Popular among mountain bikers, off-road enthusiasts, and backcountry skiers, Pearl Pass is a popular route between Aspen and Crested Butte.

The Pearl Pass/Montezuma Basin Road turns off on the right about a mile past the Pine Creek Cookhouse, at the end of the pavement on the Castle Creek Road. It climbs through steep, rocky sections and traverses wildflower meadows. About a mile past the Mace Hut, the Pearl Pass Road veers left and passes the Tagert and Green-Wilson ski huts before it crests the Elk Range at 12,700 feet. The Montezuma Road veers to the right and climbs into Montezuma Basin, ending at 12,600 feet beneath Castle Peak (the highest of the Elk Range at 14,265 feet). The higher reaches of both roads are often covered by deep snowfields through June and are rough and rocky. Both roads require high-clearance, four-wheel-drive vehicles.

HOT SPRINGS IN CONUNDRUM CREEK ⑩

CONUNDRUM CREEK is a long, straight valley full of beaver dams and avalanche chutes. It traverses the Riparian and Aspen Forest ecosystems of the Montane and Sub-Alpine life zones. The trailhead starts about five miles from Aspen up Castle Creek where Conundrum Creek flows in from the southwest. Conundrum Hot Springs is about 8.5 miles up the valley and the trail has several stream crossings, some of which can be dangerous during high runoff.

Camping at the hot springs is strictly regulated because of intense use, so heed the signs and camp only where it is allowed. A Forest Service wilderness ranger is usually on duty during summer months to ensure a measure of compliance with regulations regarding dogs and camping.

A little over a mile beyond the hot springs, Triangle Pass (12,900 feet) divides Copper Creek to the west and Conundrum Creek to the east and is a challenging route to Copper Pass, East Maroon Pass, Copper Lake, Gothic and Crested Butte through basins within the Tundra ecosystem. Conundrum Pass (12,840 feet) lies about a mile north of Triangle Pass on the same ridge, dividing East Maroon Creek and Conundrum Creek.

Conundrum Hot Springs

DANIEL BAYER

IN THE SHADOW OF PYRAMID PEAK ⑪
ON THE EAST MAROON TRAIL

PYRAMID PEAK marks the East Maroon Valley about seven miles from Aspen, where East Maroon Creek flows into Maroon Creek from the south down a long, relatively straight valley that ascends gradually to East Maroon Pass (11,820 feet), a distance of about eight miles. The trail climbs from the montane to alpine life zones, through the riparian and aspen forest ecosystems.

The East Maroon Trail follows a well-beaten track through forests and open meadows. In wet weather, sections of the trail can be extremely muddy where it crosses bogs. This popular route to Copper Lake, Gothic and Crested Butte crosses the Elk Range and is a favorite for horsepackers and hikers, but is banned to motor vehicles and bicycles due to its wilderness designation.

The trail starts downstream from the confluence with Maroon Creek and traverses through an Aspen Forest ecosystem. In a little over a mile, the Maroon Lake connector trail drops down to the right, crosses East Maroon Creek, and climbs west toward Maroon Lake. The East Maroon Trail continues climbing to the south beneath the ramparts of Pyramid Peak to the west and Highlands Ridge to the east.

East Maroon Trail

PAST THE JOHN WAYNE TUNNEL ⑫
ON THE MIDNIGHT MINE ROAD

THE TURNOFF for the Midnight Mine Road is 2.5 miles up Castle Creek from Aspen. It drops to the left into the valley, crosses Castle Creek, then climbs a steep grade up Queen's Gulch to the top of Richmond Ridge at 11,212 feet. Open to four-wheelers and mountain bikes, the road passes the tailings piles from the Midnight Mine and the John Wayne Tunnel. As the road climbs into open meadows, fields of columbines and other wildflowers appear, as does a dramatic view of Mt. Hayden.

Midnight Mine Road

RICHMOND RIDGE ON THE LITTLE ANNIE ROAD ⑬

West side of Richmond Ridge

SEVEN MILES up Castle Creek from Aspen, the Little Annie Road turns left and climbs three miles to an intersection with the Midnight Mine Road, then continues another mile and a half to the top of Richmond Ridge through Little Annie Basin. At the top of the ridge, the road connects with the Richmond Ridge road. Taylor Pass lies fifteen miles to the south and Aspen Mountain lies just to the north. This is the route of the Grand Traverse ski race from Crested Butte, a major, one-day endurance backcountry event that crosses the spine of the Elks.

ASHCROFT OVERLOOK ON THE AMERICAN LAKE TRAIL ⑭

THE AMERICAN LAKE trailhead is ten miles from Aspen up Castle Creek, directly across the road from the Elk Mountain Lodge. The trail is only three miles long, but climbs 2,000 strenuous feet to the lake and traverses two ecosystems —the Aspen Forest and the Coniferous Forest.

American Lake Trail

CATHEDRAL LAKE TRAIL/ELECTRIC PASS ⑮

Cathedral Lake

THE CATHEDRAL LAKE/ELECTRIC PASS Trail is a popular and strenuous hike, which tops out at 13,500 feet at the divide between Castle Creek and Conundrum Creek. The trailhead is about a mile beyond Ashcroft where a dirt road turns off on the right. The trail climbs to a steep, switchback ascent just below Cathedral Lake, then veers north to switchbacks leading to Electric Pass. Cathedral Peak (13,943 feet) is the high summit directly above the lake.

Electric Pass was named in the 1920s by forest ranger Len Shoemaker. While working on the pass trail, he was knocked to the ground by a bolt of lightning. He rolled down the steep tundra slopes in an effort to escape more strikes. The Hayden Survey party of 1873 also remarked on the electricity on this highest named pass in Colorado, thought to be caused by the high iron content of Electric Peak.

Miners used the pass to get from Ashcroft to Conundrum Creek in the 1880s when the route was called the Panorama Horseback Trail or Pine Creek Prospector Trail. Today, hikers are urged not to attempt crossing the pass from Castle Creek into Conundrum Creek because the trail disappears over steep and treacherous ground. From the trailhead to Electric Pass, the trail climbs through the Montane, Subalpine and Alpine life zones, and features the Aspen Forest, Coniferous Forest, Riparian and Tundra ecosystems.

FOR AN EASY STROLL through a Riparian ecosystem, follow the 1.5-mile-long Falls Loop Trail from Maroon Lake toward the Maroon Bells. A beaver pond at the upper end of Maroon Lake, complete with dam, lodge and beaver colony, is a reminder of what the early trappers looked for in the American wilderness. A small waterfall on Maroon Creek is among the scenic attractions on this pleasant mountain trail.

Continue on the Crater Lake Trail above Maroon Lake and discover one of the most popular hiking trails in the Aspen area. This trail climbs steeply enough to challenge novices and reward all hikers with outstanding mountain vistas. The trail begins at Maroon Lake and bears right at the split with the Falls Loop Trail. In about a mile the trail gains a low saddle beneath the north cirque of Pyramid Peak. This rocky saddle, which impounds water in Crater Lake, is a moraine that was pushed here by a glacier. The rocks offer protection for marmots and are nurseries for columbines and raspberry bushes.

From the grassy shores of Crater Lake the Maroon Bells rise up to the west, with Pyramid to the east. In the fall, the lake becomes a mud flat since most of the water drains out through the porous glacial debris of the glacial dam. The West Maroon Trail climbs toward the south and Buckskin Pass trail ascends to the north.

Maroon Lake

MAROON LAKE TO T-LAZY-7 ON THE MAROON CREEK TRAIL 🔟

THE MAROON CREEK TRAIL follows Maroon Creek from Maroon Lake to the T-Lazy-7 Ranch, a distance of 3.8 miles. An easy, downhill walk, the trail is within a Montane Riparian Ecosystem. Most hikers follow this trail down from Maroon Lake, through forests and open meadows, then catch the bus along the way for a ride back to Aspen. Below the East Maroon Trailhead (2.8 miles down from Maroon Lake), the Maroon Creek Trail crosses numerous major avalanche paths where the destructive force of slides can be seen in the twisted and broken trees deposited along the stream. The trail traverses Grassland and Aspen Forest ecosystems.

Maroon Creek Trail follows the line between the spruce and aspens.

CONFLUENCE ON THE RIO GRANDE TRAIL 18

The Rio Grande Trail swings around Red Butte along the Roaring Fork River.

THE RIO GRANDE TRAIL begins near the Aspen Post Office and follows the paved trail downstream on the historic Rio Grande Railroad right-of-way. The trail is paved 1.75 miles from Aspen to Cemetery Lane at Slaughterhouse Bridge, where the surface changes to crushed gravel for a five-mile stretch to Woody Creek. From Woody Creek, the trail is paved to Basalt, then returns to gravel through Emma and Carbondale, with eventual plans for completion to Glenwood Springs. The Denver & Rio Grande Western was Aspen's first railroad, and began serving the booming mining town in late 1887. Today, the trail is popular with hikers, runners and cyclists.

LOWER MAROON CREEK TRAIL 19

Maroon Creek Trail from the Wade/Terrel pedestrian bridge

THE LOWER MAROON CREEK TRAIL begins at the Aspen Golf Course parking lot, one mile downvalley from Aspen on Highway 82. Follow the dirt road that leads down to the Maroon Creek flood plain below the Highway 82 Maroon Creek Bridge, cross the pedestrian bridge over Maroon Creek (the "Bob Helm Bridge"), then follow the gorge west. The historic Maroon Creek Bridge, which passes overhead, was constructed by the Colorado Midland Railroad in 1887. A new highway bridge was built in 2006-07.

The trail is within the Riparian ecosystem in the Upper Sonoran life zone where plant species include willow, Gambel oak, chokecherry and serviceberry. Note the mix of river rock in the stream, a sampling of the geology from the upper valley. The whitish rock is porphyritic granodiorite and the red rock represents the ubiquitous Maroon Formation.

PAVED ROUTES ON ASPEN'S PEDESTRIAN/BICYCLE TRAILS 20

The longest single-span bridge in Colorado over Maroon Creek near Tiehack

THE CITY OF ASPEN provides miles of paved trails connecting town with the Marolt Property, Aspen Valley Hospital, Aspen Municipal Golf Course, Iselin Park, Aspen Highlands, the Airport Business Center (ABC), and the Owl Creek Trail to Snowmass Village. Trails also connect with Difficult Creek and Highway 82 east of town. Bridges and underpasses allow cyclists and pedestrians safe passage without crossing any busy roads.

This trail network makes Aspen a bicycle-friendly community where access to all amenities is fast and easy. Leave the car at home and explore the trails. Visit the Marolt Barn and the site of the former Holden Lixiviation Plant. The barn is owned by the Holden/Marolt Mining and Ranching Museum where late 19th century and early 20th century farming, ranching and mining equipment is on display. ❖

16 Castle, Maroon and Beyond…

CHANGE IS CONSTANT in the Castle and Maroon Creek Valleys. Erosion and tectonic activity continue to alter the landscape. Seasons mark progress on the earth's calendar. Flora and fauna follow their deeply ingrained rhythms. Human populations come and go, each wave bringing different values and reasons for being here.

Times change, and yet the mountains are very much like they were when Ferdinand Hayden studied them a hundred and thirty years ago, or, for that matter, when the Utes hunted here millennia ago. These two valleys parallel the timeline of American history: wilderness, discovery, exploitation. They reflect the boom and bust cycles and the renaissance of recreation, inspiration and conservation.

Today, beauty and adventure are the allure of these valley, whether it means climbing a Fourteener, painting a watercolor of an aspen grove, or watching a beaver building a lodge. Scenery is the draw for thousands each year who stand at the shores of Maroon Lake and take in what stands before them. Wilderness is preserved rather than tamed because it is the exception, not the rule.

Recent development has given us the Flintstones Bathrooms at Maroon Lake, the new base village at Aspen Highlands, a new Pine Creek Cookhouse, more traffic and people and impacts on the natural world. Tomorrow there could be a cable car crossing the Maroon Creek Valley connecting Highlands with Buttermilk, a four-lane highway running directly into Aspen, a gradual reduction in air quality that dims the brilliant blue of a mountain sky.

Tomorrow poses a huge question: Will Wilderness always be preserved from development, or will Congress one day rescind wilderness protection for reasons of expediency? Could the Elk Range one day be managed holistically, the way Bob Lewis envisioned, as the "Elk Mountain Preserve and National Monument"?

According to the late William Weber, one of Colorado's most noted botanists, the Elk Range, unlike most ranges in the state, is uniquely aligned east to west. This affords an unusual aspect for exposure to sun, which subtly affects flora and fauna. For this reason, said Weber, the Elks are a curiosity that deserve preservation as a study area. For decades, the Rocky Mountain Biological Laboratory (RMBL) in Gothic has been doing just that by identifying what is now recognized as a delicate environment. A new study center proposed by Lewis for Conundrum Creek may one day expand these studies to the north side of the range.

Taking the lead from the Wilderness Workshop and from the philosophy of Stuart Mace, preservation is a personal crusade. If future generations are to benefit from a legacy of wildness and rugged splendor, then current generations must adopt a mission to protect the land from the heavy hand of man. We must, each of us, listen to the message this magnificent land conveys.

Whether our revelation occurs at the summit of a Fourteener or on a picnic bench in Ashcroft, cherishing the values of wilderness is critical for preserving it. Personal commitment and community activism must form the bulwarks of lasting protection, and it all starts with the individual. It all starts with you. ❖

On a late winter afternoon, looking southeast over North Maroon Peak, lower left, to West and East Maroon Creek Valleys

BOB LEWIS · 1921–2005

BOB LEWIS was the father of this book. It was his idea, his energy that got it started, and his vision that it reflects. Without Bob Lewis, this book would not have been published. Like Stuart Mace, to whom this book is dedicated, Bob was tenacious about his stewardship of the natural world, and it was through this book, and its companion, *East of Aspen*, that he hoped to teach readers about the importance of ecological integrity in the natural world.

"I don't think of myself so much as a conservationist," reasoned Bob a few weeks before his death in the autumn of 2005, "but more as a teacher. I want to discover things and show them to people—a kind of show-and-tell. I get a lot of joy teaching because I'm able to share what I have learned. Happiness for me is sharing things with other people about nature."

After World War II, where he proudly served with the ski troops of the 10th Mountain Division, Bob Lewis moved to Aspen and taught high school biology. In this career choice he expressed Aldo Leopold's maxim: "In order to save something, you must love it, and in order to love it, you must understand it."

Independence Pass was Bob's most visible achievement. The huge rock retaining walls that have stopped the erosion that was threatening the headwaters of the Roaring Fork River were his idea. His name and life spirit are also synonymous with the Braille Trail, the Wildwood School, the Independence Pass Foundation, and the Environmental Research Group, organizations that will outlive him, thanks to the spirit in which he created them.

When Bob Lewis died, at 84, many of his plans were still left undone. His Aspen Field Biological Laboratory was still in the planning stages. His concept for a brain museum was percolating in his own labyrinthine gray matter. The idea for a Jerome B. Wheeler Society that would encourage futurist thinking in Aspen had only been fleshed out to a few friends.

On the last day of his life, Bob Lewis napped in a sunny montane meadow among wild flowers, mountain breezes and towering peaks. He lay back, as he had many times, and rocked in the familiar arms of Mother Nature. For this dedicated field biologist, connectivity with nature was always a salve. It gave him comfort to the very end. ❖

Bibliography

Author unknown .....*Glory, Glory Colorado, 1873-1876.*

Aspen Times. Willits Map of Aspen mining claims. 1883.

Bert, William Henry and Grossenheider, Richard Philip. *A Field Guide to the Mammals.* Houghton Mifflin Company. Boston. 1952.

BSCS. *Biological Science: An Ecological Approach.* Kendal Hunt Publishing, Dubuque, IA. 1992.

Bryant, Bruce. *The Geologic Story of the Aspen Region.* U.S. Geological Survey. United States Government Printing Office. Washington, D.C. 1988.

Buonpane, Vincenne. *Cross Country Nostalgia.* Snowmass Affairs Magazine. Snowmass, Colorado. March/April 1977.

Buys, Christian J. *Historic Aspen in Rare Photographs, featuring the journals of Charles S. Armstrong.* Western Reflections Publishing Company. Ouray, Colorado. 2001.

Cassells, E. Steve. *The Archaeology of Colorado.* Johnson Publishing Company, Boulder, Colorado. 1983.

Clifford, Hal. *The Falling Season: Inside the Life and Death Drama of Aspen's Mountain Rescue Team.* HarperCollins West. New York. 1995.

Clifford, Peggy. *Aspen/Dreams and Dilemmas: love letter to a small town.* Swallow Press, Chicago. 1970.

Coleman, Jon. T. *The Skeletal Shell Game: A History of a Colorado Ghost Town 1880-present.* Master's Thesis. 1992. From the archives of the Aspen Historical Society.

Conover, Ted. *Whiteout: Lost in Aspen.* Random House New York. 1991.

Cross Country Nostalgia Magazine. From the archives of the Aspen Historical Society.

Daily, Kathleen Krieger and Guenin, Gaylord T. *Aspen: The Quiet Years.* Red Ink Inc., Aspen, Colorado. 1994.

Digerness, David S. *The Mineral Belt: Volume I Old South Park—Denver to Leadville.* Sundance Books. Silverton 1977.

Frey, Ruth. *Aspen on Foot.*

Grant, Michael, C. *The Trembling Giant.* Discover. Oct. 1993.

Hayes, Mary Eshbaugh. *The Story of Aspen*. Aspen Three Publishing, Aspen, Colorado. 1996.

Helmuth, Ed and Gloria. *The Passes of Colorado: An Encyclopedia of Watershed Divides*. Pruett Publishing. Boulder, Colorado. 1994.

Katz, Joel. *Aspen Visible*. International Design Conference of Aspen research project funded by Atlantic Richfield Co. 1972.

Knoll, Charlene. *Memories Worth Saving: The Story of Ashcroft*. From the archives of the Aspen Historical Society.

Kricher, J.C. *The Ecology of Western Forests*. Peterson Field Guides. Houghton Mifflin. Boston. 1993.

Laing, David and Lampiris, Nicholas. *Aspen High Country: The Geology*. Thunder River Press, Aspen, Colorado. 1980.

National Geographic Society. *Clues to America's Past*. The National Geographic Society press, Washington, DC. 1976.

Opler, P.A. and Wright, A.B. *Western Butterflies*. Peterson Field Guides. Houghton Mifflin. Boston. 1999.

O'Rear, John and Frankie. *The Aspen Story: Including Skiing the Aspen Way*, A.S. Barnes. New York. 1966.

Rohrbough, Malcom. *Aspen: The History of a Silver Mining Town* (1979-189). Oxford Press. New York 1986.

Shoemaker, Len. *Roaring Fork Valley*. Sundance Publications, Ltd. Silverton, Colorado. 1958.

Smith, Duane. *Rocky Mountain West: Colorado, Wyoming & Montana, 1859-1915*. University of New Mexico Press. Albuquerque, New Mexico. 1992

Sprague, Marshall. *Colorado: A Bicentennial History*. W.W. Norton & Co., Inc. New York. 1976.

Spur, Joseph. *Mining Maps of Aspen*, 1894.

U.S. Forest Service. *Guide to the Maroon Bells*. Published by Rocky Mountain Nature Association in cooperation with the Aspen District, U.S. Forest Service, White River National Forest.

Wegman-French, Lysa. *The History of the Holden-Marolt Site in Aspen, Colorado*. Roaring Fork Research Scholarship Project for the Aspen Historical Society. Sponsored by Ruth Whyte. Aspen. 1990.

Wentworth, Frank. *Aspen on the Roaring Fork*. Francis Rizzari Publishing. Lakewood, Colorado. 1950.

Wolle, Muriel Sibell. *Stampede to Timberline*. Sponsor: University of Colorado. Muriel Wolle Publishing. Boulder, Colorado. 1949.

Index